The L

*Ge.*

*ISBN: 0-863811-338-0*

*Cover: Llyn Caseg
Back Cover: Llyn Tegid*

*First published in 1995 by Gwasg Carreg Gwalch,
Iard yr Orsaf, Llanrwst, Gwynedd, Wales.*

*☎ 01492 642031*

*Printed and published in Wales*

# To Ben

*The author and Ben*

*I would like to thank my family, friends and colleagues for their tolerance and support during the writing of this book. I would also like to thank Myrddin ap Dafydd of Gwasg Carreg Gwalch for taking it on board and agreeing to a weatherproof covering!*

*All photographs and the sketch map are by the author, with the exception of the above photograph, which is by Dafydd Roberts, Caerwys.*

# Contents

# ERYRI NATIONAL PARK

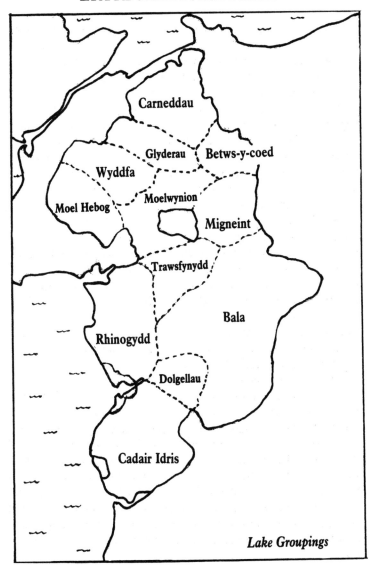

Carneddau

Glyderau   Betws-y-coed

Wyddfa

Moelwynion

Moel Hebog

Migneint

Trawsfynydd

Bala

Rhinogydd

Dolgellau

Cadair Idris

*Lake Groupings*

# Introduction

I climbed to the top of a small quartz pillar that seemed to overhang the little upland valley whose coronet ridge I had just traversed. It had been another sultry, warm day happily typical of the summer of 1994 when the pleasant scent of sun cream had prudently accompanied me around the hills. I was on one of the final few visits I deemed necessary to complete this book and already had begun to wrestle with the introduction. The car was half a mile away and eight hundred feet below, I felt content, at peace with myself and my undulating host of these last few hours. I would finish off the blackcurrant and honey mixture I always carried in my flask, be down, and away home to reflect and write upon those places I had just visited.

And then an ant like movement in the farm far down the valley caught my eye and interrupted my musings. Out of idle curiosity I raised my binoculars and trained them on a lady dressed in pink walking towards a grassless patch of grey hidden behind the farm buildings, she threw something and suddenly the grey patch was transformed into a seething chip pan! It was a secret pool of fish; not marked on the map and probably containing a higher concentration of trout per cubic foot than any other pool in Eryri.

I include this little anecdote to illustrate the difficulties I faced in deciding on a criteria for pool inclusion. Should size be the deciding factor? Should I merely cover the lakes with public access? Should I only include lakes containing fish? Should reservoirs be included? Indeed what should I include? Eventually I was guided by two main factors, the pools marked on the 1:25,000 OS map and the information I was actually able to obtain. You will therefore find a few small un-named pools marked on the map that I have passed over but I am confident that no serious omissions have occurred. You will also find in the book a few pools that no longer exist, these have been included for their interest. You will also find that the information on each lake is a mixed bag that is hopefully of interest to everyone who has made the effort to reach the lakes.

# Foreward

There can be little doubt that Frank Ward's (1931) book 'The lakes of Wales' was a significant influence and inspiration in the writing of this book. However not having Ward's time and energy I have restricted the 'catchment' area to the Eryri National Park. When the park was formed in 1952 the major slate industry areas were omitted, this was to allow their continuing development. I have included the lakes from these areas.

The 250 pools and lakes are listed in alphabetical order; each one has also been placed in a group according to their geographical location. There are ten groups which are identified on the map on page 5.

As an indirect result of the Eigiau dam disaster in 1925 a Reservoir Safety act was passed in 1930 that went some way towards ensuring a tragedy of that magnitude did not happen again. A further act was passed in 1975 which in essence stipulated that all reservoirs capable of containing 25,000 cubic metres of water would have to undergo rigorous and frequent inspections. Both these acts were obviously necessary and have doubtless averted several tragedies. As a result however they have also been the cause for many reservoirs to be deliberately breached by the owners. In the main most of these are old quarry reservoirs no longer in use.

I have used four figure grid references to pinpoint each lake whilst for more detailed locations such as caves, specific rocks etc. I have used six figure references. Lake volumes are close approximates, $m^3$ meaning cubic metres and mg meaning million gallons.

The book is not intended as a guide to the lakes and no right of way or access is implied by the inclusion of any lake in the book.

## LLYN YR ADAR
*GR 6548*
*Group: Moelwynion*
*Height: 1874'*
*Area: 10 acres*

Llyn yr Adar lies in a shallow saucer shaped depression on the long northern ridge of 'Y Cnicht' (The Welsh Matterhorn). It is surrounded by other smaller pools some of which become dry at times and have no fish. A rocky island near the middle provides a noisy sanctuary for Black Headed Gulls which no doubt explains the lake's name — Lake of Birds. Blaenau Ffestiniog angling society — Cymdeithas y Cambria holds the fishing rights and although reputed to be shy some quite respectable trout have been taken, one of 4lb was taken in 1987 for example. The small peaty stream leaving the lake meanders sluggishly for some hundred yards before being catapulted dramatically down a rocky gully whose steepness only just stops short of being a waterfall. The gully is both devoid of decent pools and the fish to fill them. At the bottom a short alluvial 'meadow' leads to Llyn Llagi. Many tales told of the colourful Blaenau poachers who would come to Llyn Adar using otterboards and other equipment permanently hidden beneath nearby rocks have by now become legendary and thanks to various angling authors over the years have become part of the fishing folklore. It has been said, most notably by W. Gallichan (1903) that these 'over the mountain' visitors made the lake their own in terms of fishing success and that the more local anglers could find no reason to consider it a good lake.

## LLYN ANAFON
*GR 6969*
*Group: Carneddau*
*Heigh: 1630'*
*Area: 13 acres*

The most northerly of the Carneddau lakes it lies tucked almost out of sight beneath Llwytmor, Foel Fras and Y Drum. Llwytmor was the scene of a very unlikely reunion in 1989 on the crash sight of a German 'Heinkel' that came down in 1941. Neither Kurt

Schlender nor Lothar Horras who survived the crash had seen each other since the accident but they were both dramatically reunited during the filming of the HTV documentary 'Adar y Drycin'. The site is reputedly haunted by the ghost of the engineer who was decapitated in the crash. Most sizeable Snowdonian lakes have been utilised by man in some way, Anafon is no exception and a well defined landrover track leads to the legacy of concrete structures by the lake outlet where Penmaenmawr and Llanfairfechan water supply begins its journey. The earthern dam was built in 1930 and gives a maximum capacity of 70,000 m³/14 million galls. An apparently new breed of 'Pondweed' was discovered here in 1883 and named after its discoverer (Potamogeton Griffithii) but is now thought to be a hybrid. There are some brown trout in both the lake and the brook leaving it with some classic little trout pools all the way down to the Pine forest above Aber. A curious arrangement once existed regarding the fishing rights to Anafon; a list of people residing within the village and confines were allowed to fish the lake and river, it is thought that the list may no longer be up to date. An old reservoir at (GR 701727) is dealt with under "Llyn y Ffridd". Some half a mile below the lake there are some ancient hut circles one of which measures twelve feet in diameter. Further evidence of ancient colonisation in the valley are plentiful; near the hut circles on the lower slopes of Foel Ganol there is an arrow stone whilst just over the hill to the north is another much larger example on the slopes leading down to Cammarnaint farm. These ancient stones were used for sharpening arrows and spears prior to going into battle or hunting or indeed there may have been ceremonial purposes. A gold cross some five inches in height was found on the actual summit of Carnedd y Ddelw above the lake in 1812 and several burial sites (Cist Feini) have been found in the area between the valley and Penmaenmawr. The lake is 10′ at the deepest part.

## LLYN ARDDU
*GR 6246*
*Group: Moelwynion*
*Height: 1200'*
*Area: 4 acres*

This small pool lies hidden in a complex series of rocky heather filled hollows on the slopes of a hill bearing the same name about a mile west of Cnicht. Despite its small size owing to its rocky bed the water level remains fairly constant and does contain smallish trout of inferior quality. In certain lights it is a sombre pool and there is a vague reference to an exorcized goblin condemned to its depths. A more detailed legend refers to a cave on the slopes nearby called (Ogof y Garreg Bengam) or (Ogof Tyrpin Lofrudd) where a dangerous highway robber would take refuge during his notorious career. Many people were said to have disappeared whilst travelling the valley and upland roads in the district. Following the discovery of a murdered traveller on Arddu a search was instigated which proved fruitless. One day however the shepherd of Cae Dafydd was out tending the sheep when he happened upon a huge man sleeping in the shelter of some rocks, he rightly assumed him to be the murderer and taking hold of the sleeping man's sword cut off his head. A cave was later found nearby containing his ill gotten gains. The actual whereabouts of the cave is not certain although the OS map has 'Ogof y Lleidr' (Robber's cave) marked at GR 618453. There is another cave some 400 yards east of the lake but that will be dealt with in Llyn yr Ogof.

## LLYN ARAN
*GR 7313*
*Group: Cadair Idris*
*Height: 1579'*
*Area: 1 acre*

An almost square shaped lake it lies on the north eastern slope of Mynydd Moel a neighbour of Cadair Idris one mile south west. There are small trout in both the lake and brook that keep to the mountain tradition of being good fighters.

On the afternoon of the 28th May 1943 a group of farmers were

*Llyn Aran, Cadair Idris*

tending their crops on Bwlch Coch farm. The sky was blue and almost cloudless but there was one large white cumulus cloud that was stubbornly clinging to the summit of Mynydd Moel above Llyn Aran. From the clear sky a Wellington bomber appeared and started circling as if attempting to identify its position, suddenly it flew into the cloud and a terrific bang was heard as it crashed into the summit rocks killing the crew instantly. One of the young men working in the field that day (Wil Fred James) recalls carrying the bodies down past Llyn Aran from the rocks. He also recalls a happier incident at the lake during those dark wartime days. They were washing the sheep in the now ruined sheep pens on the shore and were accompanied by a young 'land girl' from the city. Much light hearted banter had been directed at the girl who was not very country-wise which she accepted in the innocent spirit in which it had been intended. She had asked if she could be allowed to push the ram in and the men agreed. The ram was duly set up on its rump ready for the push and she stepped up to do the honours but just as she leaned forward to push, the ram's horns caught on her bib and in they both went!

The lake did hold some surprisingly good little trout a generation ago but they are now on the whole smaller in size and of inferior quality. Some of the locals refer to the lake as 'Caer'. Bingley in his tour round N. Wales recorded the Hairy Green Weed (Genista Pilosa) which is quite a rare plant as growing a few hundred yards N.E. of the lake. Although not thought to be there now it was re-discovered on Mynydd Moel (1901). The only other place where it is found in Wales is Pembrokeshire.

## LLYN ARENNIG FACH
*GR 8241*
*Group: Migneint*
*Height: 1487'*
*Area: 34 acres*

The lake is some 800' below and east of the mountain of its namesake Arennig Fach which rises to the north off the Bala — Trawsfynydd road. It was at one time well stocked with both Brown and Rainbow trout but it is believed their numbers to be diminishing and is now full of Perch. A metal sluice wheel covering leaning forward like a patriot missile launcher catches the eye from a long way in all directions. Closer examination shows a laddered 12' inspection shaft but the corroded state of the mechanism shows it will never work again. The earth dam topped by a dry stone wall was built sometime before 1870 and gives the lake a volume of 188,000 m$^3$/37½ mg. The dam has a maximum length of 100 yds. The rocks rising steeply to the summit of the mountain from the lake shores are called 'Creigiau'r Bleiddiau' (Wolves' Rocks) and local tradition lay claim to them as the place where the last Wolf in Snowdonia was killed. During the reign of Edgar in 959 AD local princes had to pay a tax of 300 wolf pelts per annum. Speed the mapmaker wrote in 1615 that the hills of Meirioneth were full of wolves so it may well be that these rocks were the final haunt of these feared animals. Between the foot of the cliffs and the lake a large cube shaped boulder is conspicous near the dam end of the lake. Its top is covered with a lush growth showing perhaps what the rest of the slopes would look like without sheep grazing. At the summit itself there is an interesting cairn and a round walled shelter. It is called 'Carnedd y Bachgen' (The Boy's Cairn) and was raised to remember a young shepherd boy from the farm Cae Gwernog (GR 842417) who became lost many years ago and was found dead on the summit, he was found with his cap wrapped around his bare feet. On the western side, some 600 feet below the summit is a one man shepherd shelter with perhaps room for his dog, this tiny roofed hut is in remarkably good condition and merges well with the rocks. The lake is owned by the Rhiwlas estate, Bala.

## LLYN ARENNIG FAWR
*GR 8438*
*Group: Bala*
*Height: 1326'*
*Area: 84 Acres*

Like its neighbour three miles north this lake also takes its name from the mountain rising west of it. It too was adapted as a reservoir in 1830 and continues to supply Bala with water. The 14 foot dam which consists of stone and concrete was significantly altered in 1864. Its max. volume is 1,621,000 m$^3$/324 mg. The pipeline to Bala was laid in 1879. There are some large trout here but they have the reputation of being difficult to catch, one local tradition says they can only be caught on two days a year! Andrew Foster the Head Keeper for Lord Penrhyn's estate on the Migneint paid one of his rare visits here April 1st 1882 and went away with an empty basket. The Brigands of Mawddwy came here to fill their baskets with fish. In certain atmospheric conditions strange echoes resembling piano keys being played can be heard. The 'Tylwyth Teg' or the Fairies have strong links and a tale is told of a young shepherd who discovered a bullcalf in the rushes many years ago. He took it home and looked after it and was rewarded with many fine healthy offspring. Years later whilst walking around the lake he saw a small man with a flute singing and calling his cattle back to the water. They were called Mulican, Molican, Malen and Mair and as will be seen both the story and the cows' names are very similar to other lake legends throughout the prinicpality.

The famous artists J.D. Innes and his friend Augustus John both fell in love with Arennig Fawr and numerous examples of their work portraying the area were painted in the cottage they rented at Nant Ddu in 1911, and 1912. At the time this was a wooden structure. On 4th August 1943 an American Flying Fortress crashed into the summit killing all eight of the crew, molten metal still litter the mountainside and a slate plaque in their memory has been placed at the summit. The lake is owned by Welsh Water and has a maximum depth of 127'. A handful of pools on the South ridge of Arennig Fawr (GR 8235) are semi permanent features, they do sometimes dry out and contain no fish.

## LLYN BACH (Cwm Glas)
*GR 6155*
*Group: Wyddfa*
*Height: 2,450'*
*Area: ½ acre*

This tiny pool possibly marks the 'nest site' of the Cwm Glas glacier and is one of the highest lakes in Wales. The setting is certainly a dramatic one with the high cliffs of Clogwyn y Person rearing straight up from its shore and its emptying stream cascading into the lower cwm in a series of short waterfalls. The cliffs around contain many of the rare alpine plants clinging to survival in Snowdonia. The obvious clean buttress just above is called 'The Parson's Nose' and according to tradition was first climbed by a man of the cloth whose interest was to ascend various skylines that took his fancy; in the century and a quarter since this event supposedly took placed his name has been lost. The naturalist James Fisher had earmarked a Buzzard's nest on these cliffs for a scheme he had to hatch a Golden Eagle egg and thereby re-introduce it to Snowdonia. He had even secured a promise from the RAF to fly the egg down from the Duke of Sutherland's estate, unfortunately the idea had to be shelved as it technically broke the law which does not allow the removal of protected eggs from their natural site. Years ago the pool was known as Ffynnon Felen and Bingley made a visit whilst on an ascent of Snowdon in 1798 remarking upon the numerous rare plants found in the cwm. Close by is the remains of a small 'Hone stone' quarry which was worked for a brief period. There is no fish in the pool and most winters sees it frozen for long periods.

## LLYN BACH (Dinas Mawddwy)
*GR 8319*
*Group: Dolgellau*
*Height: 2,492'*
*Area: 1/5 acre*

A very small insignificant pool whose inclusion on the OS map is justified only by its height. It is situated near the summit of Glasgwm, the most westerly peak of the Aran mountains. It is also known as 'Y Fach'. In dry summers the pool disappears leaving only a cracked peaty saucer, at best it is only a foot deep and abviously has no fish. There is another larger pool nearby called Llyn y Fign.

## LLYN BARFOG
*GR 6598*
*Group: Cadair Idris*
*Height 700'*
*Area: 3 acres*

One would almost say that this lake belongs to the 'Fairies' such is the wealth of stories concerning the little folk. It is said that they were to be seen on a fine summer's evening clad in green and accompanied by white hounds as they tended to their cattle by the lakeside. At night the hounds would bark for the souls of those who had not been babtised. Years ago a farmer from Drws y Nant caught one of these cattle and put it in with his herd. He immediately began to prosper and had a great many calves from the cow. Eventually he decided that she was too old for further use and arranged with the butcher to have her slaughtered. As the butcher was about to begin his work his arm was struck lifeless and a small voice was heard calling the cow by name to return to the lake, this she did as well as four generations of her offspring, the farmer's prosperity began to decline and he eventually died a poor man. The lake has also been linked with 'Annwn' the underworld where the mythical Gwyn ap Nudd lives, (see Llyn Gadair). King Arthur also makes an appearance in the lake's folklore when he dragged an 'afanc' (monster) out of the water with his horse and released it into Llyn Cau. His horse's hoof marks can be seen in a rock nearby called 'Craig Carn March Arthur'. Another version of the 'afanc' story is that it was Hu Gadarn's oxen that were responsible for it's removal.

There is no satisfactory explanation of the name Barfog (Bearded), it may refer to the profusion of plant growth on the lake or as Sir John Rhys suggests it may refer to a past owner. Is it a coincidence that Arthur's step-father was called Cynyr Barfog who resided a mere day's walk away? The valley containing the lake is also called 'Happy Valley' and was one of the last Catholic strongholds at the time of their oppression. There are no fish in the lake.

## LLYNNAU BARLWYD
*GR 7148*
*Group: Moelwynion*
*Height: 1450'*
*Area: 10 acres and 5 acres*

Both these lakes lie just over half a mile east of the Crimea Pass beneath Moel Farlwyd. They have both been enlarged as reservoirs, the water having been used to produce electricity for Llechwedd slate quarry. The larger of the two did have a small rocky island but due to the lowering of the lake level is now a peninsula. The lakes, like many of the Blaenau Ffestiniog waters have also been 'managed' by the flourishing Angling club in the town over the years. The first major input was the stocking in 1923 of trout reared in the nearby Barlwyd Hatchery, a further 7,000 were put in the following year. In 1925 a house was built on the lake

*Llynnau Barlwyd*

shore for the use of the local angling society 'Cymdeithas y Cambria' and up to the second world war peat was regularly cut for the fireplace. Remains of the old timber and zink 'house' can still be seen between the two lakes but comprise only of foundation bolts and a piece of the old hearth. The angling lore is strong in Blaenau and each section of shore has been baptised according to various incidents and traditions recorded over the years.

The dam between the two lakes has deteriorated dramatically in the past five years and has some deep, eroded chasms. On the north shore of the top lake a series of turf islands mark the favourite area for casting. The walls of a tiny boathouse also remains on this shore. It is generally considered that the upper lake contains the best fish.

The Crimea Pass itself is only some three hundred feet below the lakes and alongside the Horseshoe Pass in Llangollen is one of the first to close in wintry weather. The name comes from an old tavern the Crimea Arms that stood near the brow, it was closed in 1910 apparently due to rowdiness and was soon pulled down. Its remains can be seen adjacent to the layby on the south side of the road. This was Mrs Thompson's layby where for many years after the war a Mrs Thompson sold tea and snacks on green card tables. Eventually due to increasing rental charges (the council apparently needed the layby) she was forced to discontinue. On the left as you descend into Blaenau a large mound of dark material lies grassless some fifty metres from the road. This is the remains of a series of fires used to burn ex-army boots at the end of the second world war. An old character who had a market stall at Blaenau would buy mountains of war surplus equipment and have the boots patched up for re-sale, those too tatty would go on the Crimea pass bonfire. Grass has so far been reluctant to re-establish itself. One out of a crew of six survived when a Wellington bomber flew into Moel Farlwyd on 21st March 1941. On hearing the Welsh spoken by his rescuers he was convinced he had crashed in Germany and immediately surrended his pistol. The pilot of a Spitfire that crashed in the Cwm on 5th April 1942 was also killed.

The dam was built in 1888, is 30' high and when full contained 123,000 m³/24 million gallons. Following the Gwynedd earthquake in 1985 enough damage was sustained for it to be reduced by 16 feet following a 1986 inspection. This reduced the capacity to below the officially recognised reservoir level. It is owned by the Llechwedd quarry.

Another, smaller reservoir of ½ acre also provided water to the same system. This was known as Llyn Fflacs and was situated a short mile to the South (GR 707470). This had a maximum capacity of 6,000 m³ and featured in the fishing options for the local anglers.

## LLYN BEDOL (see Llyn y Dywarchen)

## LLYN Y BI
*GR 6726*
*Group: Rhinogydd*
*Height: 1,451'*
*Area: 6 acres*
The lake lies just below the col of Rhinog Fach and Y Llethr and

translated, it means Lake of the Magpie although further explanation would be guesswork. The National Trust own the lake and manage the fishing although at the time of writing it is generally believed that there are no fish in the lake due to acid rain affecting many of Wales' upland lakes. The lake was in fact cited as an example of a 'dead' lake in a National Newspaper in 1992, this, thankfully is not so. Although affected the brown trout in the lake still survive and specimens of up to ½lb can be taken. As well as the trout that were abundant it also had some 'arctic char', these rare survivors of the ice age are found only in some nine other Welsh lakes. The quality of its trout were considered to be among the best in Wales one time, having a reddish flesh and often growing up to 3lbs. There is however a splendid river draining Llyn y Bi that eventually joins the Mawddach north of Dolgellau which is full of fish. Afon Camlan has some fine trout to fill its excellent pools as it grows in size some two miles after leaving the lake. One pool called Llyn y Forwyn (GR 694249) was so named after a maid from a nearby farmhouse drowned whilst washing. Another version maintains she was drowned by her unfaithful lover, her ghost sometimes appearing in the form of a bright cloud or wheel of fire. (See Llyn Llywelyn for similiar legend.)

A smaller tarn at (GR 680269) contributes its waters to the Camlan, this one acre pool is sometimes called Llyn Cefn Cam. It has no fish. Lower down the river just above the village of Ganllwyd is a waterfall called Rhaeadr Ddu where on a nearby rock a Thomas Gray elegy has been carved in Latin; an English translation cut into slate was placed at the spot in 1973. The river makes a fine if wet approach to Llyn y Bi and the Rhinog mountain range beyond.

## LLYN BISWAIL
*GR 6447*
*Group: Moelwynion*
*Height: 1,400'*
*Area: 1½ acres*

According to the C19 dictionary of W.O. Pughe the name 'Biswail' meaning dung liquid was a popular term used as a form of insult to the English. There is also a now dried up pool with a similar 'urinal' connotation near Talyllyn (see Llyn y Tri Graeanyn). Llyn y Biswail lies just below the main north east ridge of Cnicht and does become low in dry summer. It has no fish at present but a healthy covering of vegetation and an ample water level in August 1994 does make one wonder whether it could after all sustain some brown trout. Cnicht with its sharp ridge summit is one of the popular 'small' peaks of Snowdonia. The name comes from the old word 'cnight' which was the headpiece of a suit of armour. It was the old sailors who noted the similarity as they sailed up the Glaslyn estuary in the old pre-cob days.

## BLUE LAKE
*GR 6212*
*Height: 390'*
*Group: Cadair Idris*
*Area: ½ acre*

More commonly known as the 'Blue Lagoon', this is a flooded quarry pit that has become very popular as a picnicking site over the last few years. In the sun the water becomes a brilliant blue thus explaining the name and popularity. As with all quarry pits the danger potential for swimmers is immense but is often used for this purpose nevertheless. It was the Golwern Slate Quarry which opened in 1865 and employed a maximum of six men, it closed in 1915. Half a mile east is the farm of Cyfannedd Fawr where Elliw the maid led some of Cromwell's men to their deaths, (see Llyn Cyri).

## LLYN BOCHLWYD
*GR 6559*
*Group: Glyderau*
*Height: 1,805'*
*Area: 10 acres*

Bochlwyd lies in a classic 'hanging valley' glacial cwm. The rocky cliffs of Tryfan, Glyder Fach and Y Gribin ridge close in on it on three sides whilst the stream once it escapes its rocky subterranean exit plunges over 800 feet in three quarters of a mile. The name 'grey cheek' may come from the bare, grey buttresses of Glyder Fach rising almost out of the water. Another explanation comes in the form of a tale told of the days when Welsh princes hunted these rugged slopes. An old grey buck had once been harried almost to exhaustion by the hounds when it reached the edge of a small cliff above the lake and as the hounds closed in for the kill it leapt into the water and made its escape. It would seem from the frequent references over the years that this particular area was favoured by the noblemen for their hunting, arrowheads have been found on the Tryfan slope of the lake. Bochlwyd has also had a good reputation for its fish; W. Williams, Llandegai writing in 1802 remarks that the lake is unsuitable for netting but that the trout were of excellent quality. Gallichan a century later clearly states the fish in Bochlwyd to be superior in quality to those in Idwal. Early writers on angling also remark on the ease in which a fly is lost on its rocky bed, at one time there was a boat here but a series of storms discouraged its final salvage from the lake bed. Lord Penrhyn the owner of the slate quarry at Bethesda and keen angler put some Loch Leven trout in during the last quarter of the nineteenth century. Today the trout are still there but seldom grow to more than half a pound. Fishing rights belong to Ogwen Valley Angling Association but they do not undertake a programme of stocking.

According to Taliesin's triads the 'Graves of the soldiers of Britain' Arthur's knight Bedivere is buried somewhere on Tryfan's flank. At the foot of one of Tryfan's western gullies sweeping down below the lake is a small plaque in memory of a young man killed many years ago whilst climbing. The cliffs of Glyder Fach also contain a number of rockclimbs whilst the vegetated cliffs of Y Gribin among other plants contains the 'Dryas Octopalia' a rare alpine plant found only at a handful of locations in Snowdonia. Cwm Bochlwyd is reached by a steep path from Ogwen that has seen some quite impressive improvement work during the last ten years, this is the Miner's Path which leads eventually to the Copper mines of Snowdon. The lakeside is a favourite mountain campsite for individuals and outdoor centre groups. Above the lake between the two Glyder summits a solitary peak of upthrust pinnacles of rock stands dramatically against the sky, this is Castell y Gwynt (castle of the wind). Legend says that anyone spending the night there will by the morning have either become insane or a great poet. (See also Llynnoedd Du'r Arddu, Tegid, Gadair for similar legends.)

## LLYN BODGYNYDD
*GR 7659*
*Group: Betws-y-coed*
*Height: 822'*
*Area: 14 acres*

Known locally as Bod Mawr as opposed to its smaller neighbour Bod Bach. Both lakes were reservoirs forming part of the water supply system used to turn the 68' wheel of the Pandora lead Mine. The volume of water in both lakes were considerable when they were full. A trial level was cut into the SE bank (GR 761592) but no lead was found. There are some fine brown trout in both lakes as well as eels in the old trial level. In 1970 the dam of Bod Bach was demolished and the sluice control of Bod Mawr opened by Nant Conwy Urban District Council and many fish were swept down to Geirionnydd. The level of the lake is now much lower. In the trees to the East of the lake there are 3-4 large bomb craters caused during the war when a German bomber either shed his load or mistakenly bombed Cowlyd. Whichever the reason old Griffith Pierce, Ty'n Llwyn (GR 766585) who had been in the habit of discharging his shotgun at the bombers during the 1940 campaign had the fright of life; he was convinced they were trying to get him back! The fishing lease is held by Llanrwst Fishing Club.

## LLYN BODLYN
*GR 6423*
*Group: Rhinogydd*
*Height: 1,248'*
*Area: 42 acres*

Bodlyn has supplied Barmouth and District with its water since 1894 when the 12' stone dam was built and recent improvements to the system especially the access road by Welsh Water has ensured that it will continue to do so for some time yet. One effect of the road improvement however is to allow vehicular access to the public and this previously remote lake now has to suffer the indignity of canoeing and other litter potential activities by the multitude. One of only three Welsh lakes to still naturally hold 'arctic char' (see also Cwellyn and Padarn) it also contains excellent trout. Legend has it that following a good deed done by a shepherd to the 'Fairies' they introduced the arctic char to the lake and imparted the knowledge of how to catch them to the shepherd. It is well documented that they are difficult to catch and local belief states that only one person in a hundred has the ability. Pennant (1798) commented on the quality of the char adding that they would take bait. At the time of writing there has been some concern as to whether the numbers of char are diminishing. Some local anglers swear by maggots as being the best bait, but of late the catches have certainly become fewer. Annual netting for milking trout for the hatchery has for the last two years failed to show any Torgoch. Rearing some five hundred feet up from its southern shore is 'Craig Bodlyn', a very steep and loose cliff containing much vegetation. It may have been this vegetation that attracted young William Haynes of Kenilworth to climb them in 1913 where he fell and was killed. A poignant plaque to his memory lies by the lakeside where it is said his mother made an annual pilgrimage for many years until she too passed away. Another memory plaque stands about half a mile south west of Bodlyn on the ancient London to Harlech Coach track as it traverses up out of the valley. This stone was laid by the one time Bishop of Winchester Dr. Melvyn Haigh in memory of his mother who died in 1953; the old track having been her favourite walk. Some 200 yards above the cliffs there is a miniature shepherd's house, it has two rooms and a small wall shelter with barely enough room for 3 people. The roof has caved in but it appears very much an obvious 'house' (GR 647234). At the point where the track crosses the river draining Bodlyn is a very old arched bridge called Pont Scethin which was built to carry the mail coach, a lovely old structure that somehow seems out of place in this remote valley spanning what is normally only a stream. Llyn Bodlyn has a boat house and a rather unsightly wall running all the way around it. An old building just below the lake has been a favourite bivouac for rockclimbers for a number of years. The lake is owned by Cors y Gedol (GR 600231) who also control the fishing rights which can be applied for. It has a maximum capacity of 465,000 m³/93 million gallons and has a maximum depth of 49'.

## LLYN BOWYDD
*GR 7246*
*Group: Moelwynion*
*Height: 1,550'*
*Area: 22 acres*

Lying a mere 250 yards from the designated National Park border designed in 1952 to exclude the slate industry area of Blaenau Ffestiniog Llyn Bowydd nevertheless made its contribution to this industry. It is one of over twenty lakes in this 'industrial island' which was isolated to allow the slate industry to continue its development within a National Park. Before the 13' fine stone dam was built in the 1850's to increase the lake's volume to 68,000 m³/13½ million gallons for the nearby quarry it was a much smaller lake containing some good natural trout. During the building works all the fish perished; restocking however has taken place several times since then and it still contains Brown trout. It is this industry that has also obliterated the original course of the river draining the lake for almost a mile until it re-appears on the southern extremity of Blaenau itself. It then flows relatively uninterrupted through the valley bearing the lake's name to join the Dwyryd. Water is still used by the quarry to lessen the dust created in sawing the slate. In Cwm Bowydd valley itself are the old remains of Llys Dorfil said to be the ancient fort of Derfel who fought alongside king Arthur at the battle of Camlan in 542 AD. Derfel then retired to dedicate his life to God and subsequently founded Llandderfel church near Bala. Back at the lakeside there is a vague legend concerning an old man who knew of the whereabouts of a cave that led from the lake shore down to Dolymoch.

## LLYN BRYN DU
*GR 7444*
*Group: Migneint*
*Height: 1,524'*
*Area: 1 acre*

A small lake with a few satellite pools just above Llynnau'r Gamallt on the Migneint moor. These pools invariably dry up in summer. Ward (1931) maintained that Llyn Bryn Du had also dried up and was no longer there, however, it certainly existed in October 1993. There are no fish in any of these pools including Bryn Du itself. The nature of the peaty ground, its stagnant, coloured waters may be the reason for this. A nearby stream (200 yards west) is aptly called 'Nant Drewi' (stinking stream) and probably refers to the high methane gas content in this upland bog. Curiously enough there is what appears to be a dressed stone bank forming the North Shore, giving a constant depth for some yards.

## LLYN BRYN HALL
*GR 6369*
*Group: Carneddau*
*Height: 845'*
*Area: 2 acres*

This is really an extremely deep flooded quarry pit with steep sides and is a very dangerous location. The quarry was called Bryn Hafod y Wern but is known locally as Bryn Hall from the nearby house which was converted to a Youth Hostel some years ago. Inevitably this sort of pool attracts divers and an unfortunate tragedy occurred some years ago when one failed to surface, he was never found and local belief is that he was sucked down one of the old levels which is slowly draining the pool. The pit has been used as an unofficial dump for many years including old weapons and ammunition from the second world war. The quarry was opened in 1780 by the Pennant family (later Lord Penrhyn) but the overheads were extremely high. Water was an important factor and was actually obtained from a river six miles away (see Llyn Coch), eventually the quarry closed in 1845. It re-opened almost immediately under new ownership but was forced to close in 1884 when the original owners cut off the water supply.

## LLYN BRYN MERLLYN
*GR 7324*
*Height: 700'*
*Group: Trawsfynydd*
*Area: ⅓ acre*

An inconspicuous, shallow, and fishless pool lying hidden in forestry on a hill east of the village of Ganllwyd. It merits mention more for what happened near it than for its own sake. The slopes around the pool were found at the beginning of last century to contain peat with an extremely high content of copper particles. In 1810 the Turf Mine company was formed which burnt the peat and sold the ashes to another company in Swansea for processing! It has been estimated that over £10,000 of copper was sold in this way, the scars of this almost bizzare operation can still be discerned in the area below the lake.

It may be worth mentioning that the remains of the once tallest tree in Wales can also still be seen in the grounds of Dolmelynllyn hall in the village of Ganllwyd (GR 726241).

## BRYN Y FAWNOG
*GR 775594*
*Height: 915'*
*Group: Betws-y-coed*
*Area: ½ acre*

Although originally a small natural lake it has been dridged by a hy-mac and slightly enlarged to supply water to Nant Bwlch yr Haearn Outdoor Centre owned by Clwyd LEA. There are no fish in the lake at the time of writing.

## LLYN BYCHAN
*GR 7559*
*Group: Betws-y-coed*
*Height: 867'*
*Area: 3 acres*

Llyn Bychan lies on the western periphery of the forest north of

*Llyn Bychan*

Betws-y-coed that contains some fifteen lakes. The moorland to its west is a complex upland of rocky steps, heather and bog. High above its north west shore a striking white knoll of Quartz catches the eye. Owned by the forestry commission it has always been well stocked with trout and has remained clean from copper mining pollution which has been the fate of many of the other Betws' lakes. It is one of three lakes that come under the control of Betws-y-coed Anglers' club. There is a low acidy content and Brown trout of over 3lb are frequently caught. It is one of the few true natural lakes and at one time the fishing rights were the preserve of Cobden's Hotel, Capel Curig. At the lower end a recently installed light wooden sluice gate provides some control over the level of the water. Reeds and water lilies cover much of the surface.

## LLYN CAERWYCH
*GR 6435*
*Group: Rhinogydd*
*Height: 1,350'*
*Area: 5 acres*

An ancient trackway led from Harlech in a north easterly direction for about six miles before turning east across what is now a lake to the village of Trawsfynydd. This ancient track is still a public right of way and passes through some beautiful but harsh uplands that form the northern hills of the Rhinogydd, it passes within five hundred yards of Llyn Caerwych. The area is littered with remains of ancient settlements in the form of cairns, mounds and standing stones. There is a circle of stones on Bryn Cader Faner, a hillock overlooking the lake that is thought to have contained a burial cist, the stones are about three to four feet high. Another interesting stone lies besides a branch of the track that leads down to Llandecwyn a few hundred yards north of the lake. It is known as 'Maen ôl Troed yr Ych' (Rock of the oxen's footprint). Tradition claims that a giant removed it from Llyn Caerwych and threw it to this spot, for what reason is not recorded. Careful examination (and liberal imagination) will reveal the footprints of man, bird, sheep and oxen.

Years ago the lake had the reputation for having fair sized trout and the remains of an old boat house lends testimony to this, but more recently the size of the fish are quite small although still numerous. A handful of small pools dot the hollows 200 yards north east of the lake whilst a larger but unnamed pool a 100 yards south of Bryn Cader Faner cairn is also a fairly permanent feature (GR 668351).

## LLYN CAE GORLAN
*GR 6341*
*Height: 410'*
*Group: Moelwynion*
*Area: ½ acre*

This tiny pool situated 300 yards south of the village of Rhyd is an old clay pit dug in the 1890's with the intention of producing bricks on site. The venture however was not a success, the clay was also used for lining the furnace of the foundary in Porthmadog. It is also known as Llyn y Gors Fawr.

## LLYN CASEG FRAITH
*GR 6758*
*Group: Glyderau*
*Height: 2,448'*
*Area: ½ acre*

No more than a large rain pond in reality it is the largest of a dozen pools occupying a slight hollow between Glyder Fach and Foel Goch. Shallow, peaty and exposed it does not contain any fish. It drains into Cwm Tryfan firstly by percolating through the peat before enough water is gathered to trickle down a short but steep gully. The old miner's path to the Snowdon workings passes close by leading from one pile of waymarking cairn to the next; many of these would be the original ones laid down by the miners to find their way in the mist. Higher up the western shoulder of Glyder

*Llyn Caseg Fraith*

Fach a hundred yards from the summit there is an array of rocks that deserve mention. The first pile is called 'The Mushroom garden' and lies to the right of the path leading up from the lake. They are a group of rocks that seem to spring from the ground in a sort of frozen eruption, a spectacle well suited to their name. The second group of rocks are to the left of the path, a jumbled collection of huge slabs crowned by one which overhangs most dramatically for ten feet and is known as the 'Cantilever'. A Moses Griffiths sketch which appears in Pennant's 'Tours of Wales' shows it not to have changed much in two centuries.

## LLYN CAU
*GR 7112*
*Group: Cadair Idris*
*Height: 1,552'*
*Area: 33 acres*

Llyn Cau has been cited as a perfect example of a corrie lake; indeed it is surrounded on three sides by precipitous cliffs with its only exit partially blocked by a terminal moraine that acts as a natural dam to hold the lake in the cwm. On gloomy days in mist it can be a very foreboding place, a fact that has given rise to strange traditional beliefs. It is supposed to be bottomless, fed by an underground river and to be the haunt of fabulous beasts. The 'afanc' dragged from Llyn Barfog either by Arthur or Hu Gadarn was let loose here. Another old belief was that it is the crater of an ancient volcanoe. Without doubt it is deep but this is due to the scouring actions of the glaciers that gouged away at the cwm for many thousands of years. Richard Wilson the artist immortalised the lake in 1765 making extravagant use of his artist's licence to depict the craggy cauldron like appearance of the cwm, the picture can be seen at the Tate Gallery, London. The fishing has always been excellent with many of the early anglers staying at the Ty'n Cornel Hotel, Talyllyn boasting full baskets of the natural brown trout with their characteristic shiny blue sheen. On a sunny day the lake itself takes on a kingfisher blue. Ward (1931) accuses the fish of being fickle risers and best taken late season from the eastern shore.

*Llyn Cau*

Above, on the western skyline the col separating Mynydd Pencoed and Cadair Idris is supposedly Idris' chair. Idris was a giant who lived on the mountain which he used as an observatory to view the stars. There may be some folklore confusion here between two or more legendary characters but there does exist a great many tales, features, and placenames that have been attributed to the giant. The large obvious gully on the left hand side of Mynydd Pencoed cliffs used to have a route first climbed by O.G. Jones during the gully climbing era of the Victorians but a huge rockfall has subsequently obliterated it. On the summit of Cadair Idris which is best reached from Llyn Cau via a steep, worn path called the stone chute leading up from the north western shore of the lake there is a stone hut. This is quite spacious and snug in the winter. A tale is told of an old lady who used to sell tea on the summit many years ago. Her tariffs were exorbitent and were justified by her claims that she and the donkey had to carry the water from the valley below. Some years after her death a spring was found near the summit rocks with a flat rock conveniently hiding it! There is a rare spider found on the mountain which is only found in one other location; Glyder Fawr, it is the 'Micaria Breviuscula'.

A pump storage power station was planned for this area with Llyn Cau designated as the upper storage pool with a tunnel cut through the mountain to the larger lake of Talyllyn in the valley below, a scheme similar to the Dinorwig one but thankfully it was shelved at the planning stage. In fact the Cadair Idris nature reserve was established in 1955 and finally bought by the Nature Conservancy Council in 1976.

### LLYN Y CEFN
*GR 7141*
*Height: 970'*
*Group: Moelwynion*
*Area: 1/3 acre*

A very small pool situated in the middle of the Ffestiniog 9 hole golf club. The pool may be natural as references to it go back many years although it seems to have been enlarged at one time. It has no trout but is occassionally fished for golf balls! Although very shallow (4' maximum) with a a muddy bottom several sharp slates have been encountered by bare feet. A very small quarry once operated just north. There is a rumour that someone drowned himself there many years ago. There are some very small pools on the old quarry site 200 yards north.

## LLYN CELYN
*GR 8540*
*Group: Bala*
*Height: 1,000'*
*Area: 815 acres*

Only now at the time of writing (1994) are the painted slogans 'Cofia Dryweryn' (Remember Tryweryn) on various bridges and prominent walls throughout north and mid Wales beginning to fade, 28 years after its construction. Such was the depth of feeling in the early sixties when this huge reservoir was constructed at the cost of drowning the small village of Capel Celyn. Welsh emotion was stirred as the village houses, fourteen outside the village, the chapel, its cemetery, the school, and a small community were destroyed to supply the city of Liverpool with water. One old farmstead, that of Hafod Fadog was the meeting place of the Quakers in the valley at the time of their persecution, most of them subsequently emigrated to Pennsylvania in 1682. A replacement chapel designed by R.L. Gapper stands on the roadside. There is also a plaque to remember the Quakers. A major campaign was undertaken in the late fifties when plans for the reservoir were first made public that involved many agencies and public figures, surprisingly the Quakers of Liverpool refused to back the campaign. Three young men were convicted of attempting to destroy equipment, one actually used explosives to destroy a generator, an act that was more symbolic than damaging; and although the attempt to save the cwm failed it served to unite future efforts and public awareness against other similar projects. During periods of drought, (1976 and 1984) were examples, parts of the old village re-appear. The stumps of the Yew tree avenue that led down to the chapel make a melancholy sight as does the low walled remains of the chapel itself. Ordinary little objects like the gate hinge or broken crockery are a sad reminder that this was once a living village. The 120 foot dam has been ladnscaped as much as possible with a sloping earth bank leading down to the outflow of the river Tryweryn. The original plans involved building a concrete dam and piping the water 54 miles to Liverpool, it was estimated that by taking the water out of the river at Chester instead up to £13 million was saved. It is interesting to note that plans were afoot in 1892 to build a reservoir in the cwm but were shelved at that time. It would have been along this marshy valley bottom the George Borrow continued his walk following his well documented conversation with the lady of Tai Hirion house in 1854. Between Beeching and the reservoir the old Trawsfynydd to Bala railway was doomed although a large part of the track can still be followed. On the south bank of the lake on the slopes of Mynydd Nodol an old manganese mine was worked between 1890-1913 (GR 863398). Interestingly enough some three hundred yards below the old mine and now under water is the old farmhouse Penbryn Fawr where Augustus John stayed for a while before he rented Nant Ddu, it was one Godfrey Jones from this house who was the wireless operator on the liner 'Montrose' when Dr Crippen the murderer was caught using the wireless for the first time. 'Clwb Genweirio Bala' the Angling club hold the rights and control the stocking at regular intervals. The quality of fishing seems to fluctuate from season to season. Both Brown and Rainbow trout are released. Below the dam due to regular water release as part of the Dee water level regulating scheme some excellent white water sports takes place. A White Water Centre has been established where frequent canoeing competitions are organised up to international level as well as other leisure activities like inflatable rafting for members of the public. This is one of the largest sheets of water in Snowdonia but being a 'young' lake the myths, traditions and beliefs are still very much in the making. The deepest part of the lake is 150'. Before the lake was constructed Salmon would reputedly reach as far as the tiny marshy pool where the River Celyn gathers itself (GR 831445) in their quest for spawning ground. The place was well known by poachers and attempts to safeguard the salmon in so remote a place was difficult and most unfortunate for one game-keeper who was badly beaten up.

## LLYNNAU CERRIG Y MYLLT
*GR 6347*
*Group: Moelwynion*
*Height: 1,500'*
*Area(s): 3 acres and 3 acres*

On a sunny day in late spring these two little tarns nestling as they do in rocky hollows covered in heather make an idyllic setting. The site of ancient settlements they continue to be popular with modern day campers. There is a 10 foot difference in height between the two. The lower one seems to fluctuate in level more than the upper one. When low they both exhibit a coloured collar on the bare rock making their shore, the lower lake having a reddish hue. Black headed gulls frequent the top lake. At the time of Ward's writing (1931) neither contained fish although it is quite likely that there were fish years before. Both lakes have been subsequently stocked and the fishing rights belong to Cymdeithas y Cambria, Blaenau Ffestiniog. Other interests local to the lakes include a plot of land by Berthlwyd bridge below the quarry (GR 628479) called 'clwt powlio' where sabbath games were often played between the parishes of Nanmor and Nangwynen (Nantgwynant), this was a popular custom in the old days and it was usual to set aside a piece of land next to the cemetery for these games to take place. Lifting a heavy stone and rolling it seems to have been one of the games popular here. Bwlch y Battel which is 600 yards east of the top lake will be dealt with in Llyn yr Ogof.

## LLYN CLOGWYN BRITH
*GR 6646*
*Group: Moelwynion*
*Height: 1,500'*
*Area: 1 acre*

Despite the indications given by the up to date OS map that the lake has or is drying up it is very much there. The small dam is in a remarkable state of repair and the cauldron like pool seems quite full. It is one of an impressive series of pools engineered to supply water to the Rhosydd quarry a few hundred feet below. The main reservoir was Cwm Corsiog some fifty feet higher up but Clogwyn Brith also gathered water and piped it around the corner to a gathering pool in the Cwm Corsiog stream before it continued its journey. The pipes can still be seen at intervals hugging the contour and an impressive photogenic valve juts out dramatically just below the dam. A perched block which is almost a rocking stone adds to the scene just above the dam wall. It is believed that there are no fish in this lake.

## LLYN CLYD & NEARBY POOL
*GR 6359*
*Group: Glyderau*
*Height: 2,200'*
*Area: 1 acre and ⅓ acre*

There are in fact two of these tiny tarns nestling just below the very brow of Y Garn, the one is perhaps three times as large as its neighbour fifty yards away. Both pools are drained seperately the steep tumbling streams joining some way before entering Llyn Idwal. It is incredible to think that the larger pool has numerous small trout in it. Many anglers have commented on this over the years and when one considers the size, height and access to the lake it does indeed seem a mystery. They are inferior fish with soft flesh and are hardly ever sought. The lake is technically leased to Ogwen Valley Angling Association but is largely ignored by members. February 1st 1945 saw a 'Martin Marauder' fly into the summit cliffs above the lake killing the five American aircrew instantly. Wreckage littered the slopes down to the lake as well as on the southern side of the mountain. A slate plaque in memory of the crew has been erected by the roadside near Nant Peris.

## LLYN COCH
*GR 5954*
*Group: Wyddfa*
*Height: 1,705'*
*Area: 2½ acres*

One of three lakes of this name in Snowdonia, this shallow pool shares a small cwm due west of Snowdon with two similar sized neighbours. It gets its name from the red shale and slate that has slipped from the rocks above over the years to form the lake's bed. A very prominent gully above the lake called 'Y Gwter Coch' (the Red Gully) seems to be the main chute responsible for this. There are small trout present, a fact I would not have believed had I had not seen them myself. A large number of water snails in the tiny brook connecting it with Llyn Glas higher up may be the key to their survival although a sizeable stream leaving the lake for the larger Cwm Treweirydd below does afford access for determined fish. Llyn Coch has been connected with the Tylwyth Teg where it was said they would come on certain nights of the year to sing and dance. The fairy bride legend has also been told of this lake where the young sheperd watches a group of dancing fairies and falls in love with one of them. He rushes out and seizes her imploring her to marry him, after some lengthy persuasion sometimes taking weeks in some versions she agrees to the marriage but imposes certain conditions. Most versions have these conditions as not to strike her with iron to which he readily agrees. They have many happy and prosperous years together and usually have two children, a boy and a girl. Most versions also emphasise the quality of the cattle that are introduced as a form of dowry. Eventually an accident occurs, this is usually in the form of him throwing a bridle containing an iron buckle and striking her accidently; she immediately vanishes and returns back to the lake with all the cattle. Occasionally in some versions further contact is made but usually the marriage and the story is over. This tale is extremely well documented and will receive several references throughout the book.

## LLYN COCH
*GR 6647*
*Group: Moelwynion*
*Height: 2,047'*
*Area: 1½ acres*

This is one of Wales' twenty or so named lakes lying above the two thousand foot contour, it is one of the group of lakes situated north west of Blaenau Ffestiniog near the summit of Moel Druman. A very prolonged dry summer will see the level of the water fall quite low, this coupled with the height of the lake makes it incapable of sustaining fish. It is the first of four lakes in a watershed harnessed for the use of the Rhosydd quarries but the only one to escape enlargment. A well worn path crossing over from the Gwynant valley to Blaenau passes quite close.

## LLYN COCH
*GR 6469*
*Group: Carneddau*
*Height: 1,105'*
*Area: 1 acre*

A small reservoir constructed to provide water for the Bryn Hafod y Wern slate quarry which was established around 1780. It remains a legacy both to the struggle and ingenuity of the old quarry workers. Due to land shortage water power played an important role both for slate dressing and waste removal at this small quarry. In addition to rainfall in the immediate vicinity an ingenius leat system of over six miles was cut into the mountainside and contoured all the way from the stream draining Ffynnon Caseg, it was known locally as the 'ffos ddyfn'. The quarry was forced to close in 1884 when the water supply was cut off by the Pennant family who owned Penrhyn quarry. The leat is still very much a feature in Cwm Caseg. The slopes around the lake are littered with evidence of ancient civilization with a number of hut circles, homesteads, settlements and cairns liberally marked on the map. Local fishing lore will have visitors believing the lake to be full of huge trout but in reality the brown trout present are pretty average. It is thought that Some Loch Levens were introduced here many years ago. A smaller disused reservoir below this lake is rapidly drying up. The whole area around both lakes and quarry is littered with spent cartridges, mortar bomb fins and other remnants of commando training during World War Two.

The earth dam retaining Llyn Coch is still in very good condition. Midway between the lower pool and the quarry a pipe support stands like a statue with all that remains of the original pipe sticking up like a mast in the air. Nearby, a curious boulder has an aluminium tag bolted on it with the numbers 17 and 20.

## LLYN COEDMAWR
*GR 7858*
*Height: 785'*
*Group: Betws-y-coed*
*Area: ¼ acre*

This is a very small pool which was used at one time as a reservoir to supply Penrallt lead mine with water. It lies near the junction of several forest tracks just north of the old farmhouse Coedmawr. It does not contain fish.

## COEDTY RESERVOIR
*GR 7566*
*Group: Carneddau*
*Height: 900'*
*Area: 12 acres*

Originally a holding reservoir for the waters of Eigiau to be piped down the steep slope to the Aluminium Smelting Works power plant constructed in 1907. By now thousands of youngsters and management training course trainees will be familiar with the spectacular gorge leading up to this lake. As is the case with several Eryri lakes whose exit streams have been piped to by-pass their original course the gorge normally contains only a fraction of its original water volume. This has allowed Outdoor Pursuit instructors to utilize the steep walls and clean deep pools for a variety of problem solving exercises as the group in their charges traverse through the gorge. Unfortunately there are occasions when water is suddenly released from the dam and a dangerous surge comes down the gorge, this proved fatal in 1992 when a young soldier was killed whilst climbing. The gorge saw another tragedy on the second of November 1925. Higher up the valley, another much larger reservoir (Llyn Eigiau) burst and flooded the whole valley below killing seventeen people. There is a slate plaque at the foot of the gorge amidst some huge boulders said to have been carried down by the flood. A twisted and buckled pipe from the 1925 disaster lies a short way below Coedty dam when the dam itself burst under the force of the Eigiau surge. On the southern end of the dam an impressive concrete chute allows the water to sweep down to form the river when the level is high. The dam can be walked over. The original dam had only been built a year before the disaster, it was re-built in 1926 and altered again in 1956. The volume of the lake is 300,000 cubic metres. Although providing electricity exclusively for the Aluminium works when an additional generator was added in 1918 a limited public supply was offered.

It was in fact in 1924 that water from Coedty was first used to run its own power station which was built next to the original one powered from Eigiau. In 1929 both power plants were bought off the Aluminium works by the Power Company. In 1956 the catchment area was extended by 14 square kilometres thereby increasing the efficiency of this 'low head' reservoir. 'Low head' refers to the lower catchment area of Coedty as opposed to the upper one of Cowlyd. The pipes from Coedty drop 845' and are 2 miles in length. The fishing rights are controlled by Dolgarrog Fishing Club and contains brown trout, there is no record of any stocking. It is possible that the Torgoch (Arctic Char) have found a way into the lake from other lakes in the watershed where they are known to exist.

## LLYN CONGLOG
*GR 6747*
*Group: Moelwynion*
*Height: 2,000'*
*Area: 18 acres*

The largest of the Welsh lakes lying over two thousand feet it has a dramatic setting. Along with a few satellite pools it shares an elevated basin on the very lip of an almost thousand foot drop into Cwmorthin. It drains down a rocky gully and as with Llyn Adar has carried much silt into the valley below. A conspicious peninsula juts out from the north shore lending weight to conjecture that the lake was named because of the many corners in it, translated it means 'the angular lake'.

Years ago the lake contained natural Brown Trout whose colours were slightly lighter than fish in neighbouring lakes. During the severe winter of 1947 however the lake froze to such an extent as to kill all the fish. In May 1990 an RAF helicopter was used to carry a fresh stock of young trout to re-inhabit the lake. At the time of writing (1994) it is one of the best early lakes in the districts. The Cambria Angling Society hold the rights.

## LLYN CONGLOG MAWR/CONGLOG BACH
*GR 7538*
*Group: Trawsfynydd*
*Height: 1,400'*
*Area: 8 acres and 2½ acres*

Both these lakes act as gathering pools for the rainwater blessing this wet upland area before it drains down the river Prysor and on to the lake at Trawsfynydd. There is much vegetation covering them both including white and yellow water lilies that give the lakes a picturesque look in summer. There are trout in both lakes which although numerous do not grow above the half pound. Both lakes are silting up quite significantly. A mile downriver the old Arenig gold mine which worked intermittently between 1890 and 1910 produced a total of only 47 ounces. As it burrowed beneath part of the railway viaduct it was eventually bought by the railway in order to make safe the structure. Another quarry close by the lakes provided stone for the construction of the railway viaduct crossing the river Prysor a mile due east. Tram tracks used to convey the stones can still be traced. It has nine arches and is a surprising hundred and twenty feet above the river bed! It was built in 1881 and when nearing completion a large part of it collapsed. Fortunately this happened on a Sunday when there was nobody working there and therefore no casualties. When completed it carried the 'Great Western Railway Co.' trains for 80 years, the final train running on 22 January 1961.

## LLYN CONWY
*GR 7846*
*Group: Migneint*
*Height: 1,488'*
*Area: 100 acres*

Without doubt the major lake of the Migneint mountains. It has always enjoyed an excellent reputation both for game shooting and fishing and has benefitted through generations of good management. Its 'golden era' in this respect was during the last couple of decades of last century and the first few of this one when it was owned and profesionally managed by Lord Penrhyn of Bangor. One of these 'managers' was the colourful character Andrew Foster who came down from Scotland in 1874 to become Lord Penrhyn's Head keeper for this area. Fish were plentiful in those days; one party fishing the lake in June 1880 caught 111 trout in two days whilst a month later 119 were caught in the river between the lake and Ysbyty Ifan in one day! Poaching was rife and many measures were taken to combat the problem. Nailed poles were put to float in the lake tied down with wire and weighted with rocks to prevent 'otterboarding'. Watchers were employed to keep an eye on the lake and even alarm guns were placed from 1880 onwards. The fine for fishing without permission for example was £1:15:6d. for one A. Jones of Blaenau, a hefty fine for those days. Apart from the fishing other 'managerial' inputs at this time included the transplanting of water lily roots from nearby Llyn Serw to Llyn Conwy, milking of eggs from Conwy fish for the hatchery at Llynnau'r Gamallt and the destruction of all the Great Black Backed Gulls at the lake because their diet included grouse eggs. The house near the road was called Llyn Cottage and was used frequently for night fishing by the Penrhyns and their guests. The original name for the house was 'Corlan Muriau Gwynion', (white walled fold). Another cottage (now a ruin) by the South Shore was also used for the same purpose. The boathouse at the northern shore of the lake was struck and partially destroyed by lightning on July 5th 1881 but was subsequently repaired.

Tradition has it that the lake was once owned by the knights of St

John of Jerusalem and their followers up until the dissolution of the monastries in 1536. Pennant in his Tours of Wales refers to three islands in the lake, one being the breeding ground for the Great Black Backed gulls. He then goes on to describe an incident involving a man attempting to swim to the island to procure some eggs, he was mobbed by the gulls and very nearly drowned. Borrow also passed this way in 1854 and mentions the peat diggings in the area close to the lake. Nowadays the fishing has suffered from acid rain and although attempts to neutralize the effect by the slow seepage of lime into the lake has been undertaken it is a remedy that perhaps lasts ten years. It may be of interest that a 70 yard tunnel which comprises of 28 metre deep pools in steps has been completed to help salmon by-pass the Conwy falls. This has cost an estimated £440,000 paid for mostly by the Welsh Office as compensation for any possible damage caused by the A55 Conwy Tunnel construction. It may be that the upper Conwy will as a result become the breeding ground of salmon in the not too distant future. Water from the Conwy is taken to help supply the Conwy Valley including Llanrwst and Betws-y-coed. The maximum depth is 16'. The lake is now owned by the National Trust and managed by Welsh Water. The remains of two old floodgates at (GR 779453) and a marshy depression may indicate the remains of an old hatchery or stewing pool. At the turn of the century a tragedy occurred nearby on the track. Anna Jane of Swch, Penmachno was the housekeeper for Llyn Cottage. One snowy evening, despite advise to the contrary she set off to her place of work: she succumbed to the worsening weather and died within sight of Llyn Cottage. The remains of an old shepherd's hut called Tŷ Bach Wil Ifan can be seen at GR 791462.

## COOKE'S DAM — see Llyn Nantcol

*Llyn Corn Ystwc*

## LLYN CORN YSTWC
*GR 6533*
*Group: Rhinogydd*
*Height: 1,760'*
*Area: 1 acre*

This is a small rock basin pool forming an L shape in an extremely rocky section of the north Rhinogydd. Glacial debris and score marks are abundant everywhere almost as if the glacier had only just melted. Although the pool looked to be without fish when I visited (1991) it was said to be teeming with small ones as recently as 1980. One of the handful of well worn paths connecting Harlech and Trawsfynydd comes over the col of Bwlch Gwilim which is only 300 yards to the south as it passes beneath the steep heather slopes of Clip. Other names used locally are Corn Stwc, Corn Stwy and Corn Ystwe.

## LLYN CORS Y BARCUD

**Group: Migneint**
**Height: 1,500'**
**Area: 1 acre**

## POOL S.E. OF PEN Y FOEL DDU
*GR 7639*
**Group: Migneint**
**Height: 1,710'**
**Area: 1 acre**

The name of the lake literary means Lake of the Hawk's Marsh. It is typical of the small wet area lakes dotting this southern Migneint upland, the lake shore being very spongy and ill defined. There are trout present although it is unlikely that they exist in the neighbouring pool 400 yards west on Pen y Foel Ddu which is slightly higher. The stream draining the two pools (via Cors y Barcud) is called Nant Gefail y Miners which translated means 'Stream of the Miners' tongs' a reference perhaps to the nearby gold mine (see Llynnau Conglog Bach/Mawr). The level of the lake does tend to fluctuate from season to season. The wreck of a small boat lay forlorn at the northern extremity of the lake's fenced boundary in 1994.

## LLYN CORS Y GWAED
*GR 5046*
**Group: Moel Hebog**
**Height: 763'**
**Area: 1 acre**

Cors y Gwaed means 'marsh of blood' and it seems quite likely that this is a reference to a battle or series of skirmishes that took place here many years ago. One elderly local remembers the lake being referred to as Llyn y Gwaed due to the reddish hue in the water.

In the fourth branch of the Mabinogion (a series of very old myths chronicled in the fourteenth century but far older in reality) one of the characters, Pryderi who lived in South Wales comes north to do battle. He came to put right a wrong done to him by Gwydion from Gwynedd. Gwydion had travelled south to trick Pryderi into parting with a herd of special pigs and it was this issue that was to cause the fighting. A great battle was fought with many killed on both sides, eventually terms of sorts were agreed nearby at Dolbenmaen. Further clashes however were to occur and it was finally agreed that Gwydion and Pryderi were to fight in single combat. Pryderi was killed and buried at Maentwrog, a large rounded stone on the corner of the church has been said to be his grave. There are two sites of castle remains south of the lake, one is a mile and a half away and is called 'Castell Gaerran' whilst the other is an obvious motte by the side of the main Caernarfon to Tremadog road at Garndolbenmaen. A smaller pool lies a hundred yards south of Llyn Cors y Gwaed, neither pool contains trout. There is a curious tale of an occurrence witnessed over eighty years ago by a young farm worker returning to Cae Annos one evening. He was using the path through Bwlch y Bedol and was on the mountain slopes beyond when he saw the ghosts of three shepherds standing together holding their crooks near a rock, he was never more glad of reaching his place of work. The 'shepherds' were seen at approximately (GR 513453).

## LLYN CORYN
### GR 7359
### Group: Carneddau
### Height: 1,300'
### Area: ½ acre

One of the smaller named 'lakes' in the National Park it lies a good half mile north east of Capel Curig in a rocky bowl situated on the ridge separating the Crafnant and Cowlyd watersheds. Indeed its elevated position gives a clue to its name. Corun (with an 'u') means the crown or top of the head, an apt description for the lake's site. W.O. Pughe's 1803 dictionary also gives the same explanation for coryn but uses a 'y'. It may therefore be fair to suppose that Llyn y Coryn means the lake at the top of the hill. Although quite close to a very popular walking area this boggy, rocky corner is not often visited and this was highlighted albeit in a slightly morbid way over twenty years ago when a body was discovered in a gully on the ridge. It had lain undiscovered for several months and was that of a walker who had met with an accident whilst descending to Capel Curig. The rocky summit 300 yards south of the lake is Craig y Gigfran (Raven's rock) whilst half a mile north is Clogwyn yr Eryr (Eagle's rock)! There are no fish in Llyn y Coryn at present although Ward (1931) claims there were then. There is what appears to be an artificially cut trench of some 20 yards leading into the pool. At times it becomes very low and almost dries to mud which is when it becomes a danger to sheep. A quarter of a mile south east there is a very boggy area where a gathering of streams occurr (GR 735585) at times this almost becomes a lake and there have been occasions when fish have been seen there. One of the farmers who frequents these craggy tops believes it may be possible for a lake to actually form in the near future.

## LLYN COWLYD
*GR 7262*
*Group: Carneddau*
*Height: 1,200'*
*Area: 269 acres*

At 222 feet Cowlyd is the deepest of Snowdonia's lakes. It provides water for the towns of Conwy and Colwyn Bay, the pipes needed to carry the water being over 40 miles long! A suspension bridge spanning the river Conwy between Stephenson's railway bridge and Telford's old road bridge by the castle once supported the pipes. It was built by T. B. Farrington in 1894 and had a span of 340 feet. These pipes which are below ground should not be confused with the large ones on the surface carrying water to the Dolgarrog power station which is managed by National Power. The 5'10" (1.8m.) diameter pipes carrying the water to the Dolgarrog Power Station are five miles in length. A leat runs roughly east-west at the 1,370' contour on the slopes south of the lake to channel more of the high Carneddau rainfall to maintain Cowlyd's capacity. There is also a thirty foot dam at the northern end of the lake and along with Llyn Eigiau provided water for the original Dolgarrog power station built in 1908, a new power station was constructed in 1925. A young shepherd called Wil Roberts was paid a nominal sum during the war years to check the pipeline in the valley immediately below the dam at regular intervals for bombs or other forms of sabotage by German agents. It was during one of these trips in February 1944 that he came across a crashed

Anson aircraft on the hill between Cowlyd and Eigiau, there were three survivors. A 'pipe' tunnel also connects the two reservoirs.

As would be expected of a lake of this size and age it has a collection of folk stories and traditions. There is supposed to be a water bull living in its depth that comes out with 'fiery horns and hoofs with flames issuing out of its nostrils'. Solitary wanderers have been dragged to their doom, some Irish loughs have similar water bull legends. The Tylwyth Teg have also stamped their presence with some interesting tales. A servant girl from Cowlyd farm once saw a young Tylwyth Teg mother wash three of her children by the lake's shore. Upon investigating the spot after their departure she inadvertently touched the soap and later touched her own eye. A few weeks later while she was at Llanrwst fair she saw some Tylwyth Teg stealing cakes, when she admonished them they asked her through which eye had she seen them. When she replied they touched it and immediately became invisible. A similar tale describes the servant girl hired at the fair and taken to a lucsious palace where she was told to rub some ointment daily into the children's eyes but never her own. One day she rubbed her eye with some ointment still on her finger, the whole place was suddenly transformed to a horrible den of evil demons. She asked if she could leave and permission was granted. Months later she saw her old master at the fair and nodded an acknowledgement. His response was to ask which eye had she used to see him, when told he touched it and vanished. She then lost sight of the eye for good.

Cowlyd even features in the 'Mabinogion' the most ancient of Celtic literature written in the fourteenth century in the 'Red Book of Hergest' but orally dating much further back. In one of the stories Culhwch has to complete a number of tasks for Ysbaddaden to win the hand of his daughter Olwen. One of these tasks is to find the lost Mabon son of Modron. He consults with a series of very old animals in his quest and amongst them is the 'owl of Cwm Cowlyd'. The mountain that dramatically rises from the western shore of the lake is called Pen Llithrig y Wrach (Slippery top of the witch) and would seem likely to have had an appropriate legend at one time; if there ever was one it is now lost but one can, as many writers have, conjecture. Ward (1931) offers a link with the seven foot hag from Cors Mochno that hissed like a snake before vanishing. There is a similar tale told in the Isle of Jura that concerns the 'Hag of Ben More' who captured one Mac Phie of Colonsay. When she was asleep he made his escape, but she awoke and glissaded down the scree after him leaving a feature known as the 'Hag's Slide'. The conspicuous scree running down to Cowlyd may once have had a similar tale.

There is a well worn path along the western shore and at the 'dam' end an extremely useful open building affords shelter in inclement weather. Another version is Caw-lwyd. The dam was built in 1922 and consists of an earthern embankment with a concrete core. A concrete and stone apron protects the dam from wave action which frequently occurs due to the prevailing wind sweeping the length of the lake.

The fishing is managed by Welsh Water from whom free permits may be obtained from either their Glan Conwy depot (☎ 01492 584422) or Bangor (01248 351144). The lake contains brown trout and Arctic Char removed from Llyn Peris; it is a fly fishing only lake.

## LLYN CRAFNANT
*GR 7561*
*Group: Carneddau*
*Height: 602'*
*Area: 52 acres*

The most northerly of the Betws lakes that is accessible by car. The narrow road however from the village of Trefriw in the Conwy valley leads to a cul de sac valley and in summer minor bumps and bottlenecks are frequent occurrences. Llyn Crafnant is set in a beautiful valley and rightly very popular with walkers who can reach the lake from the next valley which contains Llyn Geirionydd. An obelisk stands by the lake exit to commemorate the giving of the lake to supply water for Llanrwst by Richard

*Llyn Crafnant*

James in 1896. The actual dam was built in 1874 and gives the lake a volume of 430,000 cubic metres. It is no longer used to provide domestic water. There has always been excellent fish here with a regular programme of re-stocking that has included Loch Leven, Brown and Rainbow trout. At the time of writing there is a very active rearing and stocking scheme in operation resulting in some magnificent fish being caught. The purist will doubtless pour scorn on hooking fat, semi tame trout that have been hand fed but if it is size that counts the 14lb specimen caught in June 1991 would take some beating. Daily fishing permits can be obtained from Mr & Mrs J. Collins of the Lakeside Cafe (GR 751609), Llys Crafnant, Trefriw (☎ 01492 640818). A severe spring gale in 1994 destroyed one of the rearing cages and all the trout in that particular one made their way into the lake. It was interesting that the summer saw more than the usual number of anglers at Crafnant! Craf is an old Welsh name for garlic which in early spring fills the wooded valley containing the river and thereby offering itself as the obvious explanation for the lake's name. Jehu's 1902 survey showed a maximum depth of 71 feet.

## CRAIGLYN DYFI
*GR 8622*
*Group: Bala*
*Height: 1,905'*
*Area: 15 acres*

A lake whose immediate surroundings are steeped in myth and folklore. Aran Fawddwy the highest mountain south of Snowdon rises from its shore and is only 29 feet short of being a three thousander. The huge summit cairn was built by local people who had on one occasion been led to believe that Cadair Idris was a few feet higher and they set about to raise their own mountain! It certainly is an impressive peak as is the cliff dropping down to the lake, one can practically see the water from the actual summit cone so steep is the rock. It was in these rocks above the lake that a giant once made his home, the deep cleft that contained his cave can be seen quite clearly. He had been blessed with eternal youth provided he bathed each midsummer's morning in Craiglyn Dyfi and never brought a living captor back to his cave. Unfortunately he fell in love with a princess from a castle near Llanymawddwy and brought her to his home. Meanwhile her brother had secured a magic ladder to enable him to reach the cave and so rescue his sister. As he approached the cave entrance the 'powers' decided to act against the giant for breaking one of his conditions and both the giant and the unfortunate brother were hurled to their deaths into the lake below. Sulphur fumes began rising from the depths and a great flood was caused giving name to the foamy brook that drains the lake, (Llaethnant) which means 'milk brook'. Marks high on the walls of a small gorge just below the lake are said to be testimony of this flood. The sulphur fumes apparently still rise at times and are the given reason for the lack of fish in Craiglyn Dyfi. It is said that anyone spending a night alone amongst the rocks on a midsummer night will hear the 'Tylwyth Teg' singing a dirge at dawn. A more recent tale is told of a dispute that arose between a farmer from Nant y Barcud to the east and someone from the Mawddwy valley over the ownership of the col north of the lake. The farmer carried a sod on his back from Nant y Barcud and placed it on the col. When a meeting took place to decide the issue he stood on the sod and swore an oath that he was standing on his own land! This is called Erw y Ddafad Ddu (Acre of the Black sheep.) Another interesting explanation for the name of the river leaving the lake is that the saint 'Decho' turned it into milk for whatever purpose, an old Welsh verse refers to this. Apparently the great prince Maelgwn Gwynedd tried to have St Decho driven out of the valley and among the things he did towards this end he took away his oxen thereby depriving him of his ability to plough the land. Decho then used two wild stags, and when Maelgwn sat on a nearby rock to mock him his ankles became stuck. Decho's well is situated about a mile downstream where his thumb and finger marks can be seen in the rock. Nearby is a flat slab of rock known as Decho's bed.

The rush beds in the area around the lake were renowned in the days of rush candles for providing good quality rushes for this purpose and people would travel long distances to gather them from here. The slight col to the south of the lake is called 'Drws Bach' and has a cairn on it to commemorate one Michael Aspen of RAF St Athan Mountain Rescue Team who was struck by lightning in June 1960. A metal box inside the cairn contains a visitors book. The views from Drws bach are impressive with a 'grass cliff' falling away to the south. There are a handful of small pools some 300 yards west just before the summit ridge of Aran Fawddwy steepens.

## LLYN CRAIG Y GANLLWYD
*GR 7125*
*Group: Rhinogydd*
*Height: 960'*
*Area: 1 acre*
Ward refers to this pool as an un-named tarn and goes on to say that it contains perch. Since 1931 the area around the lake has been heavily afforested and I would be surprised if it still contained any fish. It can be approached by forest road and there is a branch leading directly to the lake, one would imagine for fire fighting purposes. There is a Forestry Visitor Centre about a mile

to the north that includes an exhibition on forestry work, a café and a shop which also acts as a starting point for numerous walks. The tracks have also become quite popular with mountain bikes. I have named the pool from the prominent hill half a mile to the west. Once the forest tracks have been left behind the going becomes very hard if the hill is to be climbed, there is a steep demoralising slope of boulders semi hidden in pillows of heather with the odd section of felled tree stump remains. The pool has very little to recommend.

### LLYN CRAIG Y TÂN and (nearby pools)
*GR 7239*
*Group: Trawsfynydd*
*Height: 1,400'*
*Area: 1 acre*
One of five small pools dotting the hillside above the remains of Braich Ddu slate quarry. The pools would have been utilised for quarry work but little evidence remains. It had the reputation of producing a good slate with an attractive coloured hue. It closed in 1868 although some extraction occurred in the 1980's by a group operating in conjunction with the Llechwedd mine in Blaenau Ffestiniog.

### LLYNNAU CREGENNEN
*GR 6614*
*Group: Cadair Idris*
*Height: 800'*
*Area: 27 acres and 13 acres*
These two lakes lie near the last junction of an old road going from Dolgellau to Tywyn 'the back way'. Two miles after this junction cars have to turn back as the 'Ffordd Ddu' deteriorates into a mountain track. The immediate area around the lakes are owned by the National Trust and have been popular picknicking and fishing sites for the visitor for a number of years. They were known at one time as the 'Arthog lakes' but now thankfully are referred to by their proper titles. The proprietor is Mr E. Lloyd, Ffridd Boedel, Arthog, nr. Fairbourne, (☎ 01341 250426) from whom

fishing permits may be obtained, there is also a water bailiff who issues permits at the lakeside. The main lake contains Brown Trout while the smaller lake has Browns, Rainbows and American Brook Trout. It is also thought that the wild fighting blood of the Loch Levens shows up occasionally. The larger lake can be fished with fly, worm or spinner whilst the smaller lake is fly only. Another variation of Cregennen is Crogenan, a name said to refer to the custom of hanging wrongdoers in the olden days. 'Crogi' meaning hanging in Welsh and a farmhouse bearing the name Crogenen stands about half a mile west of the lakes. It was the custom in days gone by for these executions to take place at crossroads, conspicuous hills and junctions and as this road was a major link between the two towns it seems likely that this lakeside junction may well have been used for such a purpose. Half a mile west are the remains of 'Llys Bradwen' (Bradwen's Court) (GR 651139); it was believed locally that an old court of law did actually stand here and was presided over by a Bradwen who came from Plas y Dre, Dolgellau at intervals to hold trials. This supposedly occurred around 1100. His son Ednowen became a great warrior bearing three silver snakes forming a triangular knot on his coat of arms, his descendants in their turn fought beside Glyndwr. Another local tradition has it that a wooden platformed dwelling house belonging to a chieftain called 'Ednowain ap Bradwen' used to stand here. Nearby the old church of 'Coel' once stood where the Welsh would come to pray and seek signs at times of conflict. Coel Codebog had a daughter called Elen who congratulated the Roman leader Cystenyn when he became Emperor. He asked her what would she have to which she replied a hundred men of arms, this she was granted. With them she went to Canaan where she secured the cross on which Jesus was crucified. It was this Coel who was later to become the subject of the nursery rhyme "Old king Cole was a merry old soul . . . " Both are attractive lakes, the larger of the two being particularly picturesque with its tree clad island. Two other small pools at (GR 663152) and (GR 665146) drain into the larger lake.

## LLYN CROESOR
*GR 6645*
*Group: Moelwynion*
*Height: 1,400'*
*Area: 5 acres*

Croesor is a tiny hamlet at the end of a cul de sac road leading up from Llanfrothen, itself a small village on the back road from Beddgelert to Penrhyndeudraeth. The lake lies at the head of the valley two miles east of the hamlet in an area surrounded by the remains of slate quarries that picked at the western extremities of the great Blaenau veins. The two quarries in this cwm began in the mid decades of the last century and closed following a big decline in the 1930's although some sporadic work took place in the 1950's. Some interesting legacies have been left, a two foot gauge tramway laid in 1864 that traversed the whole valley can still be traced. The longest tunnel in the industry for horse drawn work can be seen at (GR 647446) and the longest inclines certainly in North Wales still look impressive at the head of the cwm. The quarry even had its own hydro electric power station which was opened in 1904 under the influence of the then manager Moses Kellow. Most of its feeder pipes from Llyn Cwm y Foel are still in existence.

Llyn Croesor is a pretty lake held back by a curved twin walled dam filled with clay and peat, typical of the quarry dams. A breach midway along and general disrepair has resulted in the lowering of the lake, possibly to its original level. Another, smaller dam with a sluice chute lies on the north shore. At the upper end of the lake a series of peat hags mark the old high level of the water in its heyday. When the 22 foot dam was full it held 66,000m$^3$/13 million gallons.

The name Croesor carries with it an interesting though fanciful explanation. Elen Lueddog, the Roman leader was marching from the south along Sarn Helen 'Elen's Causeway' to meet up with her son who was marching south from Segontium (Caernarfon). It was while she and her troops were camped by the present day hamlet near a spring named after her that she received news that her son had been assasinated (see Llyn Cwellyn). In her grief she proclaimed that it was indeed a sad hour for her: 'Croes-awr' and that is why the hamlet and lake have been so called! The spring 'Ffynnon Elen' can be seen on the right of the old quarry road leaving the village (GR 629449).

## LLYN CRYCH Y WAEN
*GR 8129*
*Group: Bala*
*Height: 1,352'*
*Area: 2 acres*

Such an extensive upland saucer of open marsh it is difficult to imagine, but this tiny tarn lies in such a place. It is a gathering pool for the water that has percolated through acres of boggy peat before joining other streamlets to form the river Mawddach a name it keeps all the way to the sea. On its descent the Mawddach passes two of the famous Meirioneth gold mines. Gwynfynydd which is still operating was originally started in 1209 when Llywelyn Fawr granted the monks of Cymmer Abbey, Dolgellau permission to mine. However it was not until 1860 that anything serious was done. In 1890 a gold bar weighing over a hundredweight was made for a London exhibition, it was valued at £7,350. Just below Gwynfynydd mine the Mawddach merges with the river Cain where there are two spectacular waterfalls, Pistyll Cain and Rhaeadr Mawddach. The other mine, Bedd y Coediwr is famous for having provided the gold to make the present queen's wedding ring. The gently rising moorland east of the lake leads to another interesting site that has a gold mine, Carn Dochan (GR 850300). Folklore describes two boys playing with a shiny stone when the father of one of them who worked in a gold mine further south recognised it for what it was and thus gold was discovered at Carn Dochan. This was around 1850 and the 'shiny rock' supposedly fetched £500! Water was originally used to clean the ore but so much gold was being lost that some was even found in the Christmas goose's gizzard on the farm downstream. Work ceased in 1870 only to restart in 1889 by the company 'Browns of Chester'; they used air instead of water but the workers' health suffered and some died. Work finished in 1908. Immediately above the mine the ruins of an old castle stand dramatically above the vale, this was an old Welsh C13 fortress. A mile towards the lake there is a bluff of rock called Craig y Llestri (Rock of the Bowls) where gold bowls hidden in haste by some past occupants of the castle were found. There is another traditional belief that a golden harp has been hidden but any attempt to dig for it will result in a thunder and lightning storm.

The ruins of Twrmaen, the most solitary dwelling in Meirioneth lies about a mile to the north of the lake where it was said that during hard times the family would make and sell rush candles at the rate of 126 for a penny! Another variation of the name is Crych ar y Waun, neither version really deviating from its meaning of a wrinkle or curl on the moor. There are no fish here although Ward (1931) claims that there were at one time.

## LLYN CWELLYN
*GR 5654*
*Group: Wyddfa*
*Height: 463'*
*Area: 215 acres*

There isn't another lake in Snowdonia that has as many name variations as Cwellyn. According to one tradition the farmhouse called Cwellyn (east of the lake) was abbreviated from Cawellyn early last century which itself was a derivitive from an earlier name 'Cae uwch y Llyn' (field above the lake). Another variation is Quellyn said to be the name of an ancient family long extinct who lived on the shore. Most historians are agreed that one of the original names was in fact 'Llyn Tadderni' although on Speed's 1611 map it is spelled 'Llyntreuennyn'. Pennant (1781) gives the name as 'Llyn Torlennydd' so called due to the steepness of the banks. Whatever the name it gives food value for interest.

Alongside 'Bodlyn' and 'Padarn' it is the only other lake to still have the Arctic Char as a natural resident, indeed an old chronicle insists that Cwellyn holds the best of these enigmatic fish and this was at a time when it is believed that a few more lakes had them. It is thought that these fish became permanent residents as a result of the ice age entrapping them from their otherwise migratory lifestyles. This effectively forced an evolutionary development to adapt to their new circumstances in order to survive resulting in an almost unique species of fish. A library of folklore has developed around them including one belief that a subterranean tunnel exists between Cwellyn and Padarn of which the 'Torgoch' as they are called in Welsh have exclusive use. Another belief chronicled in 1690 was that they had been introduced to the lake by three churchmen of Rome. Early attempts to restock them in other lakes failed although they could survive for two days in a bucket if left by the side of their own lake! They are traditionally caught at a specific depth below the imposing cliffs of Castell Cidwm above the N.W. shore. It is traditional to fish for them from the shore, a pound and a half specimen was caught in 1990 which is considered to be big. The lake holds some fair sized trout and possibly pike although Ward (1931) prefers the theory that because of a dam that was built downstream in the 1920's the 'pike' are in fact land locked salmon. Daily fishing permits may be obtained from Castell Cidwm Hotel, (☎ 01286 685243) which includes the use of a boat. Bank fishing permits may be obtained from Seiont, Gwyrfai and Llyfni Anglers' Society (tel sec. 01248 670666).

Tylwyth Teg tradition is also strong at Cwellyn. The most famous of Welsh lake tales concerns a young shepherd who happens upon a group of Tylwyth Teg dancing one summer evening. He watches from his hiding place spellbound and one of the young women in particular catches his fancy. He finds himself falling in love with her and on impulse rushes out and catches her imploring her to marry him. She refuses, but following a stubborn campaign of persuasal she eventually relents on the one important condition that he never strikes her with iron. He agrees and with her dowry of quality cattle they have many happy and prosperous years together usually parenting a boy and a girl. One day however whilst trying to catch a lively horse he throws the reins and the iron buckle accidentally strikes her, she and her cattle immediately vanish back to the lake. Along with some two dozen other Welsh lakes and as many variations this tale is told of Cwellyn. An interesting variation here is that the descendants of this marriage were called 'Pellings' from her name 'Penelope' and the family were said to live in the area until the early years of the last century. Another Tylwyth Teg tale is told of a young man from Clogwyn y Gwin farm nearby who, after watching them dance on Cwellyn's shore follows them to their land where he stays for what he believes to be overnight. In fact seven years passes before he returns home to find that his parents are dead, his brothers and sisters fail to recognise him, and his sweetheart has married another, he himself then dies of a broken heart within a week.

The overhanging precipice that dominates the north west shore of the lake is called 'Castell Cidwm' and legend places a fort on its summit although no trace has ever been found of it. The rock is the haunt of rockclimbers who have more than mastered the basics; a photograph taken by Edgar Siddal of the famous Joe Brown ascending a climb called Tramgo has been used as a sign outside his two outdoor gear shops by the legendary Brown. Cidwm may have been a giant in a lost legend or he may have been the Roman Elen Lueddog's son who ambushed his half brother from the rocky summit, (see Llyn Croesor) Elen's son was bringing up the rear of a column of soldiers marching south to meet her when one of the soldiers noticed the assassin taking aim. He shouted a warning "Llech yr ola" — the last man drop, but it was too late. Llech yr ola is the name of a nearby farm. A mound in one of the fields at the lower end of the lake that stood until about a hundred and fifty years ago that was called 'Bedd y. Mab' (son's grave).

Cwellyn is 122 feet deep and has the reputation for sudden squalls, a fact commented upon by many anglers in boats! The 13 foot dam was constructed in 1976, the lake which is also fed by Gadair and Dywarchen provides water for the Caernarfon district and the supply is managed by Welsh Water.

## LLYN CWM BACH
*GR 5641*
*Group: Moel Hebog*
*Height: 580'*
*Area: 5 acres*
This reservoir site is perched in a sort of hanging valley above the

line of cliffs at Tremadog. The cliffs have become important over the last forty years as rockclimbing venues because the rock dries quickly after rain a factor that has tempted climbers from Eryri in inclement weather. Although climbed upon before the war their 'discovery' is popularly attributed to one Dave Thomas, himself a climber who spotted them whilst flying past in a bomber! There have been several major rock falls over the years with some destruction to property although thankfully with no loss of life, some of these incidents making national news. A major buttress was also blown up amidst controversy in 1963 to make it safe.

The house above where the exit stream crosses the Tremadog to Beddgelert road is called Tan yr Allt and it was here that the poet Shelley once lived. It in fact belonged to the engineer W. A. Maddocks who was responsible for building the embankment at Porthmadog thus reclaiming many hundreds of acres of land from the sea. The young poet seemed to take on board obsessions; he busied himself for instance in raising money for the repair of Maddock's embankment which had sustained storm damage soon after it was completed, this despite the fact that he himself was heavily in debt to local tradesmen. Another of his obsessions were shooting injured sheep to put them out of their misery; a combination of such factors made him unpopular with many of the locals. One night he was awakened to find someone in the house who actually shot at him before running away. The next morning he packed his belongings and left, never to return. Since 1984 Tan yr Allt has been a Steiner School. The dam, at least a hundred years old is made of stone with an earthern core, it had a capacity of 29,600 m$^3$/6 million gallons capacity of 1,950 m$^3$. Today although seemingly undamaged the reservoir is empty and no longer supplies the village of Tremadog, the marsh that is left is wadeable with wellingtons. A smaller, secondary dam some 60 yards below the main reservoir is also undamaged but empty of water. The Tannery which was based in Tremadog many years ago also received water from Cwm Bach to turn its water wheel.

## LLYN CWMBYCHAN
*GR 6431*
*Group: Rhinogydd*
*Height: 505'*
*Area: 25 acres*

Cwmbychan is famous as being the starting point for the 'Roman Steps' which is a paved path leading into the mountains (see Llyn Morwynion). Among readers of old Welsh families and military history the farmhouse sharing the lake's name at its upper end is also well known. It is said that the 'Llwyds' could trace their family tree back eight centuries to the time of 'Cynfyn' prince of North Wales and Powys. Among those who came to visit this old established family was Pennant (1781) who partook of some 'coch yr wden' (hung goat) and cheese washed down with strong home brewed ale. The ancient family cup was a dried bull's scrotum! It is claimed that one General Henry Lloyd was of the Cwmbychan lineage. He was regarded as something of a military expert and the author of books on the subject. He is said to have spied for France and the Young Pretender but it is also thought that he may have been a double agent. He was a General in Catherine the Great's army and many of his ideas were held in regard by Napolean. He died peacefully as a Chelsea pensioner in 1783. One of the Llwyds in fact made an attempt to drain the lake, fortunately he only managed to gain a few soggy acres and gave up further efforts. A layer of white mud was revealed however that according to Pennant was of a type used to treat dysentry among other ailments in Germany, it was also considered to be a good fertilizer. Since then the level of the lake has been raised to give a maximum capacity of 30,000 m$^3$/6 million gallons. Another lineage that once held influence in this region was that of Cadwgan at a time when the sword was the main settler of land ownership. There is a legend concerning one of Cadwgan's daughters. Cilwen had fallen in love with one of her father's shepherds, Merwydd Ddu. The match was not encouraged and a lot of pressure was brought to bear on the young couple to end their relationship. One day a storm broke which lasted for three days. At the end Merwydd's body was found between the south shore of the lake and a huge buttress of rock called Carreg y Saeth (arrow rock). Cilwen was heartbroken and she too was later found dead lying on his grave, they were both buried together at Carreg y Saeth. The grave is marked with a cairn and a long slab of rock. Sometimes they are seen walking arm in arm over the waters of the lake. It is also said that strange lights appear over their grave just before a storm. Carreg y Saeth is reputedly named from the old practice of using it as a vantage point when hunting deer. One face of the cliff gives an impressive echoe said to reverbrate four times. The crag is frequented by a small herd of 'feral goats' no doubt the offspring of Pennant's meal! There is a vague legend of a notorious outlaw who was pursued to this cwm through what was then called 'Drws yr Ymlid' (GR 598305) (doorway of pursuit) where he was caught and boiled to death.

The lake shore was used in August 1937 for filming scenes for 'The Drum'. This was a Rudyard Kipling story and the 25 minute footage cost an estimated £1,000,000. It was the first colour film shot by the London Film Productions company.

In addition to the natural Brown Trout a few Salmon and Sea Trout are occasionally caught but the lake is not considered a favourite with local anglers.

### LLYN CWM CORSIOG
*GR 6647*
*Group: Moelwynion*
*Height: 1,720'*
*Area: 7 acres*

Despite being a past reservoir for the Rhosydd slate quarry it is a pretty lake with large cubes of boulders littering its immediate slopes and rushes fringing its shores. The dam is in two parts seperated by a rock bluff which also provides an anchor for the two walls. The larger most easterly half appears to have been constructed in two steps and has an alarming array of steel concrete reinforcing rods sticking up out of the water by the wall, it is 14' high and 172' long. The shorter wall shows signs of recent improvement although a date of 1866 can still be discerned near one end, this is 117' long. There are trout present which are regularly stocked by the Cambrian Society and is considered a good late season lake.

## LLYN CWM DULYN
*GR 4949*
*Group: Moel Hebog*
*Height: 779'*
*Area: 34 acres*

Llyn Cwm Dulyn is the most westerly of Eryri's lakes and it lies on the final mountain slope before the Lleyn peninsula begins. A mile further west is Nebo TV mast an excellent navigation aid at night. It is a reservoir that supplies water for Llanllyfni, Talysarn, Penygroes, Nebo and Nazareth. The dam was constructed in 1901 and a seven inch iron pipe installed to carry the water. In 1971 following a fracture in the pipe which resulted in water lorries having to be used in the receiving districts, local schools closing for three days etc. some significant work was done to the dam. It received further attention in 1973. The dam is now 10 foot high and holds a maximum 25,559 cubic metres/5,030,000 gallons. It is owned by Welsh Water. For a comparatively small lake it has quite a respectable maximum depth of 97'. Dulyn is the Welsh name for Dublin and some say that the lake's name is a distant memory of the time following the Roman departure when Irish settlers did indeed come and live in parts of our country. A local legend tells of a young shepherd who went up to the cwm one day to discover a horde of Irish secretly encamped by the lakeside and preparing to march upon the community in the valley below. He ran down to the fort at Caer Engan to warn his people. The leader decided to dig some ditches and lie in wait for the Irish, this they did and following the ambush the enemy were either slain or fled. The farmhouse Rhos yr Unman (GR 474519) is said to mean the field where nobody is to be seen, a reference to the concealed ambush. Another offer is that the lake was once called Bala-Deulyn, meaning the place where two lakes issue forth or drain. It is however difficult to see where the two lakes would enter into it. It contains fine trout which are regularly stocked. An 1809 survey suggests that the Torgoch (Arctic Char) were present in the lake at the time, there was a suggestion that Cwmdulyn and Llynnau Cwmsilyn were subterraneanly linked thereby allowing the Torgoch to move freely between the lakes, this suggestion has also existed in folklore concerning Cwellyn and the Llanberis lakes. As is often the case with mountain lakes Cwm Dulyn is frequented by seagulls.

## LLYN CWMHOSAN
*GR 6627*
*Group: Rhinogydd*
*Height: 1,100'*
*Area: 1 acre*

This is a very small pool hidden in a sort of sub-cwm on the northern slope of Rhinog Fach above Bwlch Drws Ardudwy. It is also known locally as Llyn Bedol. The Bwlch was a place of some significance in ancient times being the lowest col between the coastal area of Harlech and the inland area of Trawsfynydd and beyond. The ancient path is still used by walkers, its cairn lined course easily followed. At the col itself two huge stones stand guard said to have been raised to commemorate two Britons who fought and died in the campaign against the Romans. If struck with steel they are supposed to reverbrate loudly in a tormented wail. There are also some echoe stones near the col that answer clearly when shouted at. The path west leads to the old farmhouse 'Maes y Garnedd' where the infamous Colonel John Jones was born. It was he who married Oliver Cromwell's sister Catherine and in 1648 was one of the signatories on Charles I death warrant. Although he became the Parliamentary Commissioner for Ireland he was himself executed in 1660 following the Restoration. A local tradition says that if a certain word is shouted from the summit of Rhinog Fawr the word 'celanedd' meaning slaughter will be whispered from the direction of Maes y Garnedd. A rough path leads past the lake from the col to the larger lake (Hywel) higher up. There were fish in Cwmhosan although the present situation is unknown. The stream percolates through a boulder field for the first hundred yards then becomes a tumbling brook that sometimes dries in summer before joining the larger Nantcol stream at the col. The word 'hosan' meaning sock has been offered as the name referring to the shape of the lake, another explanation might be 'arhosfan' meaning waiting place; a sort of gathering hollow for the water before it continues down. A herd of feral goats are often seen on these western slopes of the Rhinogydd.

## LLYNNAU CWMLLAN
*GR 6052*
*Group: Wyddfa*
*Height: 1,650'*
*Area: 1 acre and ¾ acre*

There are two small shallow pools lying just below the summit of the col between yr Aran and Snowdon. They are quarry reservoirs and since the quarry closed they have slowly been drying up. It seems likely that they were constructed just after 1870 when the quarry began to supply water for a dressing mill just below. In 1873 there were fifty men employed there. An old quarry track leads to Rhyd Ddu from the lakes. The actual name of the quarry was Bwlch Cwmllan, although it was known as 'Y Snowdon quarry'. It should not to be confused with its larger neighbour Cwmllan half a mile east which was known as 'Snowdon South'. It seems unlikely that there are any fish in either pool.

The original name was 'Cwm Llein' according to the Aberconwy charter of 1198 which was drawn up to give Aberconwy Abbey extensive land in Eryri by Llywelyn ap Iorwerth. There is a tale told of a midwife from Nant Gwynant who enjoyed an excellent reputation far and wide who was called out one evening by a man on a grey horse. He brought her up over this col and down to Rhyd Ddu then up to Hafod Ruffydd on the slopes beyond. She discharged her duties in a wonderful palace full of merriment and was given a purse full of gold with the instructions not to open it until she arrived home. She dutifully compiled with the request and subsequently lived a happy and prosperous life, she never saw the stranger again. Another story involving the Tylwyth Teg tells of a young shepherd tending his flock high up in Cwmllan one night. He heard crying coming from a rock crevice and saw a girl who was stuck fast. He managed to rescue her and it was then that two old men appeared and gave him a wooden staff. Every year his ewes would produce two healthy lambs and he prospered until one day in a fierce storm he lost his staff whilst crossing a swollen stream. Almost half his flock were also lost in the flood and his good fortune deserted him. It was to Cwmllan that the Prime Minister W. E. Gladstone came at the age of 83 to make a speech on the opening of the Watkin path on September 13th, 1892, there is a slate plaque on the rock commemorating the occasion. An interesting anecdote is related concerning an old farmer from Nant Gwynant who would return home from the market at Caernarfon over this col past the lakes in order to avoid paying the turnpike tolls that existed in those days. Apparently farmer Griffiths' pony knew the way when his master was the worse for wear with drink! It was also through Bwlch Cwmllan that Bingley descended on his final visit to Snowdon and came across a group of children collecting Rowan berries for the making of the drink 'diod graefel', he likened it to perry.

## LLYN CWM NANTCOL — see Llyn Nantcol

## LLYN CWMORTHIN
*GR 6746*
*Group: Moelwynion*
*Height: 1,070'*
*Area: 22 acres*
This quite sizeable lake is surrounded by slate quarries, its water having been harnessed for powering dressing sheds and its depths having been abused by slate waste. Yet it has managed to maintain an excellent reputation for its fish. Indeed it has been one of the main lakes enjoyed and controlled by the thriving 'Cambria' angling society in Blaenau Ffestiniog. Part of the lake is leased from the owner who lives in Llandrindod. The approach from Tanygrisiau ends for cars at a scenic waterfall where the path

*Llyn Cwmorthin*

continues past the relics of the quarrying activity up to the lake. As with other popular 'Blaenau' lakes the development of fishing is well documented and each section of the lake has its own unique name given by anglers over the years. It has enjoyed regular stocking, of brown trout, had a fishing house built in 1931 and two thirds of the lake was actually bought by the society in 1971. It is considered by some to be the best of the Blaenau lakes for night fishing. Sections of the shore are adorned with water lilies.

The old track passing on the west shore is an old drover's route used by drovers bringing their animals over from Llanfrothen and Croesor and some claim that it was used by the Romans centuries before that. An ancient family called Jones lived in the cwm for thirty generations and they had the reputation for living to a very old age, the last one Shon Jones died in 1863 aged a hundred. Many of them were drovers, one known as Shon Cwmorthin regularly walked sheep to Ruthin. Due to the relative inaccessibility a small community of quarry workers grew in the cwm which also boasted two chapels. In 1890 a full gale blew the roofs off the barracks in Rhosydd quarry and the men had to find their way down to the

Cwmorthin barracks many of them half naked. A recent attempt to continue with the quarrying has failed. There are plans afoot (at the time of writing) to construct a tarmac road past the lake all the way up to the Rhosydd quarries with a view to re-developing the quarry if the feasability studies prove favourable.

*Llynnau Cwm Silyn*

### LLYNNAU CWM SILYN (and nearby pool)
*GR 5150*
*Group: Moel Hebog*
*Height: 1,100'*
*Area: 15 acres and 15 acres, the nearby pool being 1 acre*
On a sunny day, viewed from Craig Cwm Silyn above, these lakes are among the most beautiful in Eryri. They both have a good supply of trout. Surprisingly the small pool lying two hundred yards east also contains fish though of an inferior quality. It is estimated that the upper of the two lakes may be two feet higher! They were known at one time as Llyn Torgochiaid' (lake of the arctic char). This no doubt indicates that these fish were once found here also. The results of a survey conducted early last century and published in 1809 by the poet Dafydd Ddu Eryri

indicates these fish to be present here at that time. The saint Peris supposedly gave some to saint Garmon for Llyn Cwellyn who in turn gave some to Gredyw sant who put them here in Cwm Silyn. It was reckoned that they were in fact smaller fish than the ones from the other lakes. Another interesting legend tells of a young fisherman who sat one dusk watching a group of Tylwyth Teg clad in green dancing on the far shore. He himself was spotted by one of them who then ran over and threw some powder into his eyes, they then vanished. Above the lake the impressive cliff has some excellent rock climbs which are much frequented by climbers in the summer months. On 20th November 1942 a Henley Target towing airplane flew straight into the cliff killing the pilot instantly, the wreck was not found until the following day. Local quarrymen helped lower the plane as the RAF mountain rescue service was not formed until 1943.

## LLYN CWM TRWSGL
*GR 5449*
*Group: Moel Hebog*
*Height: 877'*
*Area: 1 acre*

Trwsgl means lethargic or clumsy and only conjecture could offer an explanation for its application to this cwm. A tongue in cheek offer would be the state of one's legs after walking to the lake. (See Llyn Llywelyn for an elaboration.) The actual pool was a quarry reservoir and it lies at the head of the larger Cwm Pennant, a beautiful valley deservedly immortalised by the Welsh poet Eifion Wyn. Above the lake the symmetrical layout of the 'Prince of Wales' slate quarry is an impressive reminder of this past industry. The twelve years up to 1886 when it closed saw the busiest period when 200 men were employed. An old wagon left in an upper level is the only melancholy relic of any interest left at the site. The path passing the lake continues up and over the col to drop into Beddgelert forest. The name of the col is 'Bwlch y Ddwy Elor' (pass of the two biers). When someone who had moved from Beddgelert district to Pennant or vice versa to live and wished to be returned for burial it was the custom to carry the body up to this col where it was met by a group from the other district. Here the changeover took place and as two biers were required it would seem the reason for the naming of the col. The pool is unlikely to contain any fish. The slopes to the south east of the lake rise steadily to form the summit of Moel Hebog which gives one of the best views in Eryri. The old trig point on the top like all others is now disused and has been 'adopted' by the North Wales Police.

## LLYN CWMFFYNNON
*GR 6456*
*Group: Glyderau*
*Height: 1,253'*
*Area: 20 acres*

Up to and during the early years of last century it was known as 'Ffynnon Mymbyr' but once it began being referred to as Cwm Ffynnon Mymbyr it is easy to see why the Mymbyr was dropped, later on the Llyn was added and it became Llyn Cwmyffynnon. In Llywelyn ap Iorwerth's 1198 charter giving land to the abbey at Aberconwy the river leaving the lake was called Mymbyr which is further evidence that the name was once different. Ward (1931) claims that the lake was once much larger but a large part of the retaining bank burst many years ago thus reducing its size. It has always had the reputation for containing numerous small, lean hungry trout having never yielded a really big one. The fishing history is well documented in the famous Pen y Pass log book kept for many years during the hotel's golden era the last half of last century. Among the fishing experts and authors who came to Cwmyffynnon was G. J. Bennet who wrote 'A pedestrian's guide to North Wales' (1837). He was staying at Pen y Gwryd whilst he was having a rod repaired and took the opportunity to fish the lake. He describes it thus . . . "a large oval lake on which the black and sterile rocks which form inaccessible ramparts on one side are reflected in its generally unruffled surface: the scene is wild and desolate such as despair herself would select for her abode." The lake has a few rocky islets and it is near these that the best fishing is to be had. It was not uncommon to hook 2 or 3 at a time when casting, but always small hungry little fish.

On the rough heather and bouldery slopes above the lake Thomas Firbanks in his book 'I bought a mountain' describes a German who was staying at the Pen y Gwryd who fell and broke his leg. He took two days to drag himself down to the hotel where he then put himself to bed! The cwm has some fine examples of perched blocks left to balance precariously by the retreating glacier twelve thousand years ago. The most famous on the skyline between the lake and the road coming up Llanberis pass was a landmark for travellers for hundreds of years, sadly it was toppled by vandals who must have resorted to mechanical means some two decades ago. An artificial leat supplying Pen y Gwryd with water can be seen countouring the slope below the lake.

## LLYN CWMFFYNNON
*GR 5351*
*Group: Moel Hebog*
*Height: 1,320'*
*Area: ½ acre*
This is a very small tarn nestling in a deep cwm below the northern precipice of Mynydd Tal Mignedd. It contains small trout but is not considered worth the walk for fishing. The summit of Tal Mignedd has a curious, unstable looking dry stone tower about twenty feet in height, it was probably a common man's folly, an extravagant cairn.

## LLYN CWM Y FOEL
*GR 6546*
*Group: Moelwynion*
*Height: 1,100'*
*Area: 8 acres*
It was water from this reservoir that was used to generate electricity in the Croesor slate quarry power station that opened in 1904. The manager Moses Kellow has been attributed as being the driving force behind this most innovative quarry development of its time. The ten inch pipes feeding the 30 horsepower plant still lie whole

for the most part in their original bed. The power station building has now been adapted as a centre by the Urdd. The Z shaped dam now has a dramatic V breach and the narrow lake that remains has started drying up slowly. In the late 1940's it was decided to repair the dam but the logistic problems of getting the material to the site almost proved too expensive. The original path 'Llwybr y Mul' which was used for the original construction can still be seen running across the slope above the power station but the use of donkeys for the 1940's repair was impractical. Eventually a helicopter was used but on one of the delivery runs it crashed, fortunately without loss of life. Although now dwindling there are still trout in the lake and a good day's fishing can still be had. On the north east shore the site of 'Llys Dafydd y Foel' is said to be the headquarters of one of Owain Glyndwr's guerrilla leaders during his war with England. At the time when Glyndwr's support was on the wane following two significant defeats this particular group gathered here to re-organise themselves until finally the whole campaign evaporated. The main stream feeding the lake actually comes from another higher un-named pool which strangely enough is larger than its nearest neighbour which has a name, Llyn Terfyn. Cwm y Foel has Brown Trout whose fishing rights are owned by the Cambrian Angling Society of Blaenau Ffestiniog. Not often fished by the serious angler it nevertheless yields good late season trout.

## LLYN CWM Y MYNACH
*GR 6723*
*Group: Rhinogydd*
*Height: 918'*
*Area: 14 acres*

This lake used to be an extremely good lake for trout but of late the effects of acid rain seems to be depleting both the quantity and quality of its fish. It lies at the head of a beautiful valley which, with the aid of forest tracks can be reached by car. For the most part it is a shallow lake and heavily covered in reeds. The remains of a very small slate quarry can be seen 300 yards north whilst an old metal mine leaves a bigger legacy half a mile west on the slopes of

Diffwys. The area is also quite famous for its gold mines, the next valley westwards having the still working Vigra mine. Local guides to the area will recommend the 'new precipice walk' contouring westwards on the slopes of Foel Ispri, this was in fact a tramway that carried zinc blende to a point where an ariel ropeway brought it down to a mill by the side of the afon Cwm Mynach. The best and most dramatic view of the lake is obtained from the summit of Y Ddiffwys, the second highest of the Rhinogydd peaks.

## LLYN CWMYSTRADLLYN
*GR 5644*
*Group: Moel Hebog*
*Height: 642'*
*Area: 98 acres*

Other accepted variations to the name are Cwmystrallyn, Cwm Strallyn and Cwm Ystradlyn. Being relatively shallow and not a mountain lake it has with regular stocking become a popular fishing venue. It has always contained good trout but was very reedy until an earth covered dam was constructed. This gave the lake a maximum depth of 72'. For the past decade or so the lake has been leased by Pwllheli Angling Society and has been regularly stocked with Brown trout. A 4lb specimen was caught in 1991. A 125 Rainbow trout from Trawsfynydd were introduced in May 1994 and then a similar number every fortnight. An attempt to introduce Rainbows around 1980 failed when they all died overnight, American Brook trout which were introduced were also all dead within two years. Loch Levens introduced around 1970 were successful and the strain is still strong. All rod fishing methods are allowed at the time of writing. This was not the first time that the lake water had been utilised by man. In 1855 the Gorseddau quarry (GR 573453) was suddenly transformed from a small workings to a huge enterprise. In hindsight the venture was a failure but as part of the development an impressive three storey dressing mill was built at (GR 550433) called Ynys y Pandy. This was powered with water drawn by leat from the lake, which is still traceable. The mill stayed in operation for less than a decade, it was subsequently used as a village hall. At the Gorseddau quarry site which closed in 1867 there is still much to see including the old tramway which can be traced most of the way to Porthmadog. Another smaller quarry near Dinas Ddu (GR 593453) came up for sale at around the same time and an interesting tale is told of an old tenant of Dinas Ddu which is a house on the side of the Beddgelert — Porthmadog road. At the time when attempts to sell this quarry were being made this old character would do his utmost to put potential buyers off. He eventually received a solicitor's letter from the company.

The fairy bride legend (see Cwellyn) is told here with the following variation. While out in the field harvesting the corn one day the shepherd and his fairy wife are busy stacking the stooks, he throwing them to her while she loaded the cart. Unfortunately still embedded in one sheaf is the reaping hook which strikes her on the arm, she immediately vanishes. Another local belief is that Owain Glyndwr used this cwm at one time for the training and drilling of new recruits. Tradition is very strong in linking Glyndwr to this corner of Eryri (see Hafod y Llyn and Oerddwr). The dam which was built in 1959 was altered in 1976 and 1981 and is 35' high and is controlled by Welsh Water who use it to provide water for districts in the Lleyn Peninsula. The maximum volume is 2,950,000 m³/590 million gallons.

## LLYNNAU'R CŴN (3)
### GR 6648
**Group: Moelwynion**
**Height: 2,080'**
**Area: All three are 1 acre each**

The height given is an average for the three main pools on the continuing north east ridge of Cnicht from Llyn yr Adar as the next mountain summit is reached, Ysgafell Wen. They form an equilateral triangle about a hundred yards apart and have three or four 'satellite' pools nearby. All three are over the two thousand foot contour. The lowest pool did have trout of up to half a pound although the average size was much less. The middle lake also contained fish but was never regarded as being on par with the lowest. The top pool is destitute of fish and is very weedy. Salmon

Smolt were released there in the early 1970's in the hope that they would make their way down the river Edno and one day return but no evidence of success has ever been found and the scheme was never repeated. There are contradictory reports regarding the presence of fish, some locals maintain there are still a few small trout present which are generally too small to bother with whilst others claim the pools have been without fish for over 20 years. Gallichan (1903) claimed that the lower two had some big fish. Today I have been told that the top lake is fishless due to a form of natural poison rising in the water whilst some small trout occur in the others. Due to so many contradictory reports one has to conclude that sometimes there are fish in Llynnau'r Cŵn and sometimes there aren't. This particular area of the Moelwynion can be very tricky to navigate in misty conditions and over the years has become a favourite 'patch' for trainee navigators as experienced outdoor centre staff put them through their paces, in mist each lake can cloak its appearance and Llynnau'r Cŵn have often been mistaken for one another.

## LLYN Y CŴN
*GR 6358*
*Group: Glyderau*
*Height: 2,400'*
*Area: 2½ acres*

One cannot think of Llyn y Cŵn without thinking of the Devil's Kitchen two hundred yards away. Of all the lakes in Eryri this has to have the most dramatic exit for any river. The 'kitchen' is a huge steep cleft in the cliff through which the river first plunges sixty clear feet to explode in a pool which has never seen the sun. It then flows for a further two hundred feet along the floor of this black gully with steep, damp cliffs overhanging on both sides before it emerges to a further series of cascades for a thousand feet down to Llyn Idwal. The name 'Devil's Kitchen' was given to it by the sailors of last century, many of them Liverpudlians working on coasters carrying slate etc. They would have seen the mist rising from the head of Nant Ffrancon as a portent of a storm brewing out of the Devil's Kitchen. There are other tales of druids praying for

*Llyn y Cŵn*

mist to thwart the Roman invasion resulting after three days in a
terrific lightning bolt cleaving the rock into its present form. Mist
then issued forth and continued until the whole of Anglesey was
covered thereby making an invasion difficult. Quite often a tuft of
mist is seen clinging to the cleft giving the appearance of steam
issuing out of a kitchen! Large rocks which have been eroded at the
foot of the falls have also been baptised 'Devil's Bowls'. The
'kitchen' or Twll Du as it's called in Welsh was first climbed in the
severe winter of 1898 by cutting steps in a bank of snow that
reached its top, a borrowed coal hammer was used for the job! The
cliffs are also the home for the rare alpine plant the 'Lloydia
Serotina' or Snowdon Lily first discovered by Edward Llwyd in
1696. Above the cliffs the boggy plateau that contains the lake also
contains rare plants among them the rush 'Juncus Triglumis'
found only here and in Scotland. There are no fish in the lake but it
is thought that there were at one time. Williams, Llandegai (1802)
wrote that there were large trout in it "some time ago". Giraldus
Cambrensis on his 1188 tour of Wales describes the lake as

containing fish with only one eye. He said that trout, eel and perch were without the left eye and swam to one side. Hugh Derfel Hughes writing in 1866 claims the lake was so called (lake of the dogs) because the old Welsh princes regularly hunted in the area. The large plateau nearby is called Rhos Lyn y Cŵn where he says the hunting dogs and hunters would gather.

The path descending to Cwm Idwal from the plateau takes a shallow gully east of the lake, it is one of a series of similar gullies running parallel but the only one that doesn't end abruptly in a cliff. Today it is well marked by cairns but years ago it wasn't and there were instances when people took the wrong gully and fell to their deaths. Showell Styles tells one story involving a walker who set off from Ogwen for a day on the hill. When he arrived at Bochlwyd he met a camper by the lakeside and they started chatting. They both had a similar walking plan for the day so they decided to go together. They climbed Tryfan, Glyder Fach and Glyder Fawr and were descending towards Llyn y Cŵn having enjoyed the day's walk. When they arrived at the lake the walker started towards the safe path down but suddenly realized his companion for the day was holding back saying he couldn't go that way. His queer reluctance to use the path was disturbing but eventually the walker descended on his own and returned to the youth hostel at Ogwen. The next morning a party was setting off to Bochlwyd to retrieve the tent and belongings of a camper killed on the 'kitchen' cliffs two days before. Descriptions tallied and it became apparent to the walker that he had spent a whole day in the company of a ghost!

## CYFFTY RESERVOIR
*GR 7759*
*Height: 830'*
*Group: Betws-y-coed*
*Area: 2¹/₂ acres*

This was another lead mine reservoir, this time to supply water for the Cyffty water wheel. It had some excellent brown trout until one day in the mid to late 1960's. The sluice gate was for some reason left open and the lake was practically drained. Tales are told of the RAF mountain rescue lads who were in the area scooping dozens of fish into buckets and bags following the incident. Today the reservoir is fenced off and the restored water used to supply a few local houses. It had a maximum capacity of 53,280 m$^3$.

## LLYN CYNWCH
*GR 7320*
*Group: Dolgellau*
*Height: 729'*
*Area: 26 acres*

Llyn Cynwch lies in the grounds of one of the oldest estates in Wales — Nannau. A huge serpent terrorised the area around the lake many years ago and those who looked into its eyes were mesmerised and eaten. The lord of Nannau offered a reward of sixty cattle to anyone who could rid the area of it but for many years this was to no avail. Eventually a young shepherd happened upon it when it was sleeping and immediately drove a stake through its eye killing it. The serpent was buried at Carnedd Bedd y Wibr (GR 733204). Another legend tells of one of the servants of Nannau on his way one night to Dol Clochydd (GR 731214) where he was courting the maid. It was dark and he fell into Llyn Cynwch. He sank and continued to sink until as he was losing his breath he saw some light and started feeling very relaxed, he thought that he had drowned and was in heaven. At the bottom of the lake he discovered that he was in another world where there was much music, mirth and dancing. A little man with no hair asked him who he was, where had he come from etc and told him he could stay until he was tired. He stayed three days and then asked the little man if he could leave. The strange little man led him through a door in the rock and along a long corridor until they arrived at a flat rock above their heads. When the rock was moved the young servant found himself clambering out of the fireplace of Dol Clochydd! This is why local tradition has the bottom of the lake as the same height above sea level as the hearth stone of Dol Clochydd. A similar story is told of Llyn Grinwydden near Welshpool.

The lake contains trout and perch. A 3' earth bank dam was constructed in 1968 to provide water to the Dolgellau district, this provides a capacity for 73,000 m$^3$/14½ million gallons and is managed by the owners, Welsh Water. The Dolgellau Angling Association holds the lease, they have also undertaken a lively stocking programme with Brown, Rainbow and American Brook trout being present. A 7½lb Brownie was caught in 1992 and a 13½lb Rainbow was caught in 1991. The PH level is high thus counteracting the acid rain effect; this is thought to be due to a band of limestone running through the watershed. There is also some perch present. The maximum depth is 31'. The dam has recently been refurbished with an elaborate concrete structure. The house of Nannau itself was until recently a hotel but is now closed.

## LLYN CYRI
*GR 6511*
*Group: Cadair Idris*
*Height: 1,150'*
*Area: 4 acres*

Both the lake and its draining stream contain some lively dark trout with yellow bellies typical of peaty water. The land immediately surrounding the lake is very boggy and care is needed for shore fishing. There is a curious feature about half way along the stream to the road. Two parallel walls run alongside for some four hundred yards to join the ancient Ffordd Ddu running from Dolgellau to Tywyn. At one point there is a steep rocky step which makes it unlikely to have been a track although at the lake end the walls open up as if to enclose the cwm, (see also Llyn Irddyn). One could conjecture that this was a corridor through private land on to what may have been common land in the cwm. In the days when the 'ffordd ddu' was the main route between the two towns it is reasonable to suppose that animals would have been turned in to graze possibly by drovers staying overnight. This ancient track has also been suggested as a possible Roman route, artefacts found near the Dolgellau end lend support to this theory. There are some standing stones along the way one of which is found near where the stream joins the road and is called 'carreg y big'. During the Civil War an old character who was something of a bard among other things lived in Cyfannedd Fawr (GR 630122); he was also a staunch royalist. One day three of Cromwell's soldiers called by the house and enquired the way over the mountain. One of the maids who was called Elliw offered to show them part of the way and duly led off. She actually took them along the path east and then led them north to the cliff top overlooking Llyn Cyri. As they looked over the edge and were about to turn to enquire her purpose she slapped the houses' rumps and all three ran forward carrying themselves and their riders to their death.

The Tylwyth Teg or the 'little people of two worlds' are also associated with the lake having been seen standing on the cliff top above calling their cattle by name to return to the lake. As can be seen with other lake legends the theme of Tylwyth Teg cattle is often repeated. Down the southern slopes of Craig y Llyn and into the Dysynni valley the ancient castle of Bere has been re-discovered and tidied up for viewing. This was one of the last strongholds to fall to the armies of Edward the first following the Welsh collapse of 1282. A little further east the ruined cottage of Mary Jones commemorates her epic walk barefoot to Bala over twenty miles of mountain to purchase a bible in 1804. When she arrived Thomas Charles only had his own bible left but was so moved by her plight and dedication he gave it to her. The explanation of the word 'cyri' is elusive and is likely to be a verbal adaptation of another word. The nearest one can find is 'cyrio' which is a form of border or boundary possibly referring to its common land history.

## LLYN CYWION
GR 6360
*Group: Glyderau*
*Height: 2,200'*
*Area: 1/10 acre*
Llyn Cywion is merely a marshy pool, one of three similar sized

ones marked on the map. They serve only to gather the rainwater in this rather soggy cwm for the stream to begin its short journey to the Ogwen 1,500' below. Ward (1931) claims the lake was once much larger but was pessimistic about the possibilities of fish being present, the stagnant quality of the water conjurs up the same pessimism today. The lake is not easy to find in the rushy marsh.

Cywion literally means chicks and local belief claims it to be a reference to the days when the princes of North Wales came to the district to hunt and would find grouse in this particular cwm. The ridge to the north is called Llymllwyd and it too has feature called the 'Mushroom Garden' (see Llyn Caseg Fraith). Further up the ridge towards the summit of Foel Goch according to tradition there used to be a cairn marking the grave of a Druidic priest said to have been buried with a gold chain around his neck.

## LLYN DDUALLT
*GR 6742*
*Height: 600'*
*Group: Moelwynion*
*Area: ⅓ acre*
This is a very small pool enclosed within the spiral formed by the Ffestiniog narrow gauge railway as it endeavours to gain height to reach Blaenau above Llyn Tanygrisiau. The Dduallt spiral was completed in 1971 (the original route of the quarry train track now beneath Llyn Tanygrisiau). Gwilym Deudraeth a noted Welsh poet was stationmaster here during the years preceding the first world war. Dduallt manor (GR 673418) which dates back four centuries reputedly housed Oliver Cromwell during his North Wales civil war campaigns. A colonel Andrew Campbell who restored the manor in 1962 had his own steam engine. He subsidised and supervised much of the blasting required to complete the Dduallt spiral, a plaque to his memory has been mounted on a bench on the platform of his name. The pool becomes low during the summer and is not thought to contain fish. It is also known as Rhoslyn.

## LLYNNAU DIFFWYS
*GR 6546*
*Height: 1,300'*
*Group: Moelwynion*
*Area: 2 acres and 1¾ acre*

Curiously enough the most northerly of the two lakes drains at both ends, one stream running down 220' to Llyn Cwm y Foel and the other percolating through peat for a hundred yards and dropping ten foot to the southern Llyn Diffwys. They are both natural lakes, having escaped tampering by the quarries. There are fish in both lakes but they are not of a quality to attract anglers. The upper lake has a rocky islet except in dry weather when the connecting shallows becomes a causeway.

## LLYN DINAS
*GR 6149*
*Height: 175'*
*Group: Wyddfa*
*Area: 60 acres*

As it is quite a sizeable and relatively shallow lake, (30' maximum), low lying and connected to the sea by a good sized river, sea trout and salmon are both regular visitors. These are caught (if at all) around June whilst the odd early salmon in March may be tempted. A south to south east breeze is reckoned best for the local trout and May and June are the recommended months. There are two boat houses both on the north shore while the remains of an old one can be seen on the south shore near the bottom end. The south shore of the lake is leased to Glaslyn Angling Association, which was formed in 1903, and fishing permits for Mondays to Fridays are available. The lake contains Brown Trout. The point where the river Glaslyn leaves the lake was used for filming a sequence for the film 'Inn of sixth happiness' which starred Ingrid Bergman. At one time in its history the river was known as 'Y Ferlas', a riverside dwelling lower down the valley carries the same name. The small parcel of land enclosed between the river, the road and the lake was known in the old days as 'Y

*Llyn Dinas*

Geirth' and was used to gather stray goats at a time when most farmers kept them as farm animals. A hundred yards down the river, on the left bank there is a mound on top of which a small standing stone is still to be found. This is called 'Bedd Owain y Cawr' (Owain the giant's grave) (GR 611491). Owain was a giant who came to fight another giant living on the obvious rounded hill some three hundred yards across the river which is called Dinas Emrys or Dinas Ffaron (GR 606492). The contest began with stone throwing (many perched blocks on neighbouring hills have been attributed to this contest), this eventually ended in a draw. Mortal combat was next and after a long struggle the fight ended when Owain was crushed by the other giant in his own death throes having being thrown onto a sharp rock by Owain. Edward Llwyd's version was that Owen was a knight who came to fight the giant during the course of which he threw steel balls at him leaving depressions in the ground; these were apparently still visible in the C17. Another version has Owen as Owen Finddu, son of Macsen Wledig who came to drive out a tribe of Irish led by a Brynach who had settled in the valley. The mound is also known as Bryn

Diweddu and Ffedogiad y Gawres (giantess' apron load). This refers to an oft repeated legend concerning a giantess carrying an apron full of stones for the burial of her only son. When she crossed the river her apron strings broke and the stones were left where she dropped them. There was a time when an oxen would be sacrificed on this hillock every May day and a raft symbolically decorated as earth, man and woman was towed the length of the lake to the oxen feast, a huge bonfire would then be lit.

Without doubt however, it is Dinas Emrys that provides the greatest interest in the lake's immediate vicinity. Covered in deciduous trees, even today it is difficult to find a safe route to its summit and even harder to come down, it is as natural a fortress as one could find. It was here from the South of England that the British chieftain Vortigern (Gwrtheyrn) came to seek oblivion following his treacherous deal with the Saxons in 449 AD. He began to build a castle, but after each day's work was done the walls would fall in the night. This went on for some time before eventually his wise men told him to find a fair haired youth who had not been fathered. He was then to sprinkle the boy's blood on the castle site. A young boy called Myrddin Emrys was found with the necessary qualification and taken to the hilltop for the ceremony. Upon being told the reason for his death he told Vortigern that the wise men were mistaken and that he would show him the truth. Myrddin led Vortigern to the base of the hill and into a concealed cave that led deep into the hillside. At the far end there was a lake in which a stone chest contained a red dragon and a white dragon. (These were symbolic representations of the Saxons and the Britons.) He then told him that each night the two dragons awoke and fought each other and it was the tremours from this conflict that undermined the walls. He said that eventually the red dragon (Briton) would kill the white one (Saxon) and it would be then, when the hill stopped shaking that the castle could be built. The truth of Myrddin's words came to be realized and the wise men were subsequently put to death and buried in the field to the west of the hill. Myrddin had established himself as a Seer and his future was secure; Vortigern, unhappily was pursued to the Lleyn peninsula (Nant Gwrtheyrn) and from there to South Wales where he eventually received his just desserts. Myrddin made the castle his own until he too was forced to move, before he left however he hid a hoard of treasure that included the golden throne of Britain somewhere in the rocks in the valley. There are many local legends concerning the circumstances in which this treasure will eventually be found but one overriding fact is that should anyone not destined to find it come too close to its discovery a terrific storm of thunder and lightning will occur! At the summit the remains of an old stone fortress comprising of a square tower base and a few walls are still discernable while in a little hollow near the ruin is the remains of Myrddin's well. Other mythical links and traditions with Dinas Emrys include Arthur who hand-picked an elite squad of soldiers from the field opposite to embark on what was to be his final battle (see Llyn Llydaw). The field is still known as Gwaen y Gwehilion (field of the discarded), so called because the remainder of his men had to stay behind.

A sacred sow was pursued from Cornwall led a merry chase through the country babtising placenames en-route also stopped here to give birth to a wolf cub and an eaglet. There is a rock near the lake called Carreg yr Eryr (Stone of the Eagle) which is identified in the Aberconwy charter 1198 as being on the boundaries of the cantrefi of Aberconwy, Ardudwy and that of Arfon. Giraldus Cambrensis 1188 refers to this as the stone of destiny where an eagle perched on it once a week in expectation of battle between the cantrefi, a sort of Welsh 'valkyrie' perhaps.

## DOLGELLAU DAM
*GR 7316*
*Height: 530'*
*Group: Dolgellau*
*Area: 0 acres*

When full, about 40 years ago the lake was about 5' deep and held back by an earth dam. This burst around 1954 some time after the reservoir became disused. It was actually a holding pool for another smaller pool constructed of concrete in the river at (GR 738166) the feeder pipe going underground for 100 yards and passing under the road. From here a pipe ran down for ½ mile to a small power station which provided electricity for lights in Dolgellau. The remains of the valve house can still be seen where workers sometimes had to stay all night during flood to ensure leaves and other debris didn't block the pipes. Some of the locals still remember crawling along the pipe connecting the reservoirs as youngsters hunting eels in the years following the dam burst. There were trout in the lake when it existed. Today it is barely recognisable as an old reservoir although still marked on the OS map.

## LLYNNAU DIWAUNYDD
*GR 6853*
*Height: 1,207'*
*Group: Moelwynion*
*Area: 19 acres and 13 acres*

These two lakes are tucked away beneath the col seperating Moel Siabod and Mynydd Cribau to the south east. In a dry summer they become seperate lakes but for the most part retain the single characteristic 'hour-glass' shape. There are trout and minnow in both. One explanation offered for the word diwaunydd is 'dywenydd' meaning rejoicing. This is said to stem from the time when a tribe of Irish settlers ruled the Nantgwynant valley, see Llyn Dinas. They came following the departure of the Romans and were said to have stayed 129 years maintaining their seperate identity. Eventually, they were driven out following a battle near the present day PenyGwryd at a place known as Bwlch y Gwyddel (pass of the Irish). They fled over a pass called Bwlch Ehediad (pass of flight) (GR 667524) only to be caught near the lakes and slaughtered; hence the rejoicing! Another legend involving the col immediately above the lakes tells of an afanc (water beast) which lived in a large pool on the river Conwy, (GR 798547). There is some confusion over the word afanc; the modern meaning is a beaver but an older interpretation points to it having been a monster type beast, possibly a crocodile. We know that beavers existed in Wales certainly in the twelvth century but whether folk memory recalls anything more fabulous is open to conjecture. However this afanc in the Conwy was killing sheep and cattle and was generally making a nuisance of itself. It was decided to get rid of it and the plan was to tempt it out of the pool using a young girl with a sweet singing voice. When it had come out and been lulled to sleep the men rushed out of their hiding places and tied it up with chains. It was then dragged over the mountains by two oxen (see Llyn Barfog for similar legend). It was dragged past Llynnau Diwaunydd and up over the col which is called Bwlch Rhiw'r Ychain (col of the oxen's hill). The effort of dragging this huge afanc was so great that one of the oxen's eyes fell out and, coupled with its tears formed a pool on the slopes the other side called Pwll Llygad yr Ych (pool of the oxen's eye). This pool despite its small size never dries and can be seen just north of the col. Fortunately the oxen recovered and the afanc continued its reluctant journey all the way to the very brow of Snowdon where it was turned loose into Llyn Glaslyn.

Other spellings recorded are D'wennydd and Derwennydd. The lake is owned by the Weiss group, London who also own the forestry. There are brown trout and arctic char (whose recently discovered presence was a cause of some surprise). It is thought that they have been there since 1978. There are also a type of non migratory Lake Maine (USA) Salmon which were introduced in 1993 amid a lot of controversy. Diwaunedd once belonged to Cobden's Hotel, Capel Curig.

## LLYN DOLMELYNLLYN
*GR 7223*
*Height: 146'*
*Group: Rhinogydd*
*Area: 1 acre*

A garden ornamental pond that belonged to the Dolmelynllyn estate it was at one time in danger of drying up. Following repairs however it is now used as an acclimatising pool for young trout brought from the Dolgellau hatchery. They are then netted and turned into the rivers. The house, pond and grounds belong to the National Trust. There is no fishing allowed in the pool. Some fish were transferred to Llyn y Frân some years ago when this pool seemed in danger of drying up. In the grounds of the estate 300 yards north of the pool a large stump of a tree is all that remains of what was once the tallest tree in Wales, it was struck by lightning about twenty five years ago.

## DOLWYDDELAN RESERVOIR
*GR 6953*
*Height: 1,150'*
*Group: Moelwynion*
*Area: 3½ acres*

This lake provided water for the village of Dolwyddelan and like many mountain reservoirs utilised a series of leats to increase its water catchment although none actually feed the reservoir direct but rather the stream below. The dam was constructed in 1914. The pool called Merddwr Diwaunydd located some two hundred yards below the Diwaunydd lakes provides one such leat. The square towered castle of Dolwyddelan (GR 722523) is a prominent landmark feature in the valley and as well as having been occupied by Llywelyn Fawr may also have been his birthplace. Maredydd ap Ifan also made the place his home in the fifteenth century during his campaign against the Gwylliaid (Welsh bandits who were notorious in this area). Maredydd established the famous Wynns of Gwydir and reputedly came here to avoid feuding with his own family from the Lleyn. He built a new church at Dolwyddelan and succeeded to a degree in taming what was then quite a wild area. He did however have to be accompanied by twenty archers whenever he visited the church, he died in 1525 leaving twenty six children. The castle was renovated in the nineteenth century by Lord Willoughby de Eresby who made it his home.

Dolwyddelan may be a reference to Elen the Roman leader who seems to have left a legacy of placenames in Gwynedd. Ffynnon Elen in the village is said to have cured paralysis many years ago in the time when well faith healing was popular. An old hand bell dating back to the seventh century is kept in the church.

There are some quite big trout in the lake although they have the reputation of being shy and difficult to catch. The lake is owned by Bryn Goleu farm and has a depth of 11'.

There are also numerous quarry pools and minor reservoirs in the Dolwyddelan valley:

*GR 698512* — Hendre slate quarry which opened about 1840 and closed in 1900 having had a maximum workforce of six. The pool at the site was a small reservoir for the use of the quarry. The slates had a dark, almost black appearance.

*GR 700514* — Coed Mawr slate quarry. This opened around 1870 and was at one time thought to have been powered with water from the stream (Ceunant Ty'n Ddol) to its north west which may have drawn additional water from Parry's Pond, (see Llyn Edno). This too was a small intermittent operation. The pool is a flooded pit.

*GR 721522* — Chwarel Ddu slate quarry which is thought to have been started in the 1790's. It closed in 1860 and was re-opened temporarily in 1920. Recent road improvements have changed the site. The pool is a flooded pit.

*GR 736528* — It is uncertain whether his un-named pool was connected in any way to the old quarry a hundred yards south, it was called Chwarel Sion Jones and was a very small concern possibly operated by one man for the extraction of slate.

*GR 743531* — This was a reservoir used by the Prince Llywelyn slate quarry which opened in 1820, it was one of the largest in the valley employing 74 men in 1882. It closed in 1917. There is very little left of the workings due to forestry and large scale filling in, a flooded pit and some cottages are all that can be seen. The lake is now owned by Elen's Castle hotel who have had the lake stocked since 1988. The fishing which includes Browns, Perch, Tench, Carp and two quite large Rainbow trout which refuse to be caught. The local name for this pool is Ty'n Twc and fishing is exclusive for hotel guests.

## LLYN Y DRUM
*GR 7342*
*Height: 1,200'*
*Group: Moelwynion*
*Area: ³⁄₄ acre*

A very small peaty pool on the summit of a flat hill a quarter of a mile north west of Llyn Morynion on the Migneint moors. It did contain small trout until a generation ago but the effects of the acid rain has killed all fish and associated life. The small slate quarry adjacent to the lake began operation around 1860 with sporadic periods of success, at best twenty men were employed. Half a mile west the Roman route Sarn Helen can be traced while nearby there is evidence of some ancient settlements.

## LLYN Y DRUM BOETH — see Llyn Dubach.

## LLYN DRWS Y COED
*GR 5463*
*Height: 420'*
*Group: Moel Hebog*
*Area: ⅓ acre*

This tiny pool that provided water for the Drws y Coed copper miles was emptied in 1988. Following a compulsory survey under the terms of the Reservoirs Safety Act 1975 it was found to be uneconomically viable to maintain as a reservoir. There had been plans to develop it as a fishing lake. Prior to its emptying it had a capacity of 25,559 $m^3$ having a 10' masonry dam. Of interest in the valley below the dam the tiny chapel of Drws y Coed (GR 542534) was once the scene of some excitement. A huge boulder detached itself from the cliffs above, rolled down and ploughed straight through the chapel and out the other side, it can still be seen on the north side. Local tradition credits a travelling pedlar as the discoverer of copper in the valley. He apparently sat down beside some rocks on his way up the valley. In the warm sunshine he fell asleep only to be awakened by a loud bang from the nearby rocks. Upon investigation by himself and others as to the cause of this minor explosion the copper ore was discovered!

## LLYN DU
*GR 6529*
*Height: 1,800'*
*Group: Rhinogydd*
*Area: 4 acres*

One of several lakes and pools in Eryri incorporating the name 'du' (black). Most are cauldron-like pools of peaty water in the shadow of one or more steep cliffs but this one being a typical col pool doesn't suit its name. Traditionally this lake was formed by the gathering of dew. It contains small ugly trout with large heads that are obviously undernourished. Some believe that Pike are present but this seems unlikely. On the east shore an impressive slab of rock angles into the water reminiscent of Llyn Hywel two miles south. A curious feature is the exit stream which flows for some thirty yards before it disappears into the rocks. A further hundred yards east a small cliff appears with a spring at its foot, there is little doubt that this is the stream re-appearing from where it then flows quite normally. I have not witnessed this phenomena during flood, whether the stream runs above ground after rain effectively by-passing the underground section or not is uncertain. If this were the case a conceivable passage for fish would then just about be possible.

**LLYN DU**
*GR 6534*
*Height: 1,750'*
*Group: Rhinogydd*
*Area: ½ acre*
A small pool found in a rocky upland of jumbled boulders and heathery crags in the north Rhinogydd. It is reputed to contain some small trout, if so I would not envisage it being fished very often. A track passes by the lake shore and ends close by having wound its way up from the shores of Llyn Eiddew Bach, a branch also leads to Llyn y Dywarchen half a mile north. This track would undoubtedly have been connected to the mining operations undertaken on both the eastern and western slopes of Moel Ysgyfarnog for the mineral Manganese in the late Victorian years.

**LLYN DU**
*GR 5642*
*Height: 700'*
*Group: Moel Hebog*
*Area: 4 acres*
Set by the side of one of the small lanes providing an entrance to

Cwmystrallyn north of Tremadog it lies in a shallow basin of marsh. The lake itself is also shallow being largely covered in reeds. The shore is generally boggy, ill-defined and potentially dangerous. The trout caught are up to a pound, seldom more. Some locals insist that Salmons and sea Trout make it as far as the lake to spawn. Because of the surface vegetation which is prolific by the summer it is an early lake. The river also contains fish but they are not the quality they were of yore due to the effects of acid rain. The farmhouse Erwsuran lying half a mile south (GR 561415) was troubled by a ghost many years ago which took the form of a huge black cat not unlike a tiger. The hauntings became so bad that the family had to move out of the house. A well known exorcist was called who went to the house and began his preparations. He laid out a circle of salt with the form of a crucifix inside. He then stood in the circle and called upon the ghost to reveal himself, the door flew open and the ghost appeared slowly walking around the circle snarling. A terrible battle of nerve ensued which the exorcist very nearly lost, eventually the 'cat' was tamed and banished to Llyn Du where it is doomed to remain while there is water in the lake. It is part owned by Cae'r Eithin Tew farm 300 yards north of the lake.

## LLYN DUBACH
*GR 7146*
*Height: 1,350'*
*Group: Moelwynion*
*Area: 7 acres*

There are really two lakes constructed as quarry reservoirs in 1915. The Graig Ddu quarry was initially opened in 1800 as the Manod quarry but developed in 1840 and re-named Graig Ddu. Due to difficulty in obtaining water in sufficient force the main water wheel had to be buried in the ground to gain a few more feet in drop. Dubach's maximum capacity was 30,000 $m^3$. The quarry closed in 1946 having employed 110 men. Quarrying of an open cast nature re-commenced here in the 1980's. Llyn Dubach has featured in the development of fishing in the area, nine years after its construction 2,000 young trout were put in the lake. It is a spring fed lake thus minimising the effect of acid rain. A fishing house belonging to the local angling society 'Cymdeithas y Cambria' was erected there in 1926 and dozens of quarrymen would stay on to fish on a Saturday afternoon after their week's work. Although still leased the fishing is now mediocre.

Three quarry ponds which were part of the leat system for Graig Ddu are at . . . GR 716454, 716455 and 719455, the first two were known as Llynnau dŵr oer (cold water ponds). The largest of the three having had a capacity of 10,800 m$^3$. The most easterly of the three is called Llyn Glâs. Two hundred yards north of Llyn Dubach are two other 'ponds' used for the Diphwys Casson quarry whose perimeters lie some three hundred yards north west of the lake. They are at GR 718463 and 718464 and have a capacity of 2,500 m$^3$ and 4,500 m$^3$ respectively. The larger of the two is called Llyn y Drum Boeth. All seven of these pools are crown property. Llyn Dubach is sub leased by the Cambria from Barry Edge who leases the overall sporting rights.

## LLYN DUBACH (Y BONT)
*GR 7442*
*Height: 1,330'*
*Group: Moelwynion*
*Area: 3 acres*

From the point of view of size this little roadside pool must be one of the best in Eryri for yielding big trout. It is known as Dubach y Bont so as not to be confused with the other Dubach. The 'bont' is a reference to Pont yr Afon Gam, a road junction that did have the highest filling station in Wales five hundred yards south. Cymdeithas Cambria anglers have continually and regularly stocked this lake with young trout from various fisheries. The Society leases the lake from Barry Edge who has held a 20,000 acre lease on the Migneint for the past 20 years from the Crown. It is thought that the high PH reading in the pool which makes rearing fish so easy is due to its spring-fed waters. When the trout have acclimatised to the colder and peatier mountain water they would then be netted and re-stocked at larger lakes nearby whose fishing

*Llyn Dubach y Bont*

rights are owned by the Cambria. Of course not all the fish are caught and there have been occasions when very few were caught which have left them here at Llyn Dubach to grow. This, coupled with its roadside convenience has occasionally produced a huge catch. It is also known because of this use as Llyn Magu (Nursery pool). Two inch trout have been known to grow up to six inches in just one year. Above, to the north a granite quarry is at present still active while three hundred yards east, across the road the Croes y Ddwy Afon slate quarry re-opened in 1987 by workers involved in the Blaenau Ffestiniog strike. The crag 400 yards north of the lake is often used for rockclimbing and abseil practise by a local outdoor pursuit centre. From Pont yr Afon Gam westwards the afon Cynfal stream has cut a magnificent gorge down to Llan Ffestiniog with a dramatic series of waterfalls, David Cox painted the scene which is reminiscent of an alpine pass in 1836.

Its location due west of the road makes it a photogenic lake during the minutes of sunset, its proximity to the road has ensured that this quality has not been wasted by the many passing motorists.

## LLYN DULYN
*GR 6624*
*Height: 1,743'*
*Group: Rhinogydd*
*Area: 5 acres*

Llyn Dulyn lies midway between the two highest peaks of the Rhinog range, Y Llethr to the north and Diffwys to the south are both higher than the Rhinogydd themselves. The Llethr is merely a plateau with one of the many magnificent dry stone walls running along the top with a small cairn placed where the highest point appears to be. A common land grant towards the maintenance of these walls is being used by the Corsygedol estate to fill the many gaps at the time of writing. The lake's main feature is a tiny rock island in the middle which is called 'Yr Allor Goch' (the red altar). It is a curious fact that the other Dulyn in the Carneddau also had an 'allor goch' with a similar belief attached to it. Anyone wetting the stone when it is dry will cause the weather to change before nightfall. Both lakes are also virtually the same height above sea level. Other features of interest in the cwm is the presence of the

*Llyn Dulyn (Rhinogydd)*

scarce 'Narrow Buckler Fern' found by the author there in 1992. Close to the lake's southern shore there is a small shepherd's shelter with perhaps enough room for two (similar to the one on Arennig Fach). There are numerous small trout and it is generally reckoned to be a 'late' lake producing best results in July or August. There are 3-4 tiny but permanent pools on the col above the lake to the east.

## DULYN RESERVOIR
*GR 7066*
*Height: 1,747'*
*Group: Carneddau*
*Area: 33 acres*

A very dark, forbidding and sombre place, little wonder that so many superstitions and beliefs are connected to this dark cwm in the heart of the Carneddau. The lake itself is extremely deep, it reaches a depth of 189' whilst a depth of 55' was recorded by

*Dulyn Reservoir*

Jehu in his 1900 survey a mere three feet away from the shore beneath the cliffs. The cliffs rise five hundred feet sheer from the water. The area around the lake has twenty airplane wrecks and was known during the war as 'the aircraft's graveyard'. The fuselage of a Dakota that struck the cliffs on 12th November 1944 killing the crew instantly can be seen in the waters beneath the rocks. Shepherds in the old days would say that the appearance of a dove near the water heralded the timely demise of a witch whilst one shepherd claimed to have actually seen a woman who had disappeared from the district being dragged into the lake. Those who wandered alone along the lake shore who had led ungodly lives would mysteriously fall in and drown. As with the Dulyn in the Rhinogydd this lake had an 'Allor Goch' (red altar) that was believed to have magical qualities. Although the rock is no longer to be seen because of the dam built to increase the lake's volume it once stood as the furthermost rock of a causeway leading into the lake. In the seventeenth century it was widely believed that anyone bold enough to keep a solitary overnight vigil on this rock would see all who were destined to die over the following twelve months. These nights had to be one of the three special spirit nights, Mayday, Midsummer or Halloween. A further belief (see Dulyn, Rhinogydd) was that if water was splashed on the allor goch in hot weather then it would rain before nightfall.

Dulyn, in conjucntion with Melynllyn supplies Llandudno with its domestic water, the pipes leaving Plas Dulyn processing station and crossing the river Conwy at Talycafn Bridge (GR 786718) built in 1897. The original dam was built in 1881 but altered in 1932, 1947, 1953 and 1963. It is a concrete dam and stands 12'6" high. The fish at Dulyn are reputed on the one hand to have large heads and deformed bodies whilst on the other hand anglers' tales tell of huge fighting trout lurking in it depths. The truth is that the trout in the lake are quite ordinary browns that provide the angler willing to walk with a reasonable chance of some sport. Daybreak or sunset seems favourite. Since the Dinorwig pump storage scheme disrupted the fish at Llyn Peris in Llanberis a large number of its resident Torgoch (arctic char) have been re-located here at Dulyn. All the signs are that this re-location has been a success. The lake which is owned by Welsh Water can be fished with fly by obtaining a free permit from either the Bangor or Glan Conwy office. The full capacity is 418,000 m³/83½ million gallons.

## LLYN DU'R ARDDU
*GR 6055*
*Height: 1,901'*
*Group: Wyddfa*
*Area: 5 acres*

The dark, black lake seems to be the closest translation and very apt it is too nestling as it does beneath one of the biggest, steepest cliff in Eryri.

Clogwyn Du'r Arddu or 'cloggy' has been as integral a part as any cliff in the development of rockclimbing lore in Britain, all the climbing giants of the last three generations have been here where myths, legends and reputations have been created. 'The Black Cliff' by Crew, Soper and Wilson (Kaye and Ward 1971) deals with its history in a highly readable anecdotal form. The lake itself contains semi-starved trout with large, ugly heads. It was this lake that Morton the Snowdon Ranger offered to show George Borrow in 1854 ' . . . black lake where the fishes have monstrous heads and little bodies' . . . Borrow declined.

There is also the fairy bride legend (see Cwellyn) the variation here seems to have been that the marriage had actually been sanctioned by the bride's parents before it eventually ended by the accidental blow by a bridle. Amidst the huge moraine below the lake one stone stands out as being far larger than any other near it, this is Maen Du'r Arddu (GR 597560) and from earliest times has enjoyed magical qualities. Ramsay the geologist estimated its weight as being 5,000 tons! Closer inspection will reveal another smaller stone on top, a stone that Williams Llandegai (1802) claims to have been raised there by hand. Along with half a dozen other such places in Wales it is claimed that if two persons were to spend the night together on the stone then by morning one would have become a great poet while the other would have become insane.

Two travelling minstrels from long ago, Huw Belitta and Huwcyn Sion y Canu decided to try it. It would seem that Huwcyn went on to find some limited success in his chosen field of singing whereas Huw turned to the bottle and faded into obscurity. (See also Llynnoedd Tegid, Bochlwyd, Gadair.) East of the lake the remains of Clogwyn Coch copper mine litter the pathside. This mine opened towards the end of the eighteenth century and stayed in operation on a sporadic basis for some eighty years. It was worked in conjunction with the mines near the upper end on Llyn Peris (GR 598585), the miners working Clogwyn Coch only in the summer months. The copper ore was washed in the lake. Many believe there to be a connecting tunnel between the copper mines on the shore of Llyn Glaslyn (GR 616548) and Clogwyn Coch although this has never been confirmed. A story is told locally of two children who wandered off from Nant Peris and become lost. They were found three days later at Llyn Du'r Arddu, cold, hungry but safe and claim to have walked through a tunnel to get there, this was in 1934! The Cwm Brwynog valley down to Llanberis was once quite populated even having its own chapel built in 1835, Capel Hebron, that can be seen some way below the Snowdon path had a membership of 89 in 1887. Today like many other upland valleys where depopulation has taken its toll the houses are ruinous and empty with the occasional one having being converted into a holiday home. One version of the 'Hairy Man' legend (see Llyn Gwynant) is that he escaped death and came here to live out his life in yet another cave as yet unidentified.

## LLYN DWYTHWCH
*GR 5757*
*Height: 920'*
*Group: Wyddfa*
*Area: 24 acres*

According to old chronicles Llyn Dwythwch was one of three places mentioned as having the best fish. The best sea trout were to be had in the river Glaslyn below Beddgelert, the best 'torgoch' (arctic char) came from Cwellyn whilst the best trout were here in this cwm. A survey in 1352 also mentions it as a contributory factor to the wealth of Dolbadarn manor. Ward (1931) however considered the fish to be soft fleshed. Today the fishing is still attractive, both in the lake and the stream leaving it. Permits for fishing the Wild Brown Trouts contained in the lake can be obtained from the NRA who are the owners. Salmon Smolt were released but it is not known whether the experiment was successful or not. Lower down where it merges with Afon Du'r Arddu a small waterfall merits mention while even further down (GR 578593) the larger and famous Llanberis waterfall is situated. It was from the deep pool at the foot of these falls that the 50' waterwheel still to be seen in the quarry museum drew its water. Two foot diameter pipes carried it almost a mile to the dressing mill, it was replaced in 1952 by a more efficient pelton wheel. Impressive as the falls are, even more impressive perhaps is the fact that it has been descended by canoe, a feat which appeared on television! East of the lake an old rifle range is marked on the map, this has been disused for a number of years. The army took over the empty Hebron chapel (GR 584584) during the war for the storage of amunitions and it was they who created the rifle range, spent cartridges and an old bullet riddled metal plate are all that's left now.

This is another lake with a tradition of having Tylwyth Teg and local children were always told to keep away. On the ridge north of the lake are the remains of ancient settlements in the form of burnt mounds and hut circles while on the ridge south of the lake is what appears to be a 'cist faen' burial remains. It is easy to imagine that a fertile cwm such as this in its location would have been an ideal tribal home for some of our forefathers.

## LLYN DYNIEWYD
*GR 6147*
*Height: 910'*
*Group: Moelwynion*
*Area: ½ acre*

The word dyniewyd is very similar to dyniawed meaning a yearling calf and could well refer to a long forgotten incident that may have occured in this very rocky and complex upland. The pool is on National Trust land which stretches south west as far as the pass of

Aberglaslyn. Less than a mile to the west the ariel ropeway pylons of Cwm Bychan copper mine still stand by the very popular circular walk starting and finishing at Beddgelert. A mile to the east the old disused slate quarries of Berthlwyd and Gerynt lie by the roadside, they were both at their peaks around the 1880's. Below Berthlwyd quarry close to the bridge a plot of land was used in the old days for inter-parish games and recreation. This was common on the sabbath in many districts (see Arddu). Lower down the valley towards the hamlet of Nanmor an old Roman marching station once stood (GR 606461) at Beudy Newydd. At (GR 611461) the old Tŷ Mawr dwelling was converted from the old Capel Nanmor reputedly built in the reign of Henry Tudor as a result of a drowning tragedy in Traeth Bach. At the time Nanmor belonged to the parish of Llanfair, Ardudwy (1 mile south of Harlech) and it was expected that the men of Nanmor would go once a month to Llanfair church; a special door for them had actually been built in the building. One Easter Sunday whilst attempting to cross Traeth Bach the tide came in quicker than expected and the men all drowned. To prevent a re-occurrance Nanmor became part of the parish of Beddgelert and this chapel built. Cae Dafydd, the large house two miles south of the lake was traditionally the dwelling place of Dafydd Nanmor, a noted fifteenth century poet. The lake did contain small trout.

## LLYN DYRNOGYDD
*GR 6948*
*Height: 1,472'*
*Group: Moelwynion*
*Area: 1,465'*
*Area: 4½ acres*

This lake almost overlooks the summit of the Crimea pass (see Barlwyd) at the northern periphery of the Blaenau slate reserves. There are some trial scratchings to the east and north emphasising that no slate could be obtained in this direction. The two mile railway tunnel connecting Blaenau with Dolwyddelan passes beneath the hill and directly below the lake. The name Dyrnogydd is said to derive from the plural of perch and many years ago it is believed that these fish were found here. Ward (1931) wrote that large trout of up to 12lbs in weight lived in the lake, these, he added were caught through 'uncertain means'. Today the effect of the acid rain has ensured that no 12lb trout will be caught at Llyn Dyrnogydd. An old name for the lake was Llyn Danogen. The lake is owned by Mr L. Roberts, Gorddinan, Roman Bridge, Dolwyddelan from whom the lake was leased by the River Board for a short period. Salmon smolts were released in the hope that they would migrate up and down the Lledr.

## LLYN DYWARCHEN
*GR 7642*
*Height: 1,400'*
*Group: Migneint*
*Area: 7 acres*

One of three Eryri lakes bearing the name Dywarchen, this one lies on the Migneint moor and is one of the sources of the river Cynfal that drops so dramatically through the Cynfal gorge south of Ffestiniog. It would be difficult to find a wetter, boggier upland than the Migneint and the water of Dywarchen is characteristically peaty, and not ideal for trout. Before the Penrhyn estate began 'managing' this upland the lake was devoid of fish. It was in fact the autumn of 1888 that trout were first introduced to Dywarchen and it was May 1892 that the first fish was legitimately caught. These fish had come from Gamallt and Conwy lakes, both local and similar in height and makeup to ease the acclimatisation. Trout were later put in from the river Machno. A boat was put at the lake once the fish had taken. Today the acid rain has all but destroyed the fishing. At one time the lake was known locally as a habitat for gulls, notably the 'great black backed' but systematic poisoning in the early 1880's destroyed the colony. This was part of the management programme designed to ensure the safety of grouse eggs.

Half a mile due east of the lake the old boundaries between Caernarfon, Denbigh and Meirioneth met before Clwyd and Gwynedd were formed. A triangular rock marks the spot. A mile and a half south east the summit of Carnedd Iago marked the ancient boundary between three cantrefi where it is said that three cairns formed a triangle guaranteeing sanctuary to anyone standing in the middle, (GR 782406). The name dywarchen in this instance is thought to refer to the island in the lake; dywarchen meaning sod. The lake is Crown property but sporting rights for the last twenty years have been leased to Mr Barry Edge. There are no fish in the lake at the time of writing.

## LLYN DYWARCHEN
*GR 6534*
*Height: 1,800'*
*Group: Rhinogydd*
*Area: 4 acres*

Also known as Llyn y Bedol because of its horseshoe shape. A disused manganese mine has left its spoils on the north shore on the slopes of Foel Penolau and Moel Ysgyfarnog. Foel Penolau is a most interesting hill having a very square cut craggy summit, the rock has eroded and frost shattered to form peculiar triangle

*Llyn y Bedol, also known as Llyn Dywarchen*

shapes, there is an almost perfect sun dial near the top. Another old manganese mine lies south east of the summit said to have been started by the grandfather of the present farmer of Cefnclawdd (GR 678337). It is a very shallow lake almost covered in growth, the only clear corner being the north east shore. In winter sheep wade into the water to eat this vegetation and many have drowned in the process. Dywarchen is not an easy lake to fish but there are quite reasonable trout in it. Another pool at (GR 663351) is marked on the OS map but is nothing more than a rainwater pond on the east ridge of Foel Penolau.

## LLYN DYWARCHEN
*GR 5653*
*Height: 769'*
*Group: Moel Hebog*
*Area: 40 acres*

The third of the Dywarchen trilogy which lies near the village of Rhyd Ddu is steeped in Tylwyth Teg tradition. The oft told tale of the young shepherd marrying the fairy bride he fell in love with

*Llyn Dywarchen, Rhyd Ddu*

whilst watching her dance by the lake shore has a very strong tradition here. Like all the other versions (see Cwellyn) the marriage ended in sadness when he accidentally struck her with iron. There is however, an epilogue at Llyn y Dywarchen which is intertwined with another legend associated with the lake. In 1188 when Giraldus Cambrensis made his tour of Wales securing support for the Crusades he noted that there was a floating island in Llyn y Dywarchen. Five centuries on the famous astronomer Halley actually pushed it out to ascertain that the island he saw which measured 6yds x 4yds did in fact float, this was in 1698. Pennant saw it in 1786 adding that cattle and sheep would sometimes find themselves upon it in the middle of the lake. Bingley described it as being 9yds long with a small willow on it in 1798 and Ward declares it to have existed in 1931. Richard Wilson the artist even painted it placing a man standing with a pole to depict motion. The fairy bride legend (although likely to be younger than the island story) has 'adopted' the floating island as a meeting place for the young couple after the failure of their marriage. He cannot enter the lake and she cannot leave the lake but upon the island they could continue their love. The 'island' however has not been a single entity; it has been a series of different pieces of peaty bank that have broken away and kept afloat by methane gas from the decomposing roots of the vegetation. This process can be witnessed today at the eastern shore along with the numerous willows. Llyn Mynyllod (between Corwen and Bala) and Derwenwater in the Lake District are also examples of floating island lakes. The land immediately south of the lake stretching into what is now Beddgelert forest has long been regarded as belonging to the Tylwyth Teg. A local story is told of the farmer of Drws y Coed farm (GR 565527) catching one of them with a view to marriage, she consented to be his servant if he could guess her name. One day whilst on his way home from Caernarfon market he overheard some Tylwyth Teg discussing their missing kin by the name of Penelope. The story then follows the fairy bride variation adding that their offspring are still living in the Bettws Garmon area, (see Cwellyn for the Penelope link also). Since the 1870's

Llyn Dywarchen drains down to Llyn Gadair and thence to Cwellyn but its original course was through the boggy valley north and down Dyffryn Nantlle. The dam making this alteration can be seen at the northern tip of the lake. However to further confuse the reader this boggy valley used to contain another lake artificially created in 1840 for the use of the copper mines in the Nantlle valley, it was called Bwlch y Moch. Sometime between 1947 and 1959 the dam was breached, and the lake no longer exists. A curious phenomenen occured annually in this shallow lake, a small mound would begin to rise to form a tiny island in the spring of each year, by the summer this would have taken the shape of a large mushroom and by the autumn would have disappeared once again. More methane tricks? At the junction of the two lakes the old ruined cottage of Llwyn y Forwyn still merits a mention on the OS map. This was one of the early homes of Marged uch Ifan the notable athlete, fisherwoman, hunter and wrestler more associated with Llyn Padarn, Llanberis. Another possible birthplace is Hafod Ruffydd in Beddgelert forest.

The lake contains a regular stock of brown trout which are heavily fished every season. A fleet of boats are moored by the south shore dam and boat house whose use are governed by club members. The lake is owned by Seiont, Gwyrfai and Llyfni Angling Association and operate a flyfishing only policy. The prominent rocky island in the lake is a glacial 'Roche moutonee', pointing the direction of the glacier's path twelve thousand years ago. An old wooden fishing house used to grace the south shore until about 1992, a sure sign that fishing has been popular here since before the motor car. The main dam which is over a hundred years old is constructed of dry masonry with clay infill and stands 10 foot high. It holds a maximum of 100,000 cubic metres/20 million gallons.

*Llyn Edno*

## LLYN EDNO
*GR 6649*
*Height: 1,797'*
*Group: Moelwynion*
*Area: 10 acres*

The fish in Edno seem to have always had the reputation of being large but very tempremental. Among the famous to have fished here was Charles Kingsley who had to be content with his picnic of hard boiled eggs and beer. John Henry Cliffe in his 'Angling in North Wales' (1840) on the other hand was fortunate enough to catch six averaging about a pound each. Other anglers describe cannibal trout lurking in its formidable depth who prefer the flesh of their own kind to 'a well assembled fly'. Being quite a high lake it is generally reckoned that July or August is best. Afon Llynedno is also full of hungry brown trout none of which exceed half a pound. The lake has certainly secured for itself the reputation as the haunt of monster fish of 7lbs or more that need a great deal of luck to catch them.

North of the lake a long wet valley called Cwm Edno leads eventually to Dolwyddelan containing a river of the same name. A small pool on a ridge called Yr Arddu lies at (GR 672506) whilst another pool on the river itself at (GR 677522) is known as Parry's pond or Llyn Owen Parry. This merits a mention by Ward as a reasonable venue for trout, there is the remains of a dam which was used by the Coed Mawr slate quarry (GR 700514). The dam was blown up shortly after the quarry closed around 1940 because of the number of sheep that were said to have drowned in the pool. At (GR 669519) the wreck of an Aer Lingus Douglas Dakota lies buried in the peat bog. Twenty three passengers perished on the 10th January 1952, when the plane crashed, some of the bodies still lie unrecovered. A commemorative plaque has been placed on a nearby bluff of rock. The rocky slopes of Moel Meirch 400 yards north of Edno inevitably sports several small pools, a cluster of three have been marked on the OS map at (GR 659503). Interestingly enough a public footpath is also marked running east from the road at (GR 636492) to end abruptly at a point between these pools and Llyn Edno. One could surmise that a dwelling may have once existed there or that the path's purpose is to reach the old district border which also passes through at that point.

## LLYN EIDDEW BACH
*GR 6434*
*Height: 1,250'*
*Group: Rhinogydd*
*Area: 2½ acres*

Llyn Eiddew Bach lies by the side of one of the ancient tracks crossing the Rhinogydd over to Trawsfynydd. The shallow upland valley containing this particular track has a lot of evidence of ancient settlements (see Caerwych). The remains of one pocket are to be seen on the north west shore whilst an ancient cairn lies a further two hundred yards away. An old boathouse or sheep washing fold enters the water on the south east shore. The lake had good quality natural brown trout which was fished for generations but the size gradually became smaller. From the mid 1980's it was considered a 'dead' lake. A recent PH test however revealed it to be at a good level and it has recently been re-stocked by

Talsarnau and Artro District Angling Association which holds the lease. Weekly tickets are available. The lake is owned by Lord Harlech. A more recent track passes on the south side which links Eiddew Mawr, Dywarchen and Llyn Du lakes, this was constructed by the manganese mining enterprise in this area that ceased some seventy years ago.

## LLYN EIDDEW MAWR
*GR 6433*
*Height: 1,150'*
*Group: Rhinogydd*
*Area: 22 acres*

A much larger lake than its namesake nearby and some hundred feet lower, the lakes are not directly connected by stream. The trout, although numerous are not large, neither are they regarded free risers. There is a small pier type structure on its western shore, a legacy from its reservoir days. Fish are also plentiful in the brooks around the two lakes and are all regarded as good quality trout. As with its smaller neighbour it is leased by the Talsarnau and Artro District Angling Association who stock it with brown trout, the fish are considered to be slightly inferior to those at 'Fach'. It belongs to Welsh Water who constructed a small dam in 1965 to increase the volume. It is no longer used as a reservoir and the small dam/weir has been demolished, it has a depth of 42'. Numerous very small satellite pools dot the rocky hollows immediately west of the lake for a distance of some 500 yards. The word 'eiddew' means ivy presumably a reference to the abundance of this plant in the lakes' proximity at one time; this is pure conjecture.

## LLYN EIGIAU
*GR 7265*
*Height: 1,219'*
*Group: Carneddau*
*Area: 120 acres*

A slate plaque at the foot of Dolgarrog gorge (GR 768677) commemorates a disaster which happened on the second of November 1925 when the dam at Llyn Eigiau burst following 26

*The site of the 1925 Eigiau Dam Burst*

inches of rain in just five days. Seventeen lives were lost when water swept down the valley and destroyed part of the village of Dolgarrog. There were tales of unlikely survival too, one old lady was apparently swept down the Conwy clinging to an item of furniture and was subsequently rescued on her way to the sea! Among the victims was an old tramp who lived rough in the valley, his body was never found. The dam had been hurriedly built to supply water for Dolgarrog Aluminium works power station in conjunction with Cowlyd in 1911. The original engineer pulled out due to this corner cutting; it was said that complete bags of cement for example were merely thrown together into the structure and indeed pieces of neat cement can still be found at the site of the tragedy. The dam is nearly 35 foot high. Having been destroyed a new power station was built at the site of the present day aluminium works in 1925. There is a tunnel drawing water from the stream below Dulyn, another tunnel then runs to Cowlyd whilst a series of leats also channel water to Coedty reservoir as part of the overall system. The tunnels were constructed soon after

112

1929. The huge pipes leaving Cowlyd join the pipes leaving Coedty just below the dam at (GR 765672). Before the tragedy, Eigiau's surface area would have been half as much again. The retaining wall which is a structure of three quarters of a mile in length still looks very impressive but redundant whilst the sight of the actual breach always manages to provoke the imagination.

According to Edward Llwyd (1680) Eigiau in this instance refers to the shoals of fish that lived here. On Speed's 1611 map it is down as 'Llynyga'. The track to the lake continues up the valley past the disused Cedryn slate quarry (GR 719636) and up to the slightly larger quarry of Cwm Eigiau (GR 701636). Between the river and lower buildings an excellent example of a Carreg Tannau can be seen. These were usually flat rocks drilled at intervals, the holes joined by grooves. They would then be filled with explosive powder and the firework display was used by the quarrymen to commemorate any occasion of note. A smaller stone lies by its side.

In 1987 Eigiau allowed its capacity to drop below 25,000 m$^3$/5 million gallons thereby not requiring to adhere to the stringent criteria of the 1975 act. Eigiau is owned by National Grid who lease it to the Dolgarrog Fishing Club. This is a small club who pride themselves that Eigiau has never needed stocking.

Although unsubstantiated it is thought that the Torgoch (Arctic Char) released into Dulyn when Llyn Peris was emptied have found their way into Eigiau. As they are definitely in Cowlyd and Melynllyn which are also part of the system then this is quite possible. Are the old migratory instincts of the Torgoch, forced dormant for 12,000 years being re-awakened? Cedryn opened very early on in the nineteenth century and closed in 1880 whilst Cwm Eigiau opened in the 1840's and closed in 1900. Both quarries were connected to a shipping point in Dolgarrog by a five mile tramway built in the 1860's. Eigiau has a comparatively shallow depth of 32' which must also have been the depth before the dam was built. The obvious col visible from the lake at (GR 710626) is called Bwlch y Tri Marchog (pass of the three riders). It is popularly thought that this name comes from the time when three representatives from three neighbouring parishes met annually to discuss any problems that needed attention. The old 'cantref' boundary between Arfon, Nantconwy and Arllechwedd was actually two miles south west of the col. The col is also mentioned in the Aberconwy charter of 1198 as 'Bwlcherylvarthant'. Another explanation for this somewhat romantic col is that the name refers to three prominent rocks seen on the skyline nearby. One of Eigiau's claims is that is is one of the last lake in Wales to still have its own natural, brown trout. It has never been restocked and trout up to a pound are occasionally taken.

## LLYN ELSI
*GR 7855*
*Height: 732'*
*Group: Betws-y-coed*
*Area: 26 acres*

Before the lake was enlarged as a reservoir there were two lesser lakes in what must have been quite a marshy hollow, they were Llyn Rhisgog and Llyn Enoc. Enoc was supposedly a Welsh chieftain who had his hand cut off when he was caught the wrong side of Offa's Dyke. Edward Llwyd refers to the three lakes in 1698. Walter Crane the artist famous for his watercolours and illustrations in Kate Greenway's books painted 'Llyn Elsie' in 1871. It was between 1912 and 1914 that Lord Ancaster allowed the building of the 20' dam to supply Betws-y-coed with its water, this has given the lake a mere depth of 31'. A monument commemorating his generosity has been erected at (GR 784556). Water from Elsi is also drawn for the Conwy Valley and Llanrwst district. Today the surrounding area is covered with conifers and has become a popular arena for many outdoor sports that include orienteering and mountain biking. There are a couple of small tree covered island which, coupled with the intricate shoreline makes it a photogenic lake especially when viewed from the monument. A colony of Black Backed Gulls frequent the lake. It is thought that the large slate quarry of Hafod Las (GR 779562) just above Betws drew water to supply a wheel from Llyn Elsi; first along a leat and then via a two foot pipe. A recent archaeological dig has in fact shown this to be so.

Betws-y-coed Angler's Club have the lease and regularly stock the lake with Browns, Rainbows and American Brook trout. A 6lb Brownie was caught in 1992. The Brook trout were introduced in 1991 and already a 3¾ specimen has been caught. Following the Chernobyl disaster and the ongoing acid rain threat the PH level is monitored at fortnightly intervals.

## LLYN Y FAWNOG
*GR 8936*
*Height: 993'*
*Group: Bala*
*Area: 2 acres*

This is a small pool which becomes very low in dry summers. There are no fish there for this reason. Much of the surround is composed of marsh. It is privately owned and used for breeding ducks. Another local name for it is Llyn Chwid (duck lake).

## LLYN Y FEDW
*GR 6232*
*Height: 1,050'*
*Group: Rhinogydd*
*Area: 7 acres*

Harlech took its drinking water from this lake until quite recently which has very clean, clear water. The trout are also renowned for their cleanliness and fine markings and grow to quite respectable sizes. The fishing rights are leased to Talsarnau and Artro District Angling Association who ensure that the stock of brown trout are monitored. The PH level is low at present causing some concern for the future of the fishing. The middle of the lake is 10' deep but the reedy, marshy banks are shallow and often present problems for the angler. When it was decided to lower its capacity so as not to come under the 1975 reservoir act requiring regular inspection and maintenance the responsibility was then returned to its owner Lord Harlech by Welsh Water in 1992. The dam was built in 1936. The lake is situated on the western fringe of the Rhinogydd uplands amidst numerous signs of ancient settlements. The remains of a large circular fort at (GR 614325) on the summit of Moel Goedog is only one of a series of standing stones and cairn circles distributed on the western slope below to show the area's antiquity as far as population is concerned.

## LLYN Y FFRIDD
*GR 7072*
*Height: 1,050'*
*Group: Carneddau*
*Area: ¼ acre*

Really just an enlarged river pool retaining none of its reservoir size. Of interest in the immediate vicinity is an arrowstone at (GR 696733) and a stone near the track junction (GR 694723) which has been carved with a layout similar to a Nine Man Morris gameboard. Local tradition places a drover's shoeing station at this track crossroads and folklore assumes this stone to be their work. The track is actually a Roman road and possibly even older. At Bwlch y Ddeufaen (GR 715718) there are two standing stones and a cairn which are very ancient. Folklore again steps in to explain their presence. It would seem a giant and his wife were on their way to Anglesey one day, he was carrying two large stones under each arm and she had a pile of smaller boulders in her apron. Coming to meet them along the track was a cobbler carrying a pile of worn out clogs. When asked how far it was to Mona he replied that he had worn out all the clogs walking from there. In despair the giants dropped their stones where they have remained to this day (although one of the two standing stones have been re-erected a century ago). Continuing east and with the giant theme another standing stone (GR 739717) is called Ffon y Cawr (giant's stick) which carries an amusing little legend concerning a giant who threw his stick (the stone) at his dog who wasn't rounding the sheep as it should have. The dog (a greyhound) was actually sheltering under the capstone of a burial cromlech 200 yards East! Clogsan y Cawr (giant's clog) can be seen in the wall at (GR 739707) which is yet another reference to giants.

## LLYN FFRIDD CARREG Y BWCH
*GR 7454*
*Height: 725'*
*Group: Moelwynion*
*Area: 3 acres*

Two slate quarries which later merged under one ownership drew water from this purpose built reservoir. Ty'n Afallen quarry (GR 752539) was opened in the 1870's by one Joseph Kellow whose unusual surname is the same as that of Moses Kellow (see Llyn Croesor) and one therefore wonders whether they were in fact father and son. Rhiwgoch quarry (GR 749537) opened in the 1860's and took Ty'n Afallen over before they both closed in the 1900's neither having reached their expected potential. Lledr house Youth Hostel is situated just below the site by the roadside. The main stream supplying the lake draws its water from an extremely wet piece of upland composed of rock bluffs covered in heather protruding out of a soggy tussocky bog. Mynydd Cribau, whose summit has a small cairn rising out of this bog requires quite an effort to get to it. The lake is privately owned.

## LLYN FFRIDD Y BWLCH
*GR 6948*
*Height: 1,200'*
*Group: Moelwynion*
*Area: 3 acres*

This is a small quarry reservoir just below the road (west) descending into Blaenau Ffestiniog from the Crimea pass. It was created to supply the 'Welsh Slate Co.' (now called Cloddfa Ganol). The original quarry which opened in 1825 was called Cloddfa'r Weirglodd. The pass itself was called Bwlch y Weirglodd but has been known as the 'Crimea' for several generations. This came about because an old tavern by the name 'The Crimean Arms' used to stand near its summit. (See Llynnau Barlwyd.) Another explanation offered locally is that the road over the pass was actually constructed during the time of the Crimea campaign — 1854-5.

Despite its small size this little lake has played an important part in the development of the angling society 'Cymdeithas y Cambria' having enjoyed the benefit of regular stocking. It has also been used as a nursery lake in a similar way to Llyn Dubach y Bont where young trout were acclimatised and fed before being turned into some of the bigger mountain lakes held by the society. Llyn Ffridd y Bwlch was bought by Cymdeithas y Cambria in 1971. It has been traditional to allow the more elderly of the Society's members priority for fishing here.

## LLYN Y FIGN
*GR 8319*
*Height: 2,500'*
*Group: Dolgellau*
*Area: ¼ acre*

Certainly one of the highest pools in Eryri and also one of the shallowest, nowhere is it more than two feet deep. It owes its existence to the semi-circled shape of Glasgwm summit which funnels all the rainwater into the pool. It is certainly unusual to see a permanent pool of this size in such an elevated position with so little land above it. There are no fish in 'Y Fign' and it is extremely doubtful if there ever were any. The outflow stream goes south for two miles gathering strength for a dramatic series of waterfalls (GR 829174) through a forest plantation which is visible from the Dinas Mawddwy road on the approach to Bwlch yr Oerddrws. Several old mine levels are hidden in this forest where a small amount of lead was found by a series of different companies from the mid eighteenth century until the final closure in the 1850's. Gold was also unsuccessfully sought for at the site. In the 1830's during a particularly low period in lead prices a blue ochre was extracted for sheep marking, folk lore has since decreed it to be one of only three good things to come out of Dinas Mawddwy. Bwlch yr Oerddrws was supposedly used as a meeting place for Welsh leaders to try and sort out some order following the failure of Glyndwr's rebellion This was motivated by the harsh laws passed by Henry the fourth immediately after the wars.

## LLYN FIGN
*GR 8329*
*Height: 1,325'*
*Group: Bala*
*Area: 1 acre*

Although marked on the OS map as quite an interesting shaped tarn, it is in reality little more than a gathering of water to form the Afon Fwy stream. It has been described as depicting the profile of a downhill skier heading west! Improved drainage and afforestation has changed the pool's shape somewhat in recent years. Two things of note are worth mentioning. Firstly the rocks half a mile to the north east called Craig y Llestri were the scene of the discovery of some valuable bowls and plates some years ago (see Llyn Crych y Waen). Secondly the source of the Dee lies a mere mile to the south west under the cliffs of Y Dduallt. This unremarkable little spot has never received the same acclaim as the sources of the Severn and Wye that rise from Plynlumon, this, in some ways is surprising. The Dee has always played an important part in the country's history. It was once regarded as a sacred river, named Deva by the Romans it continued as an important boundary and provider throughout recorded history. Llyn Tegid itself was owned by the monks of Basinwerk Abbey, Holywell because they also had rights over the Dee, and even today millions of gallons of domestic water is taken out at Chester daily as part of the Dee scheme. A slab of rock on this cliff was once a sacrificial altar called Llech Offrwm, I have been unable to ascertain its whereabouts.

## LLYN Y FOEL
*GR 7154*
*Height: 1,756'*
*Group: Moelwynion*
*Area: 8 acres*

In 1910 this was called the best trout lake in Wales but according to Ward (1931) persistent ottering had all but destroyed this reputation in the following twenty years. There are still trout in its shallow waters but not the 'giant denizens of yore'. Being quite elevated it is a late lake, July and August being best. An otterboard

*Llyn y Foel*

attached to some flies was found on the shore during the summer of
1994. The remains of a dam on its south shore testify to it having
been a deeper lake when the 'best trout in Wales' were found there.
There are two prominent rocky islets with a number of singular
rocks depending on the season. Some writers have mistaken this
for the pool of the oxen's eye in the Afanc legend (see Llynnau
Diwaunydd), as it is almost on the route taken and also possibly
because the island in the lake may produce a resemblance to an
oxen's eye. According to one interpretation of the Aberconwy
charter (1198) 'Llegat Erych' (oxen's eye pool) is a pool in a little
stream called Afon Goch.

Behind the lake a perfect curved moraine sweeps towards the
south face of Moel Siabod whose cliffs contain some rare alpine
plants. The Holly fern was discovered here by Evan Roberts the
self taught botanist and one time warden of Cwm Idwal nature
reserve. Palmer, writing in 1937 had claimed that due to prolific
picking they had become extinct in Eryri! The path to the summit
from the lake takes a rocky but pleasant scramble up the west ridge
that encloses the cwm. On John Evans' 1795 map it was one of the

few mountains that was named, it was spelled 'Shiabod'. A Roman shield of concentric circle design was found in 1784 on these mountain slopes. A Cessna light aircraft crashed into the summit of Siabod on the eighth of June 1979 killing all six on board, a stark reminder of the dangers of the mountains even in this modern age of advanced radar and technology. Access to the lake from the east past Llyn y Rhos is only by courtesy of Rhos farm as the path is not a public right of way.

## LLYN Y FOEL BOETH
*GR 8047*
*Height: 1,630'*
*Group: Migneint*
*Area: 1 acre*

A small tarn that lies on a high plateau some two miles north east of Llyn Conwy. It is also called Llyn y Brain Gwynion (lake of the white rooks) because of the large number of seagulls that frequent it. There are numerous other smaller pools littered around the immediate vicinity. A further three miles in the same direction finds the village of Ysbyty Ifan named according to tradition because it is on land once owned by the knights of St John of Jerusalem. They established a hopsice and sanctuary here ostensibly for travellers towards the end of the twelfth century. This set up was later reinforced by Llywelyn Fawr who gave them additional land and status, this land included both Llyn Conwy and Y Foel Boeth. Unfortunately the sanctuary attracted outlaws and wrongdoers and by the fifteenth century had become notorious as a district where thieves and murderers lived in great numbers. It was not until Maredydd ap Ifan (see Dolwyddelan reservoir) came to live to the castle at Dolwyddelan that this situation was remedied. Eventually, as part of Henry the eighth's dissolution of the Monastries the hospice ceased to exist.

The old community boundary of Penmachno runs right across the lake and in the old days it was the custom to walk the boundary once a year, when the lake was reached it was deemed sufficient to throw a stone across!

On the north east slopes of Foel Boeth there is a rock called Gwely'r Lleidr (thief's bed). (GR 809484) This is a large cuboid boulder with a flat top that has a slightly raised end, this is the pillow. The story tells of a robber who would sleep on this rock. Beneath, a slight hollow allowed his dog to sleep which would alert him if anyone came near, in this way he was able to avoid capture. One day however the old dog died and that night someone managed to creep up to the rock and kill the thief as he slept. There are rocks called Cerrig Lladron (thieves' rocks) at (GR 773436) named according to tradition because a group of bandits were caught at the rocks by Maredydd ap Ifan and put to death. They were buried in the marsh nearby. Many ex-soldiers from the War of the Roses made up these 'bandits'. In the 1930's travellers might have been surprised when they reached the mountain road gate at (GR 805453) to find a rough looking individual emerging out of an equally rough roadside shelter made of turf and offering to open and close the gate, for a small fee. This was the tramp known as 'Fighting Taff', his very looks would apparently serve to persuade his 'customers' that his services were worth the nominal sum asked for. A mile to the north of the lake the old drover's road from Penmachno to Ysbyty Ifan passes in the characteristic west-east direction, this is called Ffordd Llech and crosses the river Eidda using what is considered in the district as the best built arch bridge in North Wales. Many years ago the young headteacher at Penmachno died on this track in a snow blizzard.

## LLYN Y FRÂN
*GR 7025*
*Height: 1,350'*
*Group: Rhinogydd*
*Area: 4 acres*

The rocky afforested uplands to the west of the main Trawsfynydd to Dolgellau road is amongst the most difficult walking country in Wales. Sections which are not choked with impeneterable conifers have loose, slime covered boulders hidden in drifts of heather through which rotting remnants of cut trees are constantly collapsing; the plateau beyond contains Llyn y Frân. The land to the west of the lake is owned by the National Trust the boundary actually going through the lake. There are some impressive stone walls in this region dating from the period when labour must have been very cheap. Some two hundred yards south west there is what appears to be an old Hafod which consists of a round wall structure with the remains of a walled paddock around it. It was the custom in the old days to live the winter months in the valleys in their Hendre and in the summer to move up to the hills with their flocks to their summer residences.

The lake may contain a few perch although this is open to conjecture today due to the effects of the acid rain blighting many of our mountain tarns. A few years ago trout from Dolmelynllyn were brought here as Dolmelynllyn pool seemed in danger of drying out at the time. It is not known how successful the transfer has been.

## LLYN Y FRITHGRAIG
*GR 7445*
*Height: 1,400'*
*Group: Moelwynion*
*Area: 1 acre*
There is nothing remarkable about this small tarn perched on some low hills a mile south of Tre Gynwal in Cwm Penmachno. It is a peaty pool that does not contain any fish and is surrounded by very wet ground characteristic of the Migneint moors. There are, however some interesting slate quarry remains to its north and west marking the outer edge of the Blaenau Ffestiniog veins. The Cwm Machno quarry (GR 750471) which closed in 1962 mainly due to transporting and waste disposal difficulties had a reservoir above the site (GR 748464) of which only the remains of the dam is left. Recent landscaping work has unfortunately destroyed the 'old' quarry which was impressive. Even more impressive is Rhiw Bach quarry (GR 740462) which began in earnest in 1812. This was a big operation in keeping with the tradition of Blaenau and even had a chapel and schoolroom with the men's barracks and manager's house. The most impressive feature however is the now blocked off drainage tunnel that exists at (GR 746471). This is 600 yards long

and provided access to most of the underground workings. Up until the mid 1980's it was used extensively for adventure activities by Outdoor Centres across North Wales. There are two quarry pools at (GR 741457), the quarry closed in 1953.

## FFYNNON CASEG
*GR 6765*
*Height: 2,500'*
*Group: Carneddau*
*Area: 1 acre*

Probably the most inaccessible lake in Eryri, it is hemmed in on all sides by towering cliffs with only one narrow gap for the exit stream. To the east the imposing precipices of Carnedd Llywelyn stand guard whilst to the south and west the equally impressive cliffs of yr Elen complete the enclosure. Little wonder that the mountain ponies of the Carneddau come here by tradition when it is time to foal. This is popularly believed to be the reason for the lake's name — mare's pool. The ponies which still frequent the long gentle slopes of the Carneddau are reluctant to run away but fix a wary eye on all walkers until they are well past. Years ago the travelling gypsies would come and catch a few (if they could). Today all the ponies are 'owned' albeit it by only two farms and are therefore not 'wild' in the old sense. Surprisingly enough there are some small trout in the lake due no doubt to the accessibility of the stream. A mile below the lake the stream joins the Afon Wen stream near a large sheepfold. Just above this is the start of a six mile leat that contours the hillside in a most impressive manner that was used to supply water to Bryn Hafod y Wern quarry (see Llyn Coch). Lower down the valley as it opens out the remains of ancient settlements can be seen as well as an old slate quarry popularly known as Chwarel Dr Hughes, (GR 653667). Just below this an old spring by the name of Ffynnon Ffidler (fidler's well) (GR 652666) was once marked by a stone. According to tradition this is where Idris, one of the travelling harpists of the middle ages used to come and tune his harp, he would do this by holding it above the well. Idris was also an astrologer who has been connected to both Carnedd Llywelyn and Cadair Idris. Hugh Derfel Hughes (1866) refers to a flat piece of land at the base of Carnedd Llywelyn where Idris would come to do his star gazing.

It would have been from these cliffs above the lake that the botanist Johnson had to turn back in 1639 when his guide became afraid of eagles! In winter Ffynnon Caseg is frequently frozen over for weeks at a time as it is one of the highest lakes in the country. Sulphur has reputedly been found somewhere within the tiny cwm. Afon Caseg supplies Bethesda with its domestic water whilst the neighbouring river Llafar has supplied Bangor up to 1994. An abandoned reservoir on the Llafar just below the old Manganese quarry track (GR 651654) stands testimony to an early attempt to provide Bangor, it has a monument like railing enclosure nearby. At the time of writing Norweb have plans to construct a small power station near Gwaun y Gwiail (GR 632662) using water from the Llafar.

## LLYN FFYNHONNAU
*GR 5255*
*Height: 981'*
*Group: Moel Hebog*
*Area: 2¹/₄ acres*

The broad western slopes of Mynydd Mawr levels off slightly just as it reaches the eastern perimeters of the Nantlle slate quarries, Llyn Ffynhonnau is found at this point. It also lies on the Snowdonia National Park boundary. In common with many upland lakes that happen to be close to where man has settled it has its share of stories and odd beliefs. One legend describes a fisherman one summer evening who spotted some green clad Tylwyth Teg dancing on the lake shore, he sat down to watch them. As soon as one of them realised they were being watched he ran over and threw some dust into the fisherman's eyes whereupon they vanished, (see Llynnau Cwmsilyn for almost identical legend). Another old tradition that involves the mountain Mynydd Mawr was the execution of criminals. They were apparently taken in wooden cages to the top of the cliffs overlooking the pass of Drws y Coed and thrown over to their deaths. This was a common practice by the Romans who were past masters at utilising violent death for entertainment, (see Llyn y Tri Graeanyn for a similar legend).

The lake didn't escape the poacher either as generations learnt their craft in this conveniently close pool and gave rise to many myths and exaggerations regarding methodology and success. According to Ward (1931) the poaching unfortunately culminated in the lake being artificially lowered for the purpose. There are still trout in the lake. The rock on Mynydd Mawr has examples of a peculiar dark blue crystal found only in two or three other locations in the country. The mountain is also known as Elephant mountain owing to its profile of an elephant's back when seen from the west. Locals also call it Mynydd Llus, (bilberry mountain) as the slopes around the lake is covered with these berries in spring. An interesting little anecdote concerning this populated upland is worth repeating. Many of the crofts and cottages had been built on this crown land using the once legal tradition of completing the work in a night, lighting a fire whose smoke could escape through the chimney by dawn and then claiming land as far as a hammer could be thrown. The house would then be lived in for a year before proper improvements could take place. These were known as 'Bythynod Un-nos' and represented the only way some peasants could ever own a home. In 1827 Lord Newborough tried through the Enclosure Act to stop this practice but to the locals' delight he failed. The local quarrymen contributed a cask of Welsh ale to the dinner that celebrated this failure which was held in London.

## FFYNNON LLOER
*GR 6662*
*Height: 2,225'*
*Group: Carneddau*
*Area: 6 acres*

A fisherman's courtesy path (which is not a public right of way) to the lake is evidence enough of the quality of fishing to be had here. Ward (1931) calls it the best trout lake in Wales over 2,000' having very handsome, strong fighters up to a pound. Indeed many angling authors have agreed with Ward's testimonial. Being high it is a late season lake, July and August seemingly best, and the biggest trout are beneath the rocks on the western shore. The name 'Lloer' which means moon has attracted several explanations. It is widely believed locally that the ancient people (the druids have been mentioned) would climb up to the lake to participate in some form of long forgotten pagan worship, part of which involved viewing the moon's reflection in the water. In more recent times it was the custom for young people in the area to gather at the lake on the night of the summer solstice (or Mayday) and partake in some form of party or celebration, this may be a throwback to the pagan rituals. The mountain in whose bosom the lake is cradled is known as Penyrolewen (peak of the white light) and this too has been offered as a possible link to the moon idea. The white light may have been the moon shining on the summit rocks of the mountain as seen from below. A third offer is a tenious one involving a little plant that grows in the cwm. It is the moonwort, so called because of its half moon shaped leaves, I might add that I have never been able to find the plant in this particular cwm. According to Derfel Hughes (1866) the cairns and round walled shelters on the summit of Carnedd Dafydd are the remains of an ancient temple raised by the druids in connection with the lakeside rituals below.

On a more sombre note the remains of two wartime aircraft crashes litter the slopes around the lake. In 1942 a Boston hit the scree just above the lake and incredibly one of the crew survived and was rescued after lying in pain for two days. An Anson also crashed during the war some fifty yards west of the lake killing all on board. Higher up the mountain the last remaining wing of a ventura can be seen on the 3,000′ contour, this crashed in 1943 killing all four on board.

The crag rising from the west shore has a few rockclimbs on it but is not often visited. Some round wall shelters near the path ascending Pen yr Ole Wen from the lake have been attributed to the pre Roman era.

The fishing rights are leased from the Penrhyn estate by Ogwen Valley Angling Association and the lake continues to give good sport. It is thought that a nearby band of limestone is responsible for the healthy PH level contributing to the quality of the Browns. It is a very productive lake. Fly fishing only.

## FFYNNON LLUGWY
*GR 6962*
*Height: 1,786'*
*Group: Carneddau*
*Area: 40 acres*

Ffynnon Llugwy was one of the lakes chosen to re-locate the Torgoch (arctic char) when Llyn Peris was drained as part of the pump storage scheme in Llanberis. One of the reasons chosen was because it has a maximum depth of 146'.

The Torgoch have settled well and are often seen curiously enough in the shallows. It is a mild source of annoyance and one of the comments by the local anglers is that they have to cast further to lure the larger Brown Trout. The original lake prior to the construction of the dam in 1919 would have been partly held back by the glacial moraine debris in a similar way to many other corrie lakes in Eryri. It is an earthern dam with a concrete core and there were significant alterations in 1933 and 1975. It is owned by Welsh Water and has a capacity of 56,000 $m^3$/11 million gallons from which Anglesey and Bangor now draw their supply. Prior to 1976 it was part of the Dolgarrog system but when Marchlyn Mawr was made unavailable as a public water supply due to its role in the Dinorwig Pump storage scheme Ffynnon Llugwy became the new supply source. Over eleven miles of pipes were laid down the Ogwen valley. Bangor who have taken their supply from the river Llafar up to 1994 are now to go on Llugwy's system. A holding reservoir constructed in Mynydd Llandygái will provide water for both Bangor and Bethesda. There are some particularly fine examples of these moraines here at Llugwy. The highest hearth in the parish which stood near the exit stream now is a ruin. It was called Glan Llugwy and there was a difference of over 1,700' between this tiny cottage and the lowest dwelling in the parish which was Dol Ogwen in the grounds of Penrhyn castle. An interesting view that was held about a hundred years ago was that both Ffynnon Llugwy and its neighbour Ffynnon Lloer were both old volcanoe craters and that rock spewed out in their eruptions could be found lower down the Ogwen valley at approximately (GR 640614). Derfel Hughes (1866) claims that these rocks could only have come from Llugwy and therefore subscribes to this theory. A well documented account of a climbing tragedy occuring here in 1927 appears in Thomas Firbanks' 'I bought a mountain' (1940). Following an ascent of Great Gully which is a long climb on Craig yr Ysfa (GR 693635) in atrocious weather conditions four climbers found themselves battling against exhaustion and darkness as they struggled through the snow on the shores of Llugwy. The two most experienced decided they would forge on ahead leaving the two weakest by the lakeside with the promise that they would send assistance. Giveen and Tayleur reached the safety of their accommodation but apparently made some food and took a night's sleep before organising any help for their friends. It was a full day before a party of rescuers reached the shores of Ffynnon Llugwy only to find two bodies, they had succumbed to the cold during the night. It was natural that once the facts were clarified fingers of accusations were pointed but the mystery of those missing hours and reasons for the delay were never made clear; Giveen died in a mental institute.

John Piper the artist saw fit to paint the lake in 1949.

## FFYNNON LLYFFANT
*GR 6864*
*Height: 2,725'*
*Group: Carneddau*
*Area: ½ acre*

Certainly the highest named pool in Wales to appear on the OS map, it has its own mini cwm high up on the very eyebrow of Carnedd Llywelyn, itself the second highest mountain in Wales. Llyffant is Welsh for frog and I have to say that even at this lofty height I have witnessed frogspawn in nearby pools although not in the tarn itself. It is not credited with having fish although one old

*Ffynnon Llyffant and one of the Canberra Wheels*

stalwart claims to have caught an ugly, large headed specimen in the pool many years ago. Its exit stream deteriorates into swamp some hundred yards lower down and it is hard to imagine any fish able to reach the pool let alone wishing to. The wreckage of a Canberra twin engined jet bomber which crashed into Carnedd Llywelyn while on a test flight on 9th December 1957 can be seen on the slope immediately above the lake. Part of the undercarriage and wheels are actually in the lake. Pieces of aluminium litter the stream for some three hundred yards below the lake which includes the torpedo shaped long range fuel tank in one particularly deep pool.

Pennant (1786) relates a story concerning two huge stones which 'marched' part of the way to the summit of Carnedd Llywelyn one night in 1542. One of these stones was apparently so big that a thousand yoke of oxen could not move it. They moved the distance of a bow shot and remain there to this day. Henry the eighth supposedly sent an agent to discover the truth of the matter and was subsequently convinced when the agent returned.

On the ridge leading to the summit of Carnedd Llywelyn from the lake Tristan ap Tallwch, one of Arthur's knights is supposedly buried beneath a cairn. The ridge is known locally as Y Drystan. According to tradition the 'ancients' used to sacrifice a white oxen on this cairn in times of hardship, cremated ash was discovered inside the cairn early last century. Whatever the truth, it has to be said that it is interesting that such positive beliefs and traditions survive concerning so remote a spot. Carnedd Llywelyn is one of the places credited as being the burial place of Rhitta the giant, there are three other strong claims for this dubious honour, Snowdon perhaps being the strongest. The lake is nowhere deeper than a yard.

## LLYN FFYNNON Y GWAS
*GR 5955*
*Height: 1,381'*
*Group: Wyddfa*
*Area: 10 acres*

Thousands tramp past this lake every year as they take the Snowdon Ranger path to the summit of Snowdon. Translated it means 'lake of the servant's pool' and it was given this name because a shepherd drowned here many years ago while washing his master's sheep. There is in fact quite a large sheepfold at its northern shore testimony perhaps to the possibility that the story may be true. Some three hundred yards east of the lake there also seems to be the remains of either an ancient settlement or perhaps a 'hafod' (summer residence) as was the custom of farming in the old days. A fine parallel walled dam remains from its days as a reservoir supplying the slate quarries of Rhyd Ddu. It did this in conjunction with another reservoir lower down Cwm Treweirydd (GR 588549). Both supplied water to Glan yr Afon quarry (Clogwyn y Gwin). A flood burst the banks of the lower reservoir soon after the quarry closed in 1915 and as a consequence it became a much smaller pool. There are trout in both pools although they are generally thin, hungry looking fish that do not grow very big. Llyn Ffynnon y Gwas does however get a mention in Iain Niall's fishing memories 'Trout from the Hills'. The fine stone dam was breached by a ten foot channel to lower the level and thus reduce the volume to 24,000m³/4¾ million gallons.

## LLYN Y GADAIR
*GR 7013*
*Height: 1,837'*
*Group: Cadair Idris*
*Area: 11 acres*

It was from this lake that the giant Idris washed and took his drink before settling in his 'chair' to presumably watch the stars, (see Llyn Cau, Ffynnon Caseg). On a sunny day the lake, like many of Cadair Idris' lakes takes on a deep blue and when seen from the upper eaches of the Fox's path to the summit is very photogenic. It is quite a deep lake but the trout although numerous do not grow much over half a pound and are regarded as poor quality fish. It is also a curious fact that the Gadair trout are certainly different in shape to other neighbouring lakes being more snub nosed. A fine echoe can be heard across the water from the rocks of the Cyfrwy arete west of the lake. The very obvious step in the ridge's profile is called the 'table' and the climb taking the skyline which incorporates the 'table' was first climbed solo by O. G. Jones in 1888. It was here that the famous mountaineer and skier Arnold Lunn met with a near fatal accident in 1922 whilst descending. A large block came away in his hands and he fell a full hundred feet to land on a ledge. He was rescued by his friend and the hut keeper from the summit of Cadair Idris, the incident ended his climbing career. A bell which was rung in Dolgellau church whenever news arrived of an accident on Cadair Idris was called the Cader Bell. The exit stream forms a miniature pool before finally escaping through boulders to re-appear much lower down the slope. It may have been this phenomena that gave rise to the idea that a subterranean stream joined Llyn Gadair with Llyn Cau.

Just below the lake a powerful dwarf called 'Cow Idris' built himself a dwelling with some huge boulders to guard the entrance to the central ridge, for what purpose it is not known. In the 1850's an old woman who was reputed to be quite rich but eccentric lived in this cottage and one of Cadair Idris' most famous guides, Pughe would show tourists in his charge around the cottage on their way up the mountain. Today, apart from the sheep and the walkers it is the Raven seems to be making a comeback, they frequent the cliffs in their dozens and provide free ariel acrobatics every mating season. There is a strange belief that anyone spending the night alone on the summit will by the morning have become a great poet, or have seen a great wonder or have become insane. This tradition is shared with a few other locations in North Wales, (see, Bochlwyd, Du'r Arddu, Tegid).

## LLYN Y GADAIR
*GR 5652*
*Height: 598'*
*GroupL Moel Hebog*
*Area: 50 acres*

In the sixteenth century Leland refers to the lake by its full name 'Llyn dan Gadair Eurwrychyn'. At the beginning of the eighteenth century it was known as 'Llyn Cadair yr Aur Frychin'. Two explanations have been put forward. The 'Aur Frychin' was a golden haired water beast not actually called an afanc in this instance but which did however wreak havoc locally, (see Llynnau Diwaunydd, and Glaslyn for similar legend). Things came to a head sometime in the eighteenth century when a man swimming across the lake was followed by a long trailing object which wrapped its coils around him when he was almost across and dragged him down to drown. The beast was hunted and chased up the Drws y Coed pass and eventually killed in the Nantlle valley. This story also serves to explain the name Nantlle; Nant meaning stream and llef meaning scream which the beast presumably made when it was killed! The other explanation for the lake's name is more complex. Cadair is Welsh for chair but it has also meant seat in the sense of a throne from where a district was ruled. Above the lake on the south west side there are some remains of a small community on the hill carrying the name Y Gadair. Jenkins (1898) offers a theory that Myrddin's golden throne of Britain may have been hidden on the site which could have been the earlier site of a druidic bardic centre, he quotes some of Rhys Goch Eryri's writings to support this conjecture. Nearby is the remains of Cerrig Huon, an old tavern that was last occupied in 1815. He further develops his argument for this site to have been a place of importance by claiming that Cwm Marchnad 'Cwm of the market' (GR 556518) was once an important market centre set up as part of Edward the first's policy following the English conquest. Another possibility is that the site was a fortress dwelling for an old chieftain called 'Aur Frychain'. One final tongue in cheek offer is when the lake is viewed from the north west on the ridge of Mynydd Mawr the large rocky buttress on its eastern shore looks exactly like an armchair!

The slate quarry on the south west shore which opened as a co-operative enterprise in 1885 was taken over by Glanrafon quarry in 1914 and closed in 1920. Slate waste was actually dumped in the lake for a period. The finished product was carted to Rhyd Ddu and then by train to Caernarfon. The Welsh Highland Railway whose station in the village was called the 'Snowdon Station' had a relatively short life. The Rhyd Ddu — Caernarfon branch was opened in 1877 to cater for the Glanrafon quarry, in 1922 it was extended to Beddgelert but was closed in the mid 1930's. Optimism was apparently high when the railway first came with hopes for tourist and local passenger traffic in addition to the slate. The large house oppposite the station site was actually built as a hotel but was refused a licence and has since always been a private dwelling. The old school was the birthplace of one of Wales' literary giants, Sir T. H. Parry Williams, today it is an Outdoor Centre owned by Gwynedd County Council. Half a mile along the road towards Beddgelert at (GR 575515) there are a group of boulders known as Cerrig Collwyn. Collwyn was said to be Lord of Eifionydd, Ardudwy and part of Llŷn who also gave his name to the stream running down to Beddgelert. The largest of the rocks is also called Pitt's Head. This is because one of the early travellers noticed a similarity to William Pitt the Younger's profile who became the British Prime minister in 1783 at the age of 24, an office he held for seventeen years.

There are some fine Brown trout in this shallow lake that has enjoyed some regular stocking from Seiont, Gwyrfai and Llyfni Angling Association. They are a cross between Brown and Loch Leven trout and have the reputation of being quick on the strike. Before the dam was built below Llyn Cwellyn sea trout would come up to the lake to spawn.

The lake is also on land traditionally belonging to the Tylwyth Teg (see Dywarchen) and one tale is told of a young man who lived in the farm 'Y Ffridd' (GR 575527). He was on his way home one night from Beddgelert when he happened upon some of the little folk dancing by the lakeside. As he watched transfixed with their beauty he fell asleep. When he awoke he realised that they had discovered him and tied him up in gossamer. It was not until the following evening that he was released and in his confused state he wandered all night on the slopes of 'Y Gadair' until the following day when he finally arrived home! Alas the Tylwyth Teg excuse for not coming home can longer be used by the men of Beddgelert as they have not been seen for a number of years. It is no coincidence that the belief in the little people waned at the time of the great religious revivals around the turn of the century.

## LLYN GAFR
*GR 7114*
*Height: 1,600'*
*Group: Cadair Idris*
*Area: 7 acres*

Also known locally as Llyn yr Afr, lake of the goat. Early tourists this century referred to it in the plural, ie. as the lake of the goats. Goats were common on these slopes of Eryri as domesticated animals up to the early years of last century. They were useful for grazing dangerous ledges thereby discouraging sheep from the peril and their hair was used for the making of wigs which were fashionable in high society. Castrated goats were cooked to provide 'rock venison' and as well as providing milk their tallow was used to make rush candles, there are many examples of place names incorporating the word gafr. The various herds of 'feral' goats seen in pockets around Eryri today are remnants of these old herds. It lies 450' below Llyn y Gadair on the north slope of Cadair Idris right by the side of the Fox's path. A shallow lake which has quite a lot of vegetation growing on it in the summer. The trout are small and numerous with the tendency to be temperemental. Halfway along the ridge between Pen y Gadair and Mynydd Moel the crags of Twr Du (GR 720135) form the headwall of the cwm. In these rocks the spirits of souls who were bound for hell would come to hide from the hunting hounds of Gwyn ap Nudd of the underworld. And it was on these northern slopes of Cadair that the Tylwyth Teg who gave Morgan Rhys his magic harp would come to dance on the shores of Llyn Gafr, Aran and Gadair. (See Llyn Pen Moelyn.)

## LLYNNAU GAMALLT
*GR 7443*
*Height: 1,530'*
*Group: Migneint*
*Area: 29 acres*

This is another of the Migneint moor lakes whose history is steeped in fishing lore. It was first stocked by George Casson the quarry owner who also owned the lake, he put in 15,000 Loch Leven trout in 1885. The history of its fishing is well documented by the Cymdeithas y Cambria angling society of Blaenau Ffestiniog. By 1888 the lake's reputation as a fishing centre was considerable with even the Pennants of Penrhyn estate (who owned much of the moor, see Llyn Conwy) making liberal use of Llynnau Gamallt. Regular stocking occured over the years and a fishing house was built in 1928. Although in need of some repair it is the only one of the society's to still have a roof. As with other lakes various geographical features on its shore have been babtised following incidents and beliefs in the angling world, 'Cerrig George' on one shore for instance were named after the old owner. In 1933 a particular fly constructed with seal's hair proved extremely successful, it was called the 'Fflambo' but it is a curious fact that this was the only season that it was successful. There was even a small hatchery built to rear 'home' grown trout. An ancient fish trap is believed to exist at the bottom end of the large lake where two walls were utilised in the exit stream in much the same way as a canal lock would be used. Alas the acid rains have taken their toll even in the larger upland lakes, the already acidy peat of the Migneint compounding the problem and Llynnau Gamallt were closed for fishing between 1984 and 1987 and then for a further period 1991-93. This was because the quality of fish had detiorated to an alarming degree and a study by Welsh Water was carried out. Trout from Cwmorthin lake were placed there in 1987. Then in September 1991 a report appeared in the Daily Post stating that 50 tonnes of lime was spread by helicopter over a hectare of the lake's catchment area in an effort to combat the problem. A wind powered PH monitor stands on the shore of the larger lake. The smaller of the lakes is slightly higher than the larger lake but by no more than about three feet.

The fishing rights belong to Cymdeithas y Cambria, the east shore having been sub-leased off Barry Edge who holds 20,000 acres of the Migneint moor.

## LLYN Y GARN
*GR 7637*
*Height: 1,448'*
*Group: Trawsfynydd*
*Area: 22 acres*

Llyn y Garn is situated high above the Cwm Prysor valley quite close to but steeply up from the old Trawsfynydd to Bala railway trackbed. The lake is in a rocky bowl which for the most part has steep, well defined banks. In the past it had the reputation for containing some fine perch, these have now dwindled in size generally. It was also noted for having pike. A dilapidated walled structure on its north shore may have been a boathouse. Its ownership is shared between Bryn Celynog farm (GR 75369) and Darn Gae (GR 765369). Half a mile north west the remains of the

Moel Croesau gold mine (GR 750384) can be seen on what was known by the miners as 'Welcome Hill'. This opened in 1895 and following the 1911 investiture of the Prince of Wales at Caernarfon castle when the gold for the crown was provided from this mine it was renamed 'The Prince Edward Mine'. Apart from this it never really realised the potential it had promised and shut quietly sometime in the 1930's. In 1943 a Wellington bomber struck the hill incredibly leaving two survivors out of a crew of six. One of these survivors was found up to his waist in a bog with a broken back!

Below the lake the impressive castle mound of Castell Prysor (GR 758369) stands guard over the valley. Although Roman artefacts have been found on and near the site it is generally supposed that Prysor was an old Welsh chieftain. Local farm and field names have military flavours which may indicate that this old fortress was compromised on more than one occasion.

## LLYN Y GARNEDD

*GR 6542*
*Height: 723'*
*Group: Moelwynion*
*Area: 4 acres*

## LLYN GARNEDD UCHAF

*GR 6452*
*Height: 800'*

This lake as well as a smaller one called Llyn y Garnedd Uchaf four hundred yards north is owned by Till Hill Economic forestry which is a subsidary of Gallacher's Tobacco Company pension fund. Garnedd Uchaf is little more than a marsh today. At one time Llyn Garnedd was stocked with Brown trout but any surviving fish have it all to do in what is not an ideal lake. It is very peaty and little more than 3' feet. The dam was renovated in the early 1970's and it is still a reserve source of supply for the steam trains of the Ffestiniog railway. It has a maximum capacity of 30,000 m³/6 million gallons.

## LLYN GEIRIONYDD
*GR 7660*
*Height: 616'*
*Group: Carneddau*
*Area: 45 acres*

At least three figures in Welsh culture have been linked with Llyn Geirionydd; Ieuan Glan Geirionydd (1795-1855) was born on the banks of the river draining the lake. He was a curate in Trefriw for a period and is remembered for writing poetry and hymns. David Francis (1865-1929) was a blind harpist who was born in a quarryman's cottage in Blaenau Ffestiniog and was given the name 'The blind Harpist of Meirion' at one of the many 'eisteddfodau' held on the shore of Llyn Geirionydd. It was a popular custom at one time staging eisteddfodau on lake shores (see Llyn Morynion).

The one at Geirionydd was held on the summit of a small hillock 300 yards north east of the lake above the exit stream, called Bryn y Caniadau (hill of verse). The third notable, Taliesin was a poet who lived around the sixth century whose connection with Geirionydd is apparently based on a mis-copied manuscript five hundred years ago! This error was compounded when Lady Willoughby of Gwydir castle erected a monument on the very spot where he was supposed to have been born. Apart from his poetic ability he was also a 'seer' and prophesised the death of Maelgwn Gwynedd at the hands of a yellow beast coming from the marsh; this turned out to be a yellow fever that killed a large portion of the population. (See Llyn Tegid for another legend concerning Taliesin's birth.) The monument marking the alleged spot where Taliesin was born fell in a storm some years ago but at the time of writing it is in the process of being re-built; this is a little knoll between the lake and the hillock used for the Eisteddfodau. The general opinion is that lead has been seeping into the lake rendering it fishless. These mines would no doubt have had such an effect on the lake but it has always had fish near the upper end. In 1970 when the dams were demolished at Bodgynydd many of Bod's Brown trout found their way into Geirionydd to supplement the existing (but possibly) meagre population. Locals have always carefully nurtured this 'poisoned lake' belief.

It is an extremely popular venue for picknicking and summer weekends sees the lakeside car park full. It is, thankfully the only Eryri lake where water skiing is tolerated. Recently I have noticed fish jumping at the upper end of the lake where the little stream from Llyn Bychan enters. Hopefully trout will re-establish themselves successfully then perhaps there will be more impetus to rid the lake of waterskiers.

The dam which was built in 1944 gives the lake a potential volume of 150,000 cubic metres. Jehu's 1902 survey gives the lake a maximum depth of 48 feet. One of the suggested routes for Sarn Helen the Roman north/south road passes along the east shore of Geirionydd.

## LLYN GELLI GAIN
*GR 7332*
*Height: 1,100'*
*Group: Trawsfynydd*
*Area: 12½ acres*

Edward Llwyd writing in 1698 notes that the lake 'Celligen' is full of pike and large eels, this is confirmed by Ward (1931) who adds that the pike are gradually devouring the trout. The remains of what looks like and old boathouse is to be seen near the east shore, evidence perhaps that fishing was once popular. There are also Rudd present. A small dam of 8 foot has enlarged the original lake since 1941 giving a maximum depth of 13' and the pipes that supplied Trawsfynydd can be seen now and again appearing from beneath a mound of earth running parallel to the access track. The reservoir was de-comissioned in 1993, Trawsfynydd now receiving its water from Morwynion. There is much vegetation especially near the dam end. A row of disused electric or telegraph poles lead past the lake on the hill above and 'march' across to the next hill Moel Oernant which also contains a little lake Hiraethlyn. Back where the access track joins the road two things of interest should be mentioned. At (GR 733314) there is what is thought to be a Roman's grave, Bedd Porius. It is surrounded by railings and contains a copy of the original stone which is in the National Museum. The inscription refers to Porius as a 'plain' or 'common' man and is thought to be fifth century. Two hundred yards away at (GR 733312) is another stone which is called Llech Idris. This is an almost ten foot tall standing stone tilted slightly eastwards, it is about five foot wide but only a few inches thick. Legend connects it to Idris the giant who hurled it here from his home mountain Cadair Idris. The stone's purpose is unclear but it may have been an ancient route marker where tracks from Ardudwy, Bala, and the areas to the north met. It is known that the Romans were active in this area, they had a fort at Tomen y Mur (GR 706387) and have left remains at Penystryd, less than a mile north west. They may have had mining interests or it may be that their main north/south route Sarn Helen passed close by conceivably utilising the ancient ways. In 1905 following two years at Cwm Dolgain another army invaded the area, the British army. They established the Rhiwgoch training camp, much has been written about the farms and homes that were compulsarily purchased. Today the old camp is a network of log cabins for holiday makers that includes an artificial ski slope. One incorrect local belief is that it was the soldiers who introduced the pike. Pike of up to 8lb are frequently caught.

## LLYN GLAN GORS
*GR 7760*
*Height: 900'*
*Group: Betws-y-coed*
*Area: 15 acres*
Between 1985-1988 this spring fed reservoir was the scene of some very enthusiastic and creative gamkeeping to preserve its valuable denizens. Mr Ian Woolford is a retired policeman who leased the lake and with a WDA grant rendered it escape proof for fish. He then began stocking Scottish farm Salmon in batches of 150, each one over 10lb in weight. Day permits were then issued — all year. Salmon are salt water feeders and every five weeks he would net as many as he could for the smoked salmon side of his enterprise before they lost too much weight. He would then put in another

batch and so it went on. Mr Woolford's zeal for protecting his enterprise extended to setting trip wires attached to parachute flares at key sites around the lake until one fateful day his ex-inspector arrived to advise him regarding this practise. One of these 'traps' had been set up near the gatepost as part of an experiment when the policecar arrived and drove straight through the wire, almost resulted in a burnt police car! Thereafter he toned down the poacher surprises relying instead on the reputation his traps had already generated. Following the demise of the scheme, Llanrwst angling club leased the lake for a while but at the time of writing it is privately owned and has been re-stocked with brown trout. The lake is an artifical reservoir created to supply water for the Pandora lead mine.

Sarn Helen, the Roman north/south road is thought to have passed quite close as it weaved a route from Caerhun to Caer Llugwy.

There are 5 other pools just south of Glan Gors all marked on the map. They are:-

**Ty'n yr ardd** (GR 777601). This is known locally as Llyn Bowlan and was used to supply water for Hafnau mine. It has a deep blue colour and contains no fish. It is known locally as the blue lagoon. Reservoirs (2) (GR 775601). There are in reality two pools divided by a wall. They again supplied water to the Hafnau lead mine. Reservoirs (2) (GR 770601). These two adjoining pools supplied some of the water to run the 68′ waterwheel at the Pandora lead mine. In the 1950's one Colonel Lovett leased the sporting rights for a while from the Forestry Commission. He undertook an ambitious husbandry programme which included stocking these two pools with Rainbow trout. It is not known whether there are any fish present now.

The whole of this afforested area is a popular venue for mountain cyclists and orienteers, justifiably so and most weeks will see groups of youngsters staying at the local Outdoor Education Centre learning the rudiments of navigation within its confines.

## LLYN GLAS (Treweirydd)
*GR 6054*
*Height: 1,735'*
*Group: Wyddfa*
*Area: 1 acre*

The smallest of a trio of lakes sharing a little cwm below the western summit slopes of Snowdon, the other two tarns are Coch and Nadroedd. Glas is an apt name for this pool especially when seen in the sun which produces a most exquisite shade of clear blue. It is said that this is due to the copper found in the rocks some of which was excavated many years ago. It was once thought that both this pool and Llyn Coch below were the result of this excavation. Even Ward is adamant that the large obvious mound next to the lake is 'clearly not moraine'. It seems inconceivable that such a small clear pool contains trout but it is fact full of hungry little browns that seldom grow more than a few ounzes. The little stream running from the gully into the lake is called 'ffôs Owain Glyndwr' for what reason it is not known. It is also called 'Y Gwter Las' and was the scene of a very sad occurrence in March 1891. One of the Snowdon guides known locally by his nickname 'Guto Satan' went missing on his way down from the summit having taken some supplies to the hut. It was a very stormy night and the following day a search was instigated, this continued for a few days but all efforts failed to find him. In June a letter appeared in the local paper imploring that further efforts be made and finally on the 12th he was found at the foot of this gully above Llyn Glas.

## LLYN GLAS (Cwm Glas)
*GR 6155*
*Height: 2,300'*
*Group: Wyddfa*
*Area: 1 acre*

Although tiny, this is arguably one of the lovliest tarns in Eryri. It shares the craggy dramatic Cwm Glas with another even smaller pool Llyn Bach and lies at the foot of the red shaled north ridge of Crib Goch. A small alluvial fan from the ridge is slowly filling the

*Llyn Glas, also known as Ffynnon Frech*

already shallow lake. Near its lower end a small island that contains a couple of dwarf conifers adds a pleasing touch. Years ago the name was Ffynnon Frech, meaning speckled pool. Ray (1690) refers to 'Phynon Vrech' as a Snowdon pool containing the rare 'Isoetes' growing on its shallow bottom. Bingley also makes the same reference on his ascent of Snowdon in 1798 calling it 'Ffynnon Flech'. The cliffs above also contain other rare plants that include the Holly Fern and the Lloydia. The rocky fastness of the cwm is one of the places where Merlin is thought to have hidden the golden throne of Britain when the Saxons invaded with the intention of returning to retrieve it. The Saxons stayed and the throne according to tradition is still somewhere waiting to be found, (see Llyn Dinas for another version). Cwm Glas could almost be described as a two tiered corrie, the upper tier containing both pools. At the point where the lower tier joins the main Llanberis valley years ago an old character by the name of Cady Cwm Glas lived in a rough cottage. She was a tall woman possessing enormous strength, she also had a beard. An amusing tale is told of an incident when the manager of the copper mine below Snowdon teased her about the beard. A few days later she cornered him at the mine and held him by his ankles over one of the leats running into the mill; she also chased and caught a burglar who broke into her cottage and gave him a beating. Another old woman by the name of Hetty used to spend the summer months living under one of the famous 'cromlech boulders' by the side of the road. She did this to keep an eye on her herd. An island in the middle of the stream is still known as Hetty's island, whilst the Climbers Club Hut nearby is also called Ynys Ettws.

## LLYN GLASLYN
*GR 6154*
*Height: 1,970'*
*Group: Wyddfa*
*Area: 18 acres*

An 1873 map accompanying a mine prospectus calls it 'The Green Lake', a name no doubt used by the miners due to the greenish hue caused by copper pollution. Its true name was Llyn Ffynnon Glas but over the years Glaslyn seems to have become the accepted version. Pennant called it Ffynnon Las, 'its waters dark and unfathomable whilst its edges are quite green'. It was still referred to as Ffynnon Glas in J. H. Cliffe's 1840 'Angling in North Wales'. The mines opened on a small scale as early as 1801, the early miners carrying the ore on their backs almost to the summit of Snowdon from where it was dragged by sledge to the Snowdon Ranger (then called The Saracen's Head). Soon afterwards a track to Penypass was constructed and the mine developed albeit it haphazardly under various ownerships. The causeway across Llyn Llydaw was built around 1860 and in 1898 an ariel ropeway down to Llyn Llydaw was constructed. The mine closed in 1916. It is difficult to ascertain when exactly the last fish were poisoned. There is an account of one of the miners catching an ugly toadlike fish with a large mouth using worm in 1810, apparently a fly made of wren's tail feathers had failed! The lake is 127' deep although up to the turn of the century it was believed to be bottomless. It has certainly

*Llyn Glaslyn*

always been regarded as the haunt of demons and was considered the safest place in the land for the afanc of Beaver pool in the Conwy (see Llynnau Diwaunydd). Shepherds in the eighteenth century said the afanc was a toadlike creature with wings and a tail that made shrieking sounds. There are other reports of goats and sheep that wandered too close to the shore being dragged under for ever. Edward Llwyd has been credited for first putting the Afanc legend to paper. He also refers to a difficult piece of music performed in the seventeenth century called 'cainc yr ychain bannog' which resembled the clanking of the chains and the bellowing of the oxen as the afanc was dragged. Another interesting though unsubstantiated theory is that Glaslyn is connected to an underground water system stretching as far as the north of Anglesey. An article appearing in the Anglesey Mail (March 1987) claimed that the tiny pool of Bodafon (GR 467851) would maintain its level through the driest summer despite being 300' above the sea and almost on the summit of Bodafon mountain. The article also claimed that the level of the pool had been noted to rise when rain had fallen on Snowdon but not on Anglesey! The lake has not escaped the attention of the Tylwyth Teg either. A shepherd saw an old woman by the lake shore one day who looked to be very poor, he gave her what food he had and continued with his work. When he returned to his hut he found a silver coin inside one of his clogs, this happened daily and the shepherd became quite wealthy. One night however when he had been drinking he began boasting about his fairy wealth and all the money in his pocket turned to paper, needless to say he never received another silver coin. Another legend concerns one Meurig Llwyd who was also a shepherd tending his flocks on this side of Snowdon. In the summer he would often spend some nights in a little hut by the lakeshore, one morning when he got up he saw a young girl washing her baby which was completely naked. He gave them his shirt and the next morning he too found a silver coin in his clog. As this continued Meurig Llwyd saved his wealth and eventually bought the farm of Hafod Lwyfog which is on the left of the road going down to Beddgelert from Penygwryd. Ieuan Glan Geirionydd (see Geirionydd) wrote a ballad telling the story.

Above, Clogwyn y Garnedd rises almost sheer to the summit of Snowdon the most visited summit in the kingdom. Wyddfa in Welsh it was once called Carnedd y Cawr (giant's cairn) after the giant Rhitta was slain by Arthur. Rhitta was a giant whose mythological presence occurs elsewhere (see Ffynnon Llyffant, and Lliwbran); he was a collector of men's beards, and having killed their owners he used the hair to make a cloak for himself. There are so many guides and books on Snowdon that it would be superfluous to include information here. Due south of Glaslyn the col of Bwlch y Saethau (pass of the arrows) lays its onomastic claim as being the site of Arthur's final battle. It was following a skirmish against the residents of a fort on Braich Tregalan which is just over the col (GR 613535) and Arthur and his men were pursuing the hapless enemy up the slope (possibly along what is now the Watkin path). Upon reaching the col and realising that escape was impossible the enemy let loose one last hail of arrows, it was one of these that fatally wounded Arthur. Twice he sent Bedivere to throw his sword Excalibur into the lake and twice Bedivere failed, on the third attempt the sword was received by a hand which waved it around three times before disappearing into the depths. When Arthur was carried down to the water's edge a small boat with three maidens dressed in white came for him and bore him off through the mist to the island of Afallon where his wounds could be healed. His knights went to sleep in a cave on the cliff of Lliwedd above and is called to this day the cave of the youth of Eryri. Here they sleep until such time that the nation has need of them again. The actual cave referred to is on a feature of rock called Slanting Gully and generations of rockclimbers (the author included) can unfortunately testify that they are not in that particular cave! There is a story (again concerning a shepherd) who happened upon the cave whilst looking for a lost lamb; his fright was apparently so great that his health deteriorated to such an extent that he died within a few weeks. The cairn marking the spot where Arthur was mortally struck was still in existence as recently as 1850 according to Sir John Rhys (Celtic Folklore 1901). Braich Tregalan described as a landslide by Williams, Llandegai 1802 is a glacial moraine but there is no evidence that it ever had a fort upon it. There are the remains of other small pools above Glaslyn that were constructed as part of the mining operation, the one at Pant y Lluwchfa (GR 612547) still remaining only just.

## GLOYWLYN
*GR 6429*
*Height: 1,250'*
*Group: Rhinogydd*
*Area: 8 acres*

The path leaving Cwmbychan for the 'Roman Steps' branches right after leaving the trees and leads eventually to this bright little lake. Its name, translated actually means bright lake. Surrounded with heather, bilberries and rock it is very picturesque when the heather is in bloom. Another name is 'Llawllyn' (hand lake) because it resembles the shape of a hand. It has also been referred to as Glasllyn. It has natural trout and has been fished for generations. Ward (1931) remarked on the quickness of the rising fish due to the ottering that had been taking place. Today the lake is owned by Mr J. Richards, Cwm yr Afon farm (GR 623301) from whom permits are sold. There are some good trout in the lake. Quite a lot of vegetation covers its shallow upper end.

## LLYN GODDIONDUON
*GR 7558*
*Height: 794'*
*Group: Betws-y-coed*
*Area: 10 acres*

Another of the many lakes north of Betws-y-coed in the afforested upland rising gradually to become the Carneddau. It is a natural lake and is completely surrounded with conifers with only one forestry track providing access at its northern end for water supply in the event of fire. A small patch of water lilies grace this northern corner. Ward offers an explanation for the word goddion as a meaning linked to spinning; fairy legends or insects. W.O. Pughe's 1803 dictionary gives goddau as small shrubbery whilst other similar words meaning bright may be applied with a little imagination. According to the Gossiping Guide which appeared in various reprints at the beginning of this century the lake should be called Llyn y Goeden (lake of the tree) and that it was a mistake on the OS maps that led to it being baptised Goddionduon. The lake is leased to Betws-y-coed Anglers Club who keep it stocked with Brown Trout. The PH level is quite high and fish over 3lb are caught. A large buoy dominates the centre. An old 1890 advert for Cobden's Hotel, Capel Curig boasts a lake for its residents to fish, this was Goddionduon. The Capel Curig Army Training Camp take their supply from the lake. This was the old forestry camp which was taken over by the army some two decades ago.

## LLYN Y GORS
*GR 7545*
*Height: 1,400'*
*Group: Migneint*
*Area; ½ acre*

A very small tarn on the most northerly point of the rocky ridge running north and parallel to Llynnau'r Gamallt. In dry summers it becomes a very small stagnant pool and is therefore devoid of any fish. There are three quartz rocks in the water which from a distance look like dead sheep. Apart from the short but excellent ridge walk above Llynnau'r Gamallt there is little of interest near the pool. A very small disused slate quarry half a mile east and acres of marsh seems to be the main features. The old farmhouse of Hafod Dredwydd (GR 765457) was for many years before the age of the motor car a famous beacon of welcome on these moors where neither the burning peat fire nor the hospitality was ever found wanting.

## LLYN GRAIGDDU UCHAF
*GR 677305*
*Height: 930'*
*Group: Rhinogydd*
*Area: ½ acre*

This appears to be an artificial lake excavated possibly for gravel to construct forest tracks. It is hidden in the conifers and approached through a striking avenue of overhanging branches. There are small fish; minnows or trout present as well as a great number of frogs. At the time of writing there are booms placed in the water to prevent oil and other pollutants contaminating the pool when tractors and chainsaws are used by the Forestry Commission.

## LLYN Y GRAIGWEN
*GR 7339*
*Height: 1,650'*
*Group: Trawsfynydd*
*Area: 3 acres*

This is almost an oblong shaped lake on the southern slopes of the

Migneint just south of the forestry plantation of Hafod Fawr. The north shore has a slight beach with much vegetation. Steepish banks lead along its flanks to a now breached dam. The water was harnessed for quarrying. It takes its name from the nearby hillock which is itself appropriately baptised when one considers the meaning — white rock. There are numerous large quartz boulders littering the hillside. There are trout in the lake and although not numerous do grow to a respectable size. The lake was used as a nursery lake by Prysor Angling Association and when the dam was breached many escaped down the stream. It is also known locally as Garregwen and is definitely one of those lakes that produces a wry smile on the face of any local angler when asked about its fish. Before the breach it had a capacity of 54,000 m³/11 million gallons. There is a small pool of a quarter acre two hundred yards north west which does not contain any fish.

## LLYN GRO
*GR 8154*
*Height: 800'*
*Group: Betws-y-coed*
*Area: ½ acre*

Little more than a dangerous marsh in summer it justifies its 'lake' status during the winter months. It has no fish although there may be eels present. Wild fowl also frequent the reedy little hollow containing the pool. A nearby forestry fire watch transmitter is the only real feature. Of interest nearby is the Capel Garmon burial chamber at (GR 817543). The lake is owned by Mr H. Jones, Maes y Garnedd on whose land it is situated.

## LLYN GWERNEN
*GR 7016*
*Height: 539'*
*Group: Cadair Idris*
*Area: 12 acres*

Translated, it means lake of the Alder Swamp which refers to the area to its immediate west. The lake lies by the side of the ancient 'Ffordd Ddu' which was the original way between Dolgellau and

Tywyn. The Gwernen Lake Hotel is also by the roadside where the Fox's path begins its ascent up Cader Idris. In the 1980's a flourishing fishing venture was being run at the hotel but between 1991-1994 the hotel was closed and up for sale. A sunken boat, some rotting little footbridges across the swamp and what appeared to be an old fry nursery pool were all melancholy reminders of better days when I visited in 1993. In April 1994 the hotel was taken over by hosts who are well tuned in with the environment and Llyn Gwernen is once again stocked with trout and 'managed'.

In addition to the Perch and natural Browns 2½lb Rainbows have been put in, the present catch limit being 4 fish. The lake is also a designated site of Special Scientific interest and ranks as one of the most important in its category nationwide. According to W.T. Palmer (1921) the trout in Gwernen were unique because they had had to adapt to their environment which was isolated by waterfalls and learn to eat surface food. When one looks at the lush food source in Gwernen there can be little doubt that he was in fact referring to Llyn Gadair which is much higher.

There are many versions of one particular legend concerning a green man living in the lake. It was he who in the early tourist years was blamed for the mists descending on Cadair Idris causing walkers to loose their way and fall over the cliffs. He would then rush from the lake and take their bodies back where he would eat them at his leisure. A tale is told of a number of farmers going home late one night from Dolgellau, when they arrived at the lake a large man was seen walking along the shore shouting 'the hour has come and the man has not passed!' Several people apparently saw him performing these antics. Among them was the local butcher who was startled to see a humanoid figure sprinting towards him along the road. To his relief it turned out to be someone from a nearby cottage in his white nightgown who had also heard the voice and had become agitated! The shouting man was last seen about three in the morning. When daylight came a walking stick was seen floating on the lake and then a cap, following a brief search the body of the man was then discovered in the water.

The Alder marsh was renowned years ago for its many

occurences of Will o'the Wisps or Body candles as they are known in Welsh. The sighting of this phenomenon was regarded as a portent of death, the path of the light supposedly showing the way the funeral would pass.

One of the old Cadair Idris guides by the name of Pughe was responsible for building the hut on the summit in the 1850's and he would always conduct his walks from Llyn Gwernen; almost without fail. On the hill north of the lake an old iron age fortress settlement can be seen, now merely a pile of rubble (GR 694157). A gold torque weighing half a pound and measuring 42 inches was discovered nearby in 1823 which is believed to belong to the bronze age. It is also known that the Romans used the Ffordd ddu and artefacts from their era have also been discovered near the road quite close to Dolgellau. Today, in summer the road can be very congested due to the popularity of the mountain and the Cregennen lakes found near the ancient road's tarmac limit. It then continues as a rough track south west over the mountain to Tywyn whilst the motorist has to negotiate the equally congested steep bends of the escape road down and north to Arthog.

## LLYN GWERN ENGAN
*GR 7576*
*Height: 525'*
*Group: Carneddau*
*Area: ³/₄ acre*

The small, oddly shaped pool is on common land administered by the Snowdonia National Park Committee. Fishing is free but permission must be sought. There are Rudd, Tench, Carp and Gudgeon and quite possibly Eels. This pool and another over the road (GR 747775) lie very close to the road going over the Sychnant Pass from Conway to Penmaenmawr. The road which is very old in terms of history, very narrow and twisty had tremendous usage in the last years of the 80's and early 90's when it was used by those who knew about it as a means of avoiding the bottlenecks on the A55 caused by roadworks and the town of Conway. The Sychnant Pass is very picturesque and not disimilar to a mini alpine pass.

## LLYN GWYNANT
*GR 6451*
*Height: 215'*
*Group: Wyddfa*
*Area: 85 acres*

The lake and indeed the whole valley was originally called Hwynan, Hwynen, Hoenen or Hwynein, (prefixed with the 'nant' in the case of the valley) whichever version certainly did not have the 't'. It seems that the 't' was added by the first owner and builder of Plas Gwynant (GR 631505) who wanted a touch of originality to the name. Many writers of some credibility including Sir John Rhys and even the Aberconwy Charter of 1198 testify to the 't'-less version as being the genuine one. Gwynen may have been a long forgotten saint. Plas Gwynant once had a very troublesome ghost whose activities reached a peak in the 1840's. Unexplained noises and knocks were heard sometimes all night and whenever they were investigated the noises would occur elsewhere. The owner eventually offered free accomodation to his servants if they lived in. A newly married couple took up the offer and a trouble free period followed for two years. One night however one of the other maids saw something that frightened her so much that it caused her to faint, she died a few months later without revealing the nature of what it was that she saw. The ghost finally met its match in the form of a Griffith ap Rhisiart who came to the Plas to work and refused to be frightened. Quite soon it gave up its hauntings altogether. The Plas once entertained illustrious guests like Tom Hughes and Charles Kingsley; today it is an Outdoor Pursuit centre owned by Sandwell LEA. Another ghost that once troubled the farmhouse of Hafod Lwyfog (GR 653523) for many months in the 1830's was eventually 'laid' at the bottom of the lake by an exorsist from Pwllheli. The ghost or goblin was a poltergeist who would have nocturnal clog dances, knock over milk pails, lift and drop servants' beds and even squeezed somebody's leg so that he couldn't move for a fortnight. Another tale is told locally of two goblins who were caught roasting a young girl alive one stormy night by her future husband, in trying to escape they fell over a cliff and were killéd. Yet another story concerns the disappearance of sheep, hens and food from various houses in the valley. One day an almost naked man covered in red hair was seen on the hillside by the shepherd of Bwlch Mwrchan, all attempts to capture him failed. Despite consultation with a wise man who advised them to pursue him with a red greyhound the local farmers still failed to catch him, he would usually make his escape by leaping over a cliff. One Sunday however the woman of Ty'n yr Owallt who had stayed at home from chapel heard a noise in the kitchen and upon investigating she saw a red hairy arm coming in through the window, she seized an axe and cut the hand off. The trail of blood was followed up the river Merch where it led to an inaccessible cave (GR 631518) beneath a waterfall, the hairy man was never seen again. Another version has the hairy man escaping over the mountain to take up residence in another cave by Clogwyn Du'r Arddu. Another fine old house which is near the bottom end of the lake is Bryn Gwynant (GR 640514), this was once called Penybryn and had the partial remains of what is thought to be a Roman paved path in its grounds. At one stage in its period it was a tavern called Pant Parlleni, today it is a Youth Hostel. The whole valley was once so heavily wooded that a man on a white horse could only be seen in one place from the opposite side, this spot is still known as Goleugoed. The flat meadows at the upper end of the lake have for many years been a popular campsite and boating centre where hundreds come annually. The TV series 'Trailblazers' used the lake and crag on the north shore for a canoeing and abseiling competition in 1992. An old packhorse bridge crossing the river Glaslyn at the campsite is known as the Roman bridge although it actually being Roman is highly unlikely. On the north bank of the river, half way between the bridge and the lake is a well of clear, bubbling water and nearby a rock called Pulpud John Thomas was used by an early Calvinistic Methodist preacher for open air preaching. Just above the bridge and old house by the name of Wenallt once stood, tradition has it that Madoc the discoverer of America stayed here during his preparations. The last family to live here were startled one night by a huge boulder that had rolled down the hillside and through the roof into the kitchen apparently knocking a plate out of the son's hand. The boulder was too big to move and had to be buried in place! Arthur does not escape a mention in the valley either (see also Llyn Dinas) because according to the ancient Triads one of the three most treacherous meetings took place in the valley. It was between a Medrod and Iddog Corn Prydain to plot Arthur's downfall. Above the north shore near the upper end (GR 645523) an old level cut in the search for copper came to nothing, it goes in about thirty feet. The lake is about fifty feet deep and contains trout which rather surprisingly have never enjoyed a reputation for size. There is a belief amongst anglers that a water sprite often releases the fish off the hook before they are landed! It is considered an early lake, May or June. In the past large scale netting occurred, one past owner of Plas Gwynant had a special net made that caught 1500 trout in a season!

## LLYN GWRYD
*GR 6655*
*Height: 900'*
*Group: Glyderau*
*Area: 9 acres*

Llyn Penygwryd and Llyn Lockwood are also names that have been used for this artificial lake. Unlike most of Eryri's man made lakes this one was constructed purely for fishing. Arthur Lockwood was the first manager of Cwm Dyli power station which opened in 1906, in 1921 following a short spell abroad he purchased Penygwryd hotel. He was a keen outdoor man with climbing and fishing in particular his forte. Following difficult negotiations in 1925 with Sir Richard Bulkley of the Baron Hill estate, Beaumaris who owned the land he finally secured an agreement and work on the dam was finally completed in 1927. Bulkley had kept the mineral rights and insisted on a drainage valve being installed for this purpose. Tramps, friends and casual labour were the work force and all manner of material was put into the dam, the most interesting perhaps were pieces of a German submarine being scrapped in Porthmadog! The lake froze over that winter and proved popular with guests as a skating rink, even students from as far as Bangor university came to skate on it. Lockwood apparently offered a shilling to anyone who could ride a bike across it without falling! He initially experienced problems with sphagnum moss islands lifting to the surface due to the methane gas, this also killed some of the trout he'd put in. He solved the problem by gathering the islands together and forming some permanent ones near the west shore which he secured to the lake bed. As the new lake matured the problem of methane gas went away. At its maximum the volume was in the region of 72,000 $m^3$/12 million gallons of water. In 1946 he received a grant of £50 from the River Board for setting up his own trout hatchery at the back of the hotel, this continued for many years until he became too old to manage it. He died in a nursing home in Llanrwst in 1973 aged eighty seven. It is interesting to note that the fishing fees in 1930 were 10 shillings a day plus 1 shilling per trout.

Following a period during the second world war when the Lakehouse school, Bexhill on sea were evacuated there the hotel was taken over by Chris Briggs in 1947. He was for many years active as a mountain rescuer and played host to the successful British Everest team of 1953 while they used Eryri as a training ground. Signatures of the team members as well as many other famous names can be seen on the ceiling of the bar. The hotel has fourteen bedrooms each one named after one of the fourteen peaks over three thousand feet in Wales. Penygwryd is still owned and run by the same family. One of the early owners, a John Roberts allegedly found a hoard of gold coins which he sold, the proceeds of which he used to emigrate to America. Another of the famous hosts was Harry Owen who took over in 1847 and provided welcome, comfort and advice for 44 years. He too was a local expert on fishing and kept a boat on Llyn Gwynant for his guests.

The name Gwryd is itself a subject for much conjecture. It has been offered as a man's length or armspan, a cubit or unit of measurement. It has also been suggested that it stems from a word meaning brave or valour, a reference perhaps to the battles which are said to have occurred on the site. Another avenue of thought can be followed from its spelling in the Aberconwy charter of 1198 where it appears as 'Cwmygoret' which could be Cwm agored (open corrie). In considering the version meaning 'bravery' there was certainly a Roman marching camp on the site (approximately 100 yards south west) of the hotel. The spot is also called Bwlch y Gwyddel (pass of the Irishmen) where according to tradition a battle was fought between an Irish tribe and the Britons following the departure of the Romans. It was Don the Irish king of Dublin who according to tradition struck a deal with the Romans and first came in 267 A.D. His son Gwydion ap Don is mentioned in the Triads as one of three master astronomers (alongside Idris). They stayed, maintaining their identity for 129 years their main settlement site being Muriau'r Dre (GR 655542). Eventually they were driven out when according to legend their guards were found asleep and the settlement attacked. The Irish fled over Bwlch y Rhediad (see Llynnau Diwaunydd). Among the many versions relating to this event one story describes the actual watchtower where the sleeping guards were surprised as being a round structure on a hillock called Moel y Gysgfa, (hillock of slumber). Another version describes the settlement as being a place of evil and when two visiting priests were stoned to death a shower of fire fell from the skies to destroy it. Only one young girl by the name of Anna survived, she was led to safety by angels, the place to where she was led is still called Gwastad Annas.

A hone stone quarry, now disused can still be seen above the lake on the road to Penypass (GR 655556) and waste material was extensively used to floor the yard area of the hotel. A garage and café which had become a ramshackle embarrasment and eyesore was removed in 1991, it stood between the hotel and the lake. There are still trout in the lake, some, the offspring of Arthur Lockwood's original stock, others the product of Browns travelling up the river from Llynnau Mymbyr or down with flood water from Cwmyffynnon. Although occasionally fished it is not the flourishing enterprise it once was. The hotel is steeped in mountaineering history and tradition and many artefacts from the late Victorian era are on display. Some of the equipment and indeed pieces of rock from Everest are also on display to commemorate the 1953 success and the team's personal link with Pen y Gwryd.

## HAFOD Y LLYN
*GR 5929*
*Height: 450'*
*Group: Rhinogydd*
*Area: 5 acres*

The largest of a group of three lakes about two miles south east of Harlech, there is another pool 400 yards north east. The area has been a site of human settlement for thousands of years and there are numerous antiquities marked on the OS map to show this. Altogether there are some thirty homesteads, burial chambers, hut circles, standing stones, and settlements within five miles of Hafod y Llyn including numerous ancient paths, trackways and stepping stones. Llyn Penarth and Llyn Crynu are two other names used for the lake. Penarth is a nearby farm while crynu (shivering) is because there are some very cold springs rising into the lake. There are no significant feeder streams. Penarth is an old established farm with long family traditions that can be traced back centuries. One interesting old custom that is related to the lake was the once a year washing of their household blankets in the water, they would then hang them on nearby bushes to dry.

Two boulders on the east shore that were used for this washing can still be pointed out. Near this shore the lake is nearly 30' deep, a fact borne out some years ago when a weighted plough horse rein failed to bottom. As with many of these low level farmland lakes stories and legends have grown from relatively insignificant occurrences to be elevated almost to folklore status. Two shire horses escaping from Tyddyn Du to Penarth in the winter of 1895 by walking across the frozen lake are one example. Another story includes a hare which was being enthusiastically chased by Tyddyn Du dogs and shot at by the farmer. It escaped by diving into the lake and swimming across. Meanwhile having heard the commotion one of the workers in the small Manganese mine in Penarth was waiting for the hare to finish its epic swim and promptly shot it as it came ashore. Saint Mary established a church at Llanfair (GR 576291) and on her way inland stopped by the lake to bathe with her maidens, ever since water lilies have grown there. Whilst drinking from the stream she left her finger marks in the rock (see Craiglyn Dyfi for similar legend). The Hafod y Llyn near Llyn Mair, Maentwrog also lays claim to this association. A mile to the north is Drws yr Ymlid where a notorious outlaw was once pursued, he was caught near Llyn Cwmbychan and subsequently boiled to death. There were trout, perch and pike but the trout had the unfortunate reputation for having tasteless flesh. Today the trout and pike are gone and the lake is full of Eels, Roach and Perch. It is a popular venue for holidaymakers to fish in the summer but permission must be sought from the join owners. Mr R. Jones, Penarth farm (GR 598288), Llanbedr owns the south bank whilst the north bank is owned by Tyddyn Du (GR 594298), Llanfair, Harlech.

There are three other small pools south of Hafod y Llyn. One at GR 582280 is about a third of an acre whilst another which is twice its size is at GR 582276. This is called Llyn Llety and was constructed as a sporting lake around the turn of the century. The whole area of trees belonged to the Corsygedol estate which was sold in 1858. In 1980 with the help of the World Wildlife Fund the Woodland Trust bought the Llety Walter copse and leased it to the Nature Conservancy. Unfortunately, much to the locals' chagrin the lake was drained, the twin walled clay filled dam demolished and a concrete replacement built. This, however leaked and has been unsatisfactory ever since. The lake was dry when I visited Ang, '94 but the abundant yellow water lily showed evidence of recent water. There are some mapped out nature trails around the woods and the ruins of an old boat house, a sure sign that fishing once took place. They both lie in beautiful countryside which is understandably popular in summer. Also of interest is the tiny chapel nearby where the famous 'Salem' picture was painted by Curnow Vosper. This was a picture depicting live characters inside the chapel and has become famous perhaps because a bearded face said to be that of the devil can clearly be seen formed by the folds of the old lady's shawl. Copies of the picture were given away at one time with 'sunlight' soap. A recently uncovered stone inscribed 'Llyn Bedydd' (Babtising lake) lies on the left bank of the river some 100 yards north of the chapel. The pool was used to baptise the chapel members.

Three other artificially created pools merit mention. Two small ones on Llwyn Ithel farm were constructed just over 20 years ago to prevent livestock drowning in marshy land (GR 605285) whilst another pool of ½ acre size was constructed at the same time for the same reason on land belonging to Llwyn Ithel and Wern Gron (GR 606284). John Evans of Wern Gron put in young browns from Chirk Hatchery a year after constructing the pool; they were "finger size" he recalls. A year later he caught some of half a pound. Two years later they had doubled their weight. Three years after stocking a poacher's net had cleared the pool which was 6' at its deepest. It has not been stocked since.

## HAFOD Y LLYN
*GR 6044*
*Height: 30'*
*Group: Moel Hebog*
*Area: 2 acres*

The lake was owned by the Dolfriog estate who had a wooden summer house called Llyn Du built on its shore. Both Llyn Du and the lake are now owned privately. Before 1811 when the embankment at Porthmadog was constructed the tide was able to reach the large river pool called Llyn Glas just below the bridge at Aberglaslyn. A small port with a quay had been constructed, a handful of cottages and even a tavern called Tafarn y Delyn together made up the village of 'Aber'. It was from this estuary that the Welsh explorer Madog sailed with his thirteen ships on the voyage that discovered America centuries before Columbus. If the lake was not covered by high tides at this time it would have been very close. As far back as 1625 the idea of reclaiming this estuary and the neighbouring Traeth Mawr had been mooted. Sir John Wynn of Gwydir had written to his cousin who was the engineer on the Isle of Wight reclamation project asking for his interest but received a negative reply due to the costs that it would involve.

Hafod Garegog (GR 603444) which is three hundred yards south east of the lake was once the home of Rhys Goch Eryri who was a nobleman, a bard and a friend of Owain Glyndŵr. The original house stood slightly higher than the present one. It was sometime during a wane in Glyndŵr's warring fortunes that he was being entertained by Rhys Goch, this would have been about 1409. Above the house stood a watchtower whose ruins are still to be seen. Recently renovated by the present owner the remains of the tower had been further demolished by Indian troops stationed there during the war so that they could use the long slate slabs for tethering their donkeys! It is sometimes referred to as Cadair Rhys Goch but this is almost certainly a mistake as the traditional 'chair' of Rhys Goch is believed to be above the road on the west side of Aberglaslyn pass. His 'chair' was apparently a favourite vantage point where he was inspired to write his poetry, the exact location has now been lost. From this tower one afternoon a number of soldiers were seen approaching with the obvious intention of capturing Glyndŵr. He was warned and immediately took off and supposedly swam the estuary before heading up Moel Hebog. Once over the ridge he was dismayed to find another squad of soldiers coming to meet him, escape seemed impossible. It was then through sheer desperation he noticed a slight weakness in the Moel Hebog cliffs above him, it was only half a chance, he took it and successfully completed what has been acknowledged as the first ascent of Hebog Chimney 'Simdde'r Foel'! Having escaped his pursuers he found a cave and tradition has him hidden here for some weeks kept fed by his friend Rhys Goch of Hafod Garegog.

Just above the lake in a line of low cliffs an old smuggler's cave which had been lost for many years was re-discovered about a century ago during a fox hunt but has since disappeared under a fall of rock. Half a mile north east of the lake (GR 603456) is a small innocuous monument in the middle of some scrubland with an englyn written on it. The englyn, which is a four lined verse in a strict metre was written by Eben Fardd in memory of young David Davies of Hendre Fychan who was struck by lightning on October

1st 1853. An amusing legend concerning the building of Aberglaslyn bridge is told which is also recited of numerous other bridges throughout the country, the most notable perhaps being Devil's Bridge in Dyfed. The local version concerns Robin Ddu Eryri who had the reputation of being a bit of a dabbler in the occult. He had commissioned the devil to build the bridge due to the difficulty in the terrain. The devil had asked for the first soul to cross the bridge as his fee. When the work was finished he sent word to Robin who was at the time partaking in some refreshment in Tafarn y Delyn. He arose and taking a piece of bread off the table took the tavern's dog with him and made his way to the bridge where the devil was waiting. Asking aloud whether the bridge was strong enough he threw the bread across and the dog immediately ran after it thereby becoming the first soul to cross the bridge; he was thus able to confound the devil! A treaty of commerce was once signed on Aberglaslyn bridge between Britain and France, it came about in this way. The British Minister, Lord Thurlow was holidaying in Beddgelert when his French counterpart arrived with the prepared treaty, they met on the bridge and both put their signatures to the document on the parapet.

The old disused Welsh Highland Railway passes close by the lake and had an official stop there called the Hafod y Llyn halt. It is a shallow lake containing a few trout. A designated site of Special Scientific Interest the present owner ensures that the lake and its environs are protected from casual or accidental damage. Various studies on its butterfly population have been carried out by University teams.

**HAFOD Y LLYN**
*GR 6441*
*Height: 412'*
*Group: Moelwynion*
*Area: 4 acres*
The upper end of the lake is covered in vegetation and is almost unfishable, the lower end is quite clear and trout and perch are fished. It was stocked with brownies over ten years ago by the

owners of the trees and land, Economic Forest. No stocking has taken place in recent years. The lake is hidden in conifers belonging to the Til Hill Economic Forest Co. and surrounded with bogland. It is possible that this was the lake originally referred to in the Saint Mary legend (see Hafod y Llyn, Rhinogydd) because a nearby lake is actually called Llyn Mair. It this were so then the original lake would have been much smaller. Hafod y Llyn was enlarged artificially in order to maintain the water level in Llyn Mair which was used to power a saw mill. The Ffestiniog narrow gauge railway passes within 100 yards but the lake is not visible from the train because of the trees. The railway was built in 1834 for carrying slate from the huge quarries of Blaenau Ffestiniog to Porthmadog and originally relied on gravity with horses pulling the empty wagons back up to the quarry. It was not until 1863 that steam was introduced. In 1946 due to more effective road transport the track was abandoned but fortunately not dismantled. Following a campaign to generate interest the Ffestiniog Railway Trust was formed and restoration work began in 1954, it is now a thriving tourist and local passenger line. The cast iron bridge three hundred yards north east of the lake built in 1854 is best appreciated from the road. Less than a mile south east is the Tanybwlch National Park study centre administered by Gwynedd County Council. There is much National Trust property in the area around the lake including the woods which are designated National Nature Reserve. Always popular with walkers, some of whom use the Tanybwlch station for the start of their walks there are also some Nature Trails laid out in the woodland around. The dam was built in 1887 and has a capacity of 50,000 cubic metres/10 million gallons. It was completely renovated in the early 1970's.

## HENDRE DDU QUARRY RESERVOIR
*GR 7912*
*Height: 1,200'*
*Group: Dolgellau*
*Area: 1½ acres*
This lake was constructed to supply water for the Hendre Ddu

slate quarry which is spread quite extensively over the slopes half a mile below. It is still registered as a reservoir of 25,000m3 capacity requiring regular inspections. The whole site is now afforested. The quarry opened in 1850 and despite the many levels and chambers output was never great, 31 men worked here in 1883. The quarry finally closed in 1940. The PH level is quite low and there are no fish in this lake. Another smaller reservoir can be found at GR 786124 which provided water for Ratgoed slate quarry. Unfortunately it is now little more than a river pool, the dam having been breached. Less than a generation ago some fine sea trout could be caught here. There is still quite a lot of remains to be seen at Ratgoed although the site is afforested. A workforce of 25 men worked here in 1882, the quarry closed in 1953.

## LLYN HESGYN
*GR 8844*
*Height: 1,389'*
*Group: Bala*
*Area: 5 acres*

Forming an almost perfect circle this lake is in a hollow on the east slope of Carnedd y Filiast, the highest peak on these hills between Llyn Celyn and the A5. There are no reports of there being trout but pike are known to feed off the minnows and perch living there. The pike are large lean creatures with huge heads exhibiting the classic signs of underfed fish. It is also known as Hesgen and Hesgin and is privately owned.

## LLYN HIRAETHLYN
*GR 7436*
*Height: 1,050'*
*Group: Trawsfynydd*
*Area: 11 acres*

As long ago as 1584 when Humphrey Llwyd visited the lake it was known for having a peculiar kind of perch with a twist or bend in their tail. These perch are not found anywhere else in this country but are found in some lakes in Norway. At that time there were also trout but these have now gone. The 'deformed' perch were still occasionally caught in Ward's time (1931) but it seems that only smallish ordinary perch are there now. Pennant (1781) calls it Llyn Rathlyn and he also refers to the 'deformed' perch adding that similar fish are found in Lake Fahlun, Sweden. Edward Llwyd calls the lake Llyn yr Ithyn in 1698 and today it is referred to as Rhullyn, or Rhithlyn by the locals. It has always been considered a dangerous lake to bathe in due to some very cold springs rising from its bed. According to local tradition it was these springs in an indirect way that were responsible for the naming of the lake which means 'lake of longing'. A young man who had lost his sweetheart some years ago apparently wandered across the lake when it was frozen, his mind pre-occupied with his grief. When he was in the middle the ice broke and he fell through and was drowned. The ice was thin at that point because of the spring rising beneath.

The old Bala to Trawsfynydd railway passes close by and there is a fine old bridge carrying it over the public path leading to the lake which exhibits the sturdy brickwork characteristic of the railway bridges at that time. Lower down towards the valley about ¾ mile east and significantly above the valley floor the site of the old Castell Prysor remains a very impressive mound, (GR 758369). It is thought that the Romans used the site due to the number of coins, urns and other artefacts found in the immediate vicinity but it is believed that the mound built as it is on a natural rocky hillock is Welsh in origin. It may have been the 'capital' of the commote of Ardudwy.

**LLYN HIRAETHLYN (Moel Oernant)**
*GR 745340*
*Height: 1,590'*
*Group: Trawsfynydd*
*Area: ¾ acre*

Little more than a rain pond in reality it does however command an excellent view perched as it is virtually on a saddle on Moel Oernant. If one was able to stand on someone's shoulder it would just about be possible to get the two Hiraethlyn lakes in one photograph. A trail of disused electric poles lead across the hill towards Llyn Gelli Gain. There are no fish in this pool which in many ways is reminiscent of Llyn Caseg Fraith.

## LLYN HORON (and nearby pool)
*GR 6196*
*Height: 425'*
*Group: Cadair Idris*
*Area: 1 acre and ½ acre*

A Dr Tibort Davies stocked this little lake with brown trout about 40 years ago for private fishing. When this ceased the lake was largely left unattended receiving attention only from local youngsters. Then between 1968-1976 some work was carried out under the supervision of Dr Graham Harris involving the release of sea trout fry. The lake had to be netted first if only to dispel rumours that monster fish lived there. Using a Gill net under the supervision of Mr Emyr Lewis (keeper) they were surprised to catch a male brownie of 3lb 10ozs and a female of 5lb 12ozs both in their fifteenth year. These are thought to be amongst the oldest recorded trout. At the time of writing it is not thought to contain anything other than Eels.

Although Dr Davies' trout grew well, when the lake was netted sometime after the 'fry' release not a single one was found. The farmer of Tyddyn Rhys y Gader (GR 615965) however assured me that he often caught the smell of frying fish wafting across his fields form the nearby holiday camp.

Apparently experiments carried out with dye some years ago seemed to indicate beyond reasonable doubt that the water supplying this spring fed lake came from a point near Bryneglwys quarry, Abergynolwyn (see Llyn Pont Llaeron). The lake is known locally as Llyn Penoro'. A small brick lined reservoir north of Horon (GR 613970) supplied Aberdovey with water up to 1992.

## LLYN HYWEL
*GR 6626*
*Height: 1,784'*
*Group: Rhinogydd*
*Area: 13 acres*

It has been rather unfairly dubbed as one of the three most sombre lakes in Wales. It is certainly well contained on three sides but it certainly isn't a gloomy cwm to compare with say Dulyn, Idwal or

*Llyn Hywel*

Cau. A spectacular three hundred foot slab sweeps into the water at the eastern end whose angle is enough to give an easy rockclimb. It has been misinterpreted as Giraldus Cambrensis' one eyed fish lake (see Llyn Cŵn). Pennant gives it a mention (1781) as a lake containing "a race of trouts with the most deformed heads, thick, flatted and toad shaped". Ward (1931) concedes them to be dark, with large heads and prominent eyes; classic mountain trout which are not feeding properly. There are many small, lean trout in the lake which are obviously underfed, they have large oversized heads whose flesh do not keep very long before going off. The lake is also known as Llyn Cwm Howel. Hywel was supposedly a young farm worker who was on his way from Bont Ddu to Nantcol when he somehow got lost in the mist and the dark. Initially when he didn't turn up home and a token search made it was presumed that he had emigrated to America. Many months later his body was found on the shore of the lake. His mother in her bitterness is credited to have said that were it one of Corsygedol's dogs that had gone missing it would have been found a long time before. Corsygedol was the home of the Vaughn family, a lineage that produced at least

one member of parliament. Seen from the summit of Rhinog Fach
Llyn Hywel is a very photogenic lake.

## LLYN IDWAL
*GR 6459*
*Height; 1,223'*
*Group: Glyderau*
*Area: 28 acres*

One of the most popular corries in the country for geography field
trips concerned with glaciation. There are lateral moraines,
terminal moraines, striation marks, perched blocks, roche
moutonees and other glacial evidence all very obvious to pick out
and study. It is incredible therefore to think that Charles Darwin
accompanied by Professor Adam Sedgwick actually failed to notice
these signs during his first visit in 1831, it was to be many years
before he returned to see this evidence and begin the
documentation that formed the basis of our understanding of the
subject. Gallichan as recent as 1903 describes the lake as being an
old volcanoe crater. On the western shore of the lake huge
moraines thought to be formed by the bulldozing effect of the
glacier from Cwm Cneifion (GR 6458) run parallel to the lake. No
doubt some of these mounds were moraines formed by the Idwal
glacier. The largest is known as Bedd y Cawr (giant's grave) where
a huge giant called Idwal is buried. Tales of his exploits have been
lost and attempts to connect the other mounds with famous
warriors' graves have also by today become vague. Another Idwal
lays claim to the naming of the lake; he was the son of Cadwaladr
the last of the Briton kings who abdicated to Rome in the eighth
century. Rhodri Molwynog murdered Idwal and had his body
thrown in the lake, he was then able to claim his estate said to be
based where the modern day Penrhyn castle stands. Another
version has Idwal as Owain Gwynedd's son entrusted to Nefydd
Hardd of Nant Conwy while Owain was away. Nefydd was his
uncle and having two sons of his own contrived to cause a hunting
accident in Cwm Idwal so that his own sons Rhun and Dunawt
would inherit Owain's estate. Derfel Hughes (1866) relates how
Idwal was killed for striking Dunawt who had claimed Idwal's

falcon kill for his own. For this deed Nefydd was demoted to bondsman and his other son Rhun later gave land and money to establish the church at Llanrwst. It is said that since this sad incident no bird of the land will fly across the lake. There is no tradition of Tylwyth Teg in this sombre cwm but the devil has given his name to the dark chasm in the cliffs above (GR 638588) see Llyn Cŵn for the legend). The cliff is one of the few places where the Snowdon Lily grows. According to one Thomas Champion who toured Snowdonia in 1735 the Devil's Kitchen had been haunted by a spirit which had recently been tamed. The cliffs used to be known as Trigyfylchau. A lone boulder lying some distance from the south shore (GR 643591) is called the 'Parson's Boulder' and has an amusing tale. A parson many years ago during the then fashionable pastime of plant collecting came up to Cwm Idwal and sat at this spot to eat his lunch, it was quite still and misty. Suddenly he heard a low murmur which gradually grew louder and became a roar, at this point the ground started shaking and one can only imagine how terrified the poor parson would have been. Then out of the mist this huge boulder bounced and rolled to a stop merely feet away from him; he apparently ran and never returned! Pennant who toured in 1781 declared the lake to be the haunt of demons and that no bird dare fly across its waters. Above and to the south the long graceful Idwal slabs continue to provide generations of inexperienced rockclimbers with developed characters and dry mouths. There is even a very long Showell Styles ballad written involving the slabs in a humorous tale of love and rivalry which is usually left for recital at climbing club dinners. Noel Odell the last man to see Mallory and Irvine as they strived for the summit of Everest in 1924 made one first ascent here in 1919 and named the climb after the footwear he wore — Tennis Shoe! Today the cwm is owned by the National Trust and is a Nature Reserve, various plots of fenced off areas indicate studies that are in progress to help our overall understanding of the environment and therefore its long term conservation. The small rocky island near the east shore gives an indication of the sort of vegetative growth that could be expected were it not for the sheep which constantly graze the slopes.

Last century the cwm was owned by the Bethesda quarry magnate Lord Penrhyn who also happened to be a keen angler. The lake was well 'managed' in this respect and in addition to the native trout which were of the highest quality he introduced Loch Leven trout. The Ogwen Valley Angling Association who hold the present rights have not stocked the lake for a number of years but every now and then the flash of a silver belly having taken the fly heralds the beginning of an epic fight from one of the offspring of Penrhyn's Loch Leven, they are excellent fighters. Among the Association's Anglers Idwal has a reputation for being a good consistent lake. The lake is at its deepest (38′) just off the rocks on its west shore although a pool surrounded with weeds near its upper end is known as 'Y Llygad Glas' (blue eye) is also deemed a dangerous place. During a lull in the quarry production Penrhyn had some of his workmen construct the track leading from Ogwen to the lake, it was never properly finished so it is doubtful whether he was in fact able to use his pony and trap to reach Llyn Idwal as was the intention. A large double ended boat was kept in a boathouse the ruins of which can be seen near the bottom end of the lake on the east shore. On a still day, wearing polaroid sunglasses the actual boat can also be seen in the water a few yards away from the shore. The lake is held back by a large moraine which has piled up on to the bedrock; the shore at this point is composed of a shallow shingle beach which is very popular with walkers bathing tired feet in the summer. Large shoals of minnows are frequently seen at this end of the lake. The late Evan Roberts, a self taught Botanist of some esteem was the first warden in the Cwm.

## LLYN IRDDYN
*GR 6322*
*Height: 1,029′*
*Group: Rhinogydd*
*Area: 23 acres*

In keeping with most of this west coast of Ardudwy, burial chambers, hut circles and cairns dot the countryside as evidence that man has settled here since very ancient times. A particularly fine example of a cromlech can be seen by the side of the track that provides access to the lake. Corsygedol Cromlech (GR 603228) comprises of a huge slab of rock resting on one large boulder with what is left of the original pile of smaller boulders scattered by its foot, it is also known as Arthur's Quoit. It was the custom of burying the burnt ashes of chieftains and prominent citizens in these cromlechs, they would then be covered with rock and soil. One school of thought believe that these structures may have been constructed for other more ancient purposes first. A very old arched bridge called Pont Fadog (GR 607225) which is reminiscent of Pont Scethin (see Bodlyn) crosses the river after passing Corsygedol. The words SAER and the date 1762 can clearly be seen on it. An old British settlement is thought to have stood on the west shore of the lake. There is certainly a Tylwyth Teg tradition which casts an ominous light on the 'fair folk' of Llyn Irddyn. It was thought prudent to either walk on grass, carry some or even chew on a stalk when walking the shore of the lake, this was to prevent being dragged in by the Tylwyth Teg. That they should be considered capable of doing this is interesting and quite rare in Welsh mythology. It is also interesting that grass should be a form of talisman against them in much the same way as garlic is against the vampire. The lake is also known as Llyn y Derwydd (lake of the druid) and in tradition there are vague references to Mayday rites and rituals having taken place in connection with the Druids. The larger of the boulders along the lake shore have been linked to these rites. The water was considered to be beneficial by the Druids and it is thought that they had a crude fish trap on the south shore. It has always been fished for trout and remains quite popular. A curious double walled access corridor of common land leads to the east shore which is reminiscent of a similar arrangement at Llyn Cyri. The boundaries of six farms as well as the common land meet at the lake.

About half a mile to the west is the old drovers' route over to Bontddu which was quite a steep but important communication link in the old days. It was over this ridge that Richard Vaughn of Corsygedol was carried twice a year by his tenants as part of an agreement tied in with their tenancy. Vaughn was a member of parliament which neccessitated his attendance at Westminister, he was also extremely fat and it was for this reason that he had to be carried (presumably by a Sedan chair arrangement) to where a coach could then take him to London. He supposedly entertained Charles the second at Corsygedol. He died following surgery in an attempt to remove some of the fat. A mile and a half along this ridge of Llawlech is the pass of Bwlch y Rhiwgyr, a very ancient route to and from Ardudwy. It was from this pass that the 'seer' Rhys Ifans was lifted into the air by unseen forces and brought down unharmed but having been gifted with the ability to foretell the future. He is said to have predicted the great fire of London almost forty years before it happened. Just below the col a white rock represents the spirit of a noble lady who was murdered nearby. Another spirit is said to haunt a sheepfold (GR 636219), it is that of a baby who was also murdered. Dafydd Las who was the resident bard at Nannau composed a tune named after this spot 'Pant Corlan yr Ŵyn' (the hollow of the lambs' fold). An interesting old belief states that when a person standing on the col can see the chimney of Sylfaen farmhouse (GR 633212) with one eye and the bell house of Llanenddwyn church (GR 583234) with the other then he is close to a hidden cave containing treasure! An old cast iron pipe of some 6″ diameter leaves the lake and runs parallel to the stream for some way. It is damaged and obviously has not been used for its original purpose for some time.

## LLYN IWERDDON
*GR 6847*
*Height: 550′*
*Group: Moelwynion*
*Area: ³/₄ acre*

This is one of many small quarry reservoirs that were constructed during the slate boom of the second half of the nineteenth century. Water power was important to operate the quarry mills and all manner of leats and small retaining pools were engineered to increase the water catchment for this purpose. It has two retaining walls which is unusual for so small a reservoir, an indication perhaps of the magnitude of need that existed for this water. Its use as a quarry reservoir ceased in 1969 when the quarry closed. The lake has also been called Llyn Bwlch y Moch. Moch is Welsh for pigs but an old Welsh word no longer used meaning swift or early is also spelled moch. There are two other examples in Eryri of Bwlch y Moch, and all three because of their geography lend credence to the idea of moch as meaning a short cut. A look at the OS map would show that anyone wishing to travel from the Nantlle valley to the Cwellyn valley would be quicker to cut through Bwlch y Moch (GR 560550) rather than follow what is now the present day road. The same is true of the route the Pyg track takes from Penypass to reach the long cwm of Llyn Llydaw. Here it is also a quicker route for anyone walking from Blaenau to the cwms beyond than through Cwmorthin or up the Crimea pass. There are Brown trout in the lake at the time of writing although there have also been periods in recent years when it was thought to be empty of fish. An unsubstantiated rumour amongst local anglers (1994) has it as containing some stocked torgoch (arctic char).

| **LLYN JERICHO** | **and nearby pool** |
|---|---|
| *GR 6616* | *6717* |
| *Height: 100'* | *50'* |
| *Group: Cadair Idris* | *Cadair Idris* |
| *Area: ½ acre* | *1 acre* |

Years ago there were perch in this tiny pool but since a council tip was opened nearby some fifteen years ago it is thought that the water has now been contaminated.

**LLYN LLAGI**
*GR 6448*
*Height: 1,238'*
*Group: Moelwynion*
*Area: 8 acres*

This has always been a good fishing lake for brown trout although both feeder and exit streams are disappointing from the point of view of decent pools. The Blaenau Ffestiniog fishing society 'Cymdeithas y Cambria' holds the fishing rights at the time of writing. The best fish are found in the deep water below the cliffs. James Spooner the architect responsible for the building of the Ffestiniog railway once used a coracle to fish this lake. Ward (1931) refers to a "curious bubbling sound" heard at the lake and seems to think it may be gases escaping from rotting vegetation, the lake bed is generally muddy, a state which may support his theory. Gallichan (1903) also maintains the view that the best bank is below the cliff which is also where the larger trout of up to ¾lb lie. At that time the fish were extremly wary and difficult to hook due to the otterboarding that occurred there too often. The remains of an old settlement can be found on the north west shore which could possibly have been a 'crannog' type set up. Crannogs were artificial islands or structures constructed in and above the water which gave the added security from wild beasts and other enemies. They were generally used by the 'Beaker People' who had not discovered iron. Being a fair haired race many historians support the theory that they were the original Tylwyth Teg whose fear of iron was generated when tribes bearing metal weapons came over from the continent and slowly conquered them. The inevitably flawed folk memory of thirty centuries of tales told thousands of times eventually produced the little people. It was to be this image that remained when their mirth and magical exploits were set into print.

## LLYN LLENNYRCH
*GR 6537*
*Height: 700'*
*Group: Rhinogydd*
*Area: 6 acres*

There is also a farmhouse, a woodland and a gorge named Llennyrch on this northern section of the Rhinogydd above the village of Maentwrog. The gorge carries the water of Afon Prysor when it leaves Llyn Trawsfynydd, that is, the water that is not piped to run the power station at Maentwrog. Before the lake at Trawsfynydd was built Ceunant Llennyrch in flood must have been an awesome sight. A path that meanders its way up from the power station to the vicinity of Llyn Llennyrch and the farmhouse was the scene of a mysterious murder back in 1838. William Evans who lived in the farmhouse of Llennyrch also owned other property and it was his custom to collect the rents at regular intervals. One November evening following a day's rent collecting he had stayed longer than usual in one of the taverns of Maentwrog and it was quite dark when he set off up the path. He was never to reach his home. Two men lay in wait behind what has since become known as William Evans' tree, nobody knows the details of what happened only that his body was found in the morning a little below the path and the empty money bag neatly folded nearby. Scratch marks on the tree were said to have been made in the struggle as were some indentations in the ground. He had apparently dug his heels into the ground in an attempt to prevent himself being thrown down the mountainside. His assailants were never brought to justice and curiously enough no grass has ever grown in his heel marks! The tree can be seen to the left of the path on the way up at (GR 654392). A little higher up and close to where the path veers right there are some stones that were used at one time for strength testing games by local youths. They are called 'cerrig gorchest' and numerous examples of these rocks and sites of the activities that usually occured on the 'Sabbath' can be found throughout Wales (see Llyn yr Arddu). The lake is full of small trout that become very lively on a balmy summer evening. Talsarnau and Artro Angling Association did have the lease and the lake was stocked but is now in private hands. Three tiny pools marked on the map 400 yards west of Llennyrch become very low in the summer, the largest of the three which is linked by stream to Llennyrch contains small trout and minnows. The small chapel which is some two hundred yards from the lake has now been converted into a house.

**LLYN LLETY — see Hafod Y Llyn (Rhinogydd)**

## LLYN LLIWBRAN
*GR 8725*
*Height: 1,450'*
*Group: Bala*
*Area: 11 acres*

Edward Llwyd wrote to his cousin David Lloyd in 1686 informing him that rare plants were to be found on Aran Benllyn in particular "above Llyn Llymbran". Many locals still insist the lake is Llymbran. It is also referred to as Llyn Bran, Llyn Aran and Llyn Aran Benllyn. According to the Gossiping Guide (1891) a printing error on the part of the Ordnance Survey was responsible for the Lliwbran version which has become the accepted one by now. Gallichan (1903) calls it Llyn Aran. A small disused slate quarry lies three hundred yards north of the lake which opened around 1775 and then worked with fluctuating success for around a hundred and fifty years. Slate from the quarry can still be seen on the roof of Talardd (GR 894269). Hywel Harries an early pioneer of the Methodist movement stayed overnight at Talardd during one of his visits to the area. At the time of writing the only electricity in the house is generated from the river which powers the lights only. The road from Llanuwchllyn continues uphill to the famous Bwlch y Groes Pass where a junction leads left down to Llyn Efyrnwy or right down to Dinas Mawddwy. Just below this road (GR 908236) is a mound said to be the grave of Rhitta the Giant killed by King Arthur following an epic fight that began near the rocks on the road above. (See also Ffynnon Llyffant and Glaslyn).

The lake was well known for its attractive golden trout and has featured in many books and articles, Ward speaks highly of the lake as does Bollam in the early decades of this century. An interesting account is given by A.G. Bradley in his book 'In praise of North Wales' (1925). He describes a day at the beginning of the century when he aquires an 'urchin' from the school in Llanuwchllyn to carry his net. A most derogatory and condescending account of the boy's attentiveness follows which seem to be linked to the fish not biting. When they do finally bite

177

the boy is nowhere to be seen and Bradley seems more concerned with having to carry his own tackle than the possibility that the boy may have drowned. The lad as it turned out had understandably decided to go home; he probably didn't like Bradley's company. There was a time when a bull in the access field played a part in the fishing lore of Lliwbran with many a close shave story told by the old anglers. Today the lake is well stocked and owned by the farm of Tŷ Mawr. The cliffs above the lake are very steep and over the years a large number of sheep have fallen to their deaths. It has seen some human tragedy as well, climbers and plant collectors mainly; people who conciously took the risk in following their chosen activity. But a few years ago a young woman from Nant y Llyn farmhouse in the valley below was out walking with her husband. The exact circumstances are not known but she too was killed on Craig y Llyn. About four hundred yards downstream of Nant y Llyn a very old arched bridge without a parapet lies almost hidden in trees and ivy, (GR 891261) this is Pont y Gilfach. It is very old and is known in the valley as the Roman Bridge but is more likely to be seventeenth century. Today it is only used by the sheep and the shepherd but on the 20th June 1781 a handful of some very grateful people gingerly crossed Pont y Gilfach. A terrible storm had broken over the Aran resulting in some severe flooding that killed fifteen people, dozens of cattle and sheep, destroyed many homes and every bridge in the watershed, all except this one. The small group of cold, wet people that used it that terrible night had walked over five miles to cross the river to get to their home which at the beginning of their detour was only yards away. The bridge was to survive two other major floods; one in 1880 and one in 1926. Above the bridge almost on the skyline of the steep slope rising to the east is a singular quartz pinnacle called 'Y Maen Bras'. Opposite the long ridge that joins Aran Benllyn with Aran Fawddwy sweeps south from Llyn Lliwbran. A faint weakness line can be discerned rising from a point just south of the lake diagonally to the summit of Benllyn, this is Llwybr Leusa (Leusa's path). Various tales are told to explain its name. One story has Leusa as an old lady who had bought a cow in the market and brought it home this way. Another story tells of a thief from Dolgellau who came this way to steal half an ox which had been salted and was hanging from one of the beams of Nant y Barcud farmhouse. Other references to a shepherd who could ride his horse this way and a character who could run the path occur but nobody can say with any conviction who Leusa really was.

## LLYN LLYDAW
*GR 6354*
*Height: 1,430'*
*Group: Wyddfa*
*Area: 110 acres*

According to Sir John Rhys Llydaw is Welsh for Armorica and W. O. Pughe's 1803 Dictionary has it as 'extending along the water'. The geologist, Ramsay believed it to be a derivitive of 'lludw' (ash) because of the ash like deposits found along the shore. Llydaw is also the Welsh for Brittany where a similar language is still spoken, and where there can be no denying a historical link exists between the two countries. Folklore will insist that the settlers of Brittany came originally from Wales or certainly shared a common root. Is it not possible that some of the people who lived on the shores of this lake took the name with them in much the same way as the Welsh who emigrated to Patagonia last century did? There is evidence that a Crannog settlement (see Llagi) did exist here. It is a larger than usual corrie lake and has a fine moraine dam at the eastern end, it has a maximum depth of 190' which makes it amongst the deepest of Eryri's lakes. Although next to no mining took place on the shore, the lake certainly suffered from the copper waste from the Snowdon mines near Glaslyn above in that they poisoned the fish. J. H. Cliffe writing in 1840 describes an incident when one of the colts followed him and Harry Owen of Penypass into the water and had to be rescued, this means that there must have been fish in the water at that time for Cliffe to even be in a boat. W. M. Gallichan writing in 1903 describes the trout in Llydaw as being large and keeping near the middle. They apparently only rise near the surface for a few minutes ever hour. Baiting with worm was considered a good bet near the upper end of the lake. The large stepped Brittania crushing mills on the north shore (GR 629545) were built in 1898 to process the copper ore from Cwm Glaslyn above. The ruins are still to be seen as well as the huge 'piano' shaped crushing hammers lying by the side of the track. The lake then apparently took on a greenish hue along the shoreline as early as 1899 due to the copper washings. The mines closed in 1916 but there was obviously so much seepage from the works that it was bound to continue for many years. Arthur Lockwood (see Llyn Gwryd) put a score of trout in sometime in the 1930's but his optimism was not rewarded, they lived their lives out but did not reproduce and the lake remains without fish. It seems ironic that during most of the period when mining occured fish continued to survive but during the final few years leading to the mine's closure the waters became polluted, a legacy that has continued to the present day. The fine track that leaves Penypass and skirts the north shore is called the Miner's Track and was constructed during the first decade of last century soon after the mines opened. Originally the ore was carted along the track and rafted across the narrow eastern end of the lake where the causeway is today. In or around 1853 however one of the rafts capsized and despite the only casualty being a tethered horse it was decided to build a causeway. A David Jones of the Prince Llywelyn hotel, Beddgelert was given the contract. During the work that entailed lowering the lake by 12′ an ancient dugout canoe was found in the silt, further evidence that settlements once adorned the lake shore. The canoe was oak and measured 10′ X 2′ and was sold to a Dr Griffiths who paid £5 and costs for the workmen to carry it down to Beddgelert. He wrote an article on it to the Cambrian Journal in 1862; the canoe is now on display at the National Museum, Cardiff. In 1906 Cwm Dyli Hydro electric power station was built, the first on the National Grid and the level of Llydaw was raised slightly, possibly to its original level. The catchment area for the power station is only 4 square kilometres but with an average rainfall of 13 feet is obviously able to maintain its efficiency. Initially the elctricity was for the slate quarries, there were even plans to build an electric railway at one stage. In 1988 the last two of the four pelton wheel turbines which had been working since 1906 producing 5 megawatts of electricity were removed and replaced with the more efficient Francis turbines. Cwm Dyli is computer controlled and is operated from Dolgarrog, (see Llyn Coedty). The twin pipes that effectively bisected Cwm Dyli and were both an eyesore and a landmark for almost eighty five years have now been replaced by a single pipe. There was a suggestion and a hope that this new pipe may have been buried but it too lies on the surface. Since the power station was built three generations of walkers have had the dubious pleasure of occasionally having to wade across the causeway. This depended of course on whether electricity was being generated or not, if it was then the lake level would be low and the causeway uncovered, but if not then the lake level would be maintained as high as possible which usually meant that at least a foot of water covered the causeway. This has not happened now for many years but up until the mid seventies the semi-expected surprise of having to walk through water could be built into any day's outing that involved returning along the Miner's Track. The lake's capacity is 765 million gallons.

## LLYN LLYWELYN
*GR 5650*
*Height: 796'*
*Group: Moel Hebog*
*Area: 6 acres*

The col and rocky hillock above the lake a mile to the west are both called 'trwsgl', a name that defies all obvious explanation (see Llyn Cwm Trwsgl). But there is also another spot with this strange name a mile downstream of the lake to the east and this has a legend which both involves the lake and attempts to explain trwsgl. Llam Trwsgl (GR 574504) is the name of a gap between two rocks through which the river Colwyn flows, it is thought to be the place where the river was crossed years ago. Below this mini gorge a long deep pool known as Llyn Nad y Forwyn (pool of the maiden's cry) has its own legend. Many years ago two giants had an argument;

they were both convinced that each one could outjump the other. After some time spent arguing they decided to hold a jumping competition. It was held on a particular rock which can be seen on the eastern side of the road. The first one jumped and only just made it across the river and the mark made by his foot as he landed can still be seen on the rock. The other giant fared better, he managed to jump all the way up into the cwm, the spot where he landed was quite soft and the large hollow he made was soon filled with water to form Llyn Llywelyn. Trwsgl meaning clumsy presumably refers to the first of the two giants. Llyn Nad y Forwyn is so called because tradition tells us that a young maiden was pushed into the pool one stormy night by her fiance who had fallen in love with another. The maiden's ghost has been seen rising out of the water on some nights whilst at other times wheels of fire have been seen running the length of the pool, (see Llyn y Bi), sad wailings and moaning sounds have also been heard on certain nights of the year. The ghost is known as 'Bwgan Pen Pwll Coch', Pwll Coch being the pool immediately above Llyn Nad y Forwyn and where the giant's footprint can be seen. Sea trout have been caught in this river Colwyn.

The stream leaving Llyn Llywelyn is called Afon Hafod Ruffydd Isaf because it flows through a farm of that name just before it joins the Colwyn. At the beginning of the nineteenth century a very skilful midwife whose services were much sought after lived in Hafod Ruffydd. One night when the little stream was swollen with rain she fell in whilst trying to cross just below the lake and was drowned; her memory has been perpetuated in poetry. In 1794 a brass shield weighing four pounds and just over 2' wide was found in the marsh near the lake, it had twenty seven concentric circles on the front. Pennant was given the opportunity to view it when he toured in 1781. The next cwm to the south is called Cwm Meillionen and although the forestry now covers most of its slopes it too once had a handful of dwellings. The house of Meillionen itself was once occupied by two batchelors who, one day received a visitor. The visitor had come as a result of a dream; in the dream he had seen a ruin called Hafod Ernallt near Meillionen and hidden beneath a certain stone in this ruin there was a hoard of treasure. The two wily old batchelors managed to convince him that it was Meillionydd in the Lleyn that he was after and in the morning saw him on his way. They in turn went up to where the old ruin was situated (GR 573484) and found the stone in question. Beneath, exactly as the dream had said they found a hoard of treasure and became very rich. A small room having neither door or window which is entered via a small hole described by Jenkins (1899) was still evident in 1994, the main ruin almost completely covered in moss. Just above the old ruin is one of the two sites put forward as Glyndŵr's cave (see Hafod y Llyn). A large horizontal fault crosses the impressive cliff of Moel yr Ogof (GR 560478), this is called Ogof Elen and is generally regarded as where Glyndŵr hid for a brief time. It involves a tricky scramble across the face of the cliff to reach what is only a shallow depression affording little shelter. At the beginning of the scramble another, more obvious cave is often mistaken for it; this is in fact an old asbestos mine, said to be the only one in the country. The whitish grey seam can be seen on the right wall. Another notable, one Ieuan ap Rhobert of Gesail Gyfarch supposedly hid here during the Wars of the Roses. At (GR 572473) in a small boulder field in the cwm there is another cave formed by the chance meeting of two rocks that also has a strong claim to be Glyndŵr's cave. It is drier, comfier and close to a spring which is known as Ffynnon Glyndŵr.

According to Ward (1931) the lake was much larger at one time but had diminshed in size to little more than a marshy pool containing a few very small trout. Since then it has been slightly enlarged with a dam but it is doubtful if the quality of fishing has improved. The forestry contains a fine camping site which has attracted other activities like pony trecking, orienteering and mountain biking through the forest tracks, fishing permits may be obtained at the campsite.

## LLYN MAENDERYN
*GR 6052*
*Height: 1,850'*
*Group: Wyddfa*
*Area: 1 acre*

This tiny tarn lies just off the south ridge of Y Wyddfa some 500 yards north of Bwlch Cwmllan. It is very exposed and shallow and is devoid of fish. Just over the ridge to the north a Mosquito crashed into the rocks on 31st July 1948 after being hit by lightning and breaking up. The pilot and a passenger were killed. A doll found at the scene was apparently being taken by the passenger,to see his wife who had just given birth to twins. This ridge is an excellent approach to the summit of Y Wyddfa which requires care in windy conditions.

## LLYN MAES Y PANDY
*GR 6908*
*Height: 175'*
*Group: Cadair Idris*
*Area: 0 acre*

One of two lakes included in the book which do not exist! It was a small spring fed pool at (GR 699087) measuring perhaps quarter of an acre. Also known as Llyn Bach and Llyn Y Garnedd it was drained some forty years ago. The spring and stream still flow and a large cairn of rocks which stood out of the lake like an island is still there. Maesypandy farm nearby was once owned by the Vaughns of Nannau and although of a later and different lineage one John Lloyd became the High Sheriff of Meirionnydd in 1644. Folklore tells us that many years ago the second wife of one of the farmers of Maesypandy took her own and her husband's son (by his first marriage) to the pool to bathe them. Somehow the eldest son was drowned thereby leaving her own son the only heir; although suspicious nothing could be proved contrary to her account of it being an accident and matters were uneasily allowed to pass. However the spirit of the drowned boy did not allow matters to rest and for many generation he haunted her descendants and caused some of them to drown in the same pool. The spirit was eventually exorcised and put into a sealed earthen jar which was buried beneath the cairn in the pool.

## LLYN MAIR
*GR 6541*
*Height: 258'*
*Group: Moelwynion*
*Area: 14 acres*

Thousands stop to enjoy the roadside beauty of Llyn Mair every year. It is a very fertile lake, its banks a chaos of growth whilst seagulls and a variety of water birds including swans add the variety to this much photographed lake. It is a shallow lake, being no deeper than 5'. It has been vaguely connected with Saint Mary (see Hafodyllyn, Harlech) because the name Mair is the Welsh version of Mary and also because its nearest neighbour is called Hafod y Llyn. Llyn Tal y Bwlch is another name that has been used for it. Plas Tan y Bwlch which has belonged to Gwynedd County Council since 1975 and run as a Study centre was the home of the Oakeley family who owned many of the quarries in Blaenau Ffestiniog until the early 1960's. The original house was built in the fifteenth century, its previous name being Plas Madog. There are trout in the lake and at one time was renowned for its pike but it is thought that they are no longer there. A generation ago 2/6 half a crown (12½p) was offered for each pike caught. According to tradition it was approximately a mile to the south near Felinrhyd that Pryderi was killed by Gwydion in single combat, this came about following the failure of peace talks. The story occurs in the Mabinogion (see Llyn Cors y Gwaed). A rounded boulder forming a part of the corner of Maentwrog church has been said to be his gravestone. The boulder is actually called Maen-Twrog (Twrog's stone) and may be linked to a seventh century saint of that name. An earth embankment with a masonry lining on the water face was built in 1780 to give a capacity of 63,000 cubic metres. The water was used to power a saw mill believed to have been at (GR 659409).

## LLYN Y MANOD
*GR 7144*
*Height: 1,400'*
*Group: Moelwynion*
*Area: 16 acres*

The lake lies halfway between Manod Mawr and Manod Bach on the saddle formed by the two mountains. It has been described as a deep, dark lake containing trout that grow up to eight pounds. Its angling traditions have always been strong with regular stocking taking place under the management of Cymdeithas y Cambria, Blaenau Ffestiniog's fishing club. Fishing rights were first obtained by the club in 1894, the rent being £1 a year paid to the crown! By 1898 the first of two boathouses had been built and the lake's reputation steadily grew season by season as the management programme developed. A total of 5,000 young trout reared in the hatchery nearby were put in in 1924 whilst in 1931 5,000 water snails were put in to improve the food supply. There is a legend of a young girl discovering a cave on the slopes by the lake but because the entrance was slippery she decided to fetch her father before venturing inside. When they returned the cave was nowhere to be seen and has not been seen since. Half a mile to the north east the highest slate quarry in Wales can be found. Graig Ddu was mainly open cast and opened around 1800. In 1882 there were 110 men working here some of them living in barracks. The quarry closed in the 1940's and later attempts to extract slate in the 1980's using untopping methods have to a large extent destroyed the remains of the 'old' quarry. The quarry workers used a particular red clay found in one of the local dingles called Ceunant Sych to hold their candles and a specific type of moss was used to clean the bore holes in preparation for blasting, they were occasionally given half a day off to gather these natural resources. Some of the Blaenau quarrymen preferred clay taken from the shore at Talsarnau.

## LLYN MARCHLYN BACH
*GR 6062*
*Height: 1,600'*
*Group: Glyderau*
*Area: 12½ acres*

Considering its size this is quite a deep little reservoir of 97' which has been extended from an already existing lake. The first dam of any substance was constructed by the Vaenol estate in 1960 and this provided water for the Gwyrfai district. There were other alterations in 1969, 1971, 1978 and 1985. Granite blocks from Gwalchmai quarry helps protect the dam rim from wave action. At present the dam is 26' and it has a capacity of 350,000m³/70 million gallons. It is used as a stand-by reservoir and supplements the areas normally covered by Ffynnon Llugwy. The approach is along a modern tarmac road which continues past to its larger neighbour Marchlyn Mawr. The extensive quarry remains just below and north of the lake were an attempt to obtain cheaper slate in the world slump in prices which occured in the 1950's. Although thousands of tons were lorried out the venture didn't solve the problems and closed in 1969 at the same time as Dinorwig — the mother quarry. The huge expanse of wet moorland stretching north of the lake once dubbed 'the great soggy yonder' by an off-route mountain biker was the traditional spot of a great battle. Brwydr Gwaun Cynfi. According to Hugh Derfel Hughes (1866) the battle took place against the Irish in 396 A.D. Other historians prefer the theory that Edward the first crossed over from Anglesey in 1295 to crush the first real resistance shown by the Welsh since Llywelyn was killed in 1282. He was making for Dolgellau where his army was to do battle with Madog ap Llywelyn when he was ambushed here at Gwaun Cynfi. A coin bearing the head of Edward has apparently been found. There are numerous other myths and heresays regarding other battles which coupled with swords, weapons and place names in the area lend weight to the theory that there may have been several skirmishes here over the centuries. Another battle that was settled some three hundred yards below the lake was according to locals, fought in court. The bold, well maintained wall that runs north west from Marchlyn Mawr past Marchlyn Bach was the boundary between the two powerful estates of the Vaenol (Ashetton-Smith) and the Penrhyn (Pennant) who owned the Dinorwig and the Penrhyn slate quarries respectively. It would seem that a dispute arose over the use of the stream draining Marchlyn Bach. Water was a very important commodity for quarries in those days and the problems arose when one or other of the two parties diverted the stream for his own exclusive use thereby depriving the other of water. The stream actually meandered in and out of both estates. This sort of occurrence was not uncommon in those days (see Llyn Coch, Carneddau). The matter was finally settled in court when it was decided to install a 'Carreg Rhannu' (dividing stone) in the wall at the point where the stream crossed. This large diamond shaped stone, in conjunction with iron grills set into the wall effectively shared the water; up to the 1940's it would receive a weekly visit to ensure that the grills were not blocked. The OS map shows the unusual phenomena of a stream dividing at (GR 604630) each branch then flowing down two separate valleys, this is the site of the 'Carreg Rhannu'.

Early OS maps show Elidyr Fawr as Carnedd Elidyr while Elidyr Fach is a nameless spur but it is interesting that Pennant (1781) refers to them as Llider Vawr and Llider Vach. Marchlyn Bach was called Marchlyn Isaf in 1802. It has always been known to contain trout although never large ones and despite the quarrying both the lake and the stream below still has small brownies.

## LLYN MARCHLYN MAWR
*GR 6162*
*Height: 1,979'*
*Group: Glyderau*
*Area: 52 acres*

A lake steeped in legends and half recorded myths. Marchlyn means the lake of the horse and there is a legend that anyone wandering the lake shore by themselves in mist risks the danger of being scooped onto the back of a huge black stallion which will then gallop three times around the lake and plunge into its depths. Williams Llandegai (1802) refers to a tract of land nearby called Rhos Marchlyn where young horses were turned out for the summer. Elidir Fawr the mountain towering above also has a stake in the horse connection. It is said that Elidir was a chieftain who came from the north country to marry Maelgwn Gwynedd's daughter Eurgain. He arrived on a horse so big it could carry seven and a half people, the half being his jester who ran alongside with his hand on the saddle! Geoffrey of Monmouth refers to three Elidirs who were prominent leaders in Britain, 286, 272 and 261 B.C. he may have been one of these. The lake was traditionally the place where evil spirits were sent in byegone days by those with the gift for banishing them. There is a somewhat confused story of a shepherd stumbling across a cave beneath the Creigiau Cwrwgl cliffs south west of the lake. Inside were Arthur's treasures, when he turned he saw a coracle with three beautiful women being rowed by a figure so terrible and hideous that he lost all sense of direction and could never find the cave again. A fisherman apparently saw a strange sight many years ago. He was fishing the lake when a heavy mist descended, it cleared briefly, enough for him to see a small man thatching a hay stack on a ladder, the bottom of the ladder was resting on the water! Creigiau Cwrwgl (coracle rocks) contain a fine pillar called the Pillar of Elidir which has some difficult rockclimbs. Elidir Fawr is the only one of the three thousanders to be composed of Cambrian rock, the second oldest in the world. Somewhere on the slopes beneath the lake (the spot is unknown to the author) there is a rock which has been inscribed with 'Lewis Bishop of Bangor' and a cross.

Water from the lake was used for raising the slate from the depths of Penrhyn quarry and as a result the level of the lake was frequently quite low which ruined the quality of the fishing. Before the days of the quarry there were supposedly two trout types found in the lake. Dark coloured ones with largish heads were caught beneath the rocks on the south west shore whilst lighter, prettier trout were found on the opposite shore. The lake was also used to supply water to the public. In March 1976 the lake was drained as part of the work in constructing the Dinorwig Pump Storage Scheme, the largest in Europe. Ffynnon Llugwy was made available to make up for this loss of public water. A series of tunnels were cut through Elidir Fawr from the lake bed and a power station installed deep in the mountain. The water having turned the turbines then continues into Llyn Peris where it is stored until off peak electricity pumps it back up to Marchlyn Mawr. All the fish were removed to Llyn Padarn. The lake was allowed to start refilling in October 1979. The construction work that included a huge dam to increase the lake's volume also involved building the tarmac road leading to the lake. The dam is 117' high and consists of a rock filled embankment with asphalt and concrete facing which gives a capacity of 700,000m$^3$/140 million gallons. During this work it was rumoured that several otter boards and other poaching implements hidden beneath various rocks were discovered. They will never be needed here again as no fish could be put in and expected to survive the dramatic fluctuating levels of the lake and what must be a terrific current generated when the power station is on. The maximum level of the lake was raised by 113' by the construction of the new dam which was specifically engineered to cope with a 'tidal' fluctuation of over a 100'. This represents the volume of water used (maximum) to generate electricity which would then be pumped back up. On June 12th 1991 a private helicopter was filming above the lake when it was caught in a strong downdraught and crashed into the water. Both occupants survived but electricity generating was held up for two days while the wreckage was salvaged.

## LLYN MELYNLLYN
*GR 7065*
*Height: 2,094'*
*Group: Carneddau*
*Area: 18½ acres*

The largest of the four lakes in the Carneddau to be over two thousand feet above sea level; Melynllyn means yellow lake.

Although it has a small dam which was deliberately breached in 1970 built at its northern end in 1887 the lake is kept back by a large obvious moraine with some huge boulders. Despite its sombre appearance with the cliffs of Craig Fawr providing a sinister backdrop it is a relatively shallow lake. There are Brown trout although never large which are traditionally taken at sunset. Arctic Char from Llyn Peris have also been relocated here. It is a fly fishing only lake, permits for which can be obtained from Welsh Water PLC, Penrhosgarnedd, Bangor (☎ 01248 351144). In January 1943 an Anson airplane crashed into the summit of Foel Grach, the pilot took over 17 hours to stumble down to Rowlyn Uchaf farm (GR 747681) for help. Amateur divers found the wreckage of another plane in 1968 lying in the deepest part of the lake. At the time it was thought to be an unrecorded wreck but is now believed to be part of the Canberra which struck the summit of Carnedd Llywelyn in 1957, (see Ffynnon Llyffant). South of the lake an old 'hone' stone quarry spread over two sites now lies disused. The slate which would be soaked in oil for two days were extensively used for sharpening chisels, planes and other tools. The short tramway leading from the quarry face to a dressing mill at (GR 706656) can still be traced. A leat cut from the lake was used to power a water wheel can also be traced, the huge flywheel is still in situ inside the collapsed building. During the many rescues involving wartime planes in this particular area the old mill was used as an advanced base. The quarry track which is still in remarkably good condition leads to the Eigiau road (GR 732664). The peat bog just below the lake has an abundance of ancient Birch stumps and branches from the old forests which covered Eryri up to two thousand feet over forty centuries ago. Along with Dulyn, Melynllyn provides water for the Llandudno district and is owned by Welsh Water.

## LLYN MORWYNION
*GR 6530*
*Height: 1,500'*
*Group: Rhinogydd*
*Area: 5 acres*

There has been some confusion between this lake and the next in the context of legends. A few authors have linked the maidens of Dyffryn Clwyd story to this lake, possibly because it is nearer Ardudwy but most sources place the legend at Llyn Morynion, the next lake. It is interesting to note that the correct grammatical plural of 'morwyn' namely 'morynion' has not been applied to this lake whereas the lake on the Migneint has been blessed with this dignity. The famous 'Roman Steps' pass within two hundred yards to the south as they lead over Bwlch Tyddiad. They do continue for a short distance beyond the Bwlch but peter out to become an ordinary path as the conifers are approached. These 'steps' have puzzled historians for many years; they are in fact a series of large slabs paving the path leading up from Cwmbychan. A similar though not as well publicised series of 'path steps' lead from Cwm Nantcol to Bwlch Drws Ardudwy (GR 645273). They were popularly thought to be a route for Roman slaves to carry the gold from the mines of Trawsfynydd to waiting galleons at Harlech but various other theories have been put forward regarding their origin. They have been dated as pre-Roman as well as post-Pennant (due to the fact that he did not mention them in 1781). They were in all probability medieval trading routes and not mentioned by Pennant because they weren't regarded as anything more special than any other 'attended' track through wet moorland. There are some smallish trout in the lake.

## LLYN MORYNION
*GR 7342*
*Height: 1,300'*
*Group: Migneint*
*Area: 28 acres*

There are two popular legends to explain this lake's name which means lake of the maidens. Many years ago there was an apparent scarcity of women in the commote of Ardudwy so the men of the coast decided to raid Dyffryn Clwyd in the hope of taking some young maidens back with them. They came at night and surprised the valley community and by dawn were on their way over Hiraethog. A large group of armed men swiftly followed them and caught them up near this lake high up on the Migneint moor. A battle followed which resulted in all the men of Ardudwy being killed. They were buried near the old Sarn Helen Roman road (GR 722425) about a mile to the west of the lake. Another version has three Ardudwy youths who captured three Clwydian maidens, they were pursued and caught by the fathers and brothers who then killed them. There were apparently thirty mounds but most if not all have disappeared, all that is left now is some undulations and uneven ground. The skirmish occured at a place called Bwlch y Wae (pass of woe) and the name of the farm is Tŷ Nant y Beddau (house of the stream of the graves). The legend then continues to describe how the maidens then threw themselves into the lake to drown. This was presumably because they had accepted their new husbands with relish and couldn't face the prospect of returning having done so. The second legend comes out of the Mabinogion and involves Gwydion the sorcerer who pursues Blodeuwedd his own creation (see Llyn yr Oerfel for the story). She flees with her maidens from the fort at Tomen y Mur but are constantly looking back at their pursuers, this proves to be their undoing because they all fall headlong into the lake and are drowned, all except Blodeuwedd who is transformed into an owl by Gwydion.

It is a very popular lake for fishing having been an integral part of Cambria's development plans since their inaugeration in 1885. The east bank is sub-leased off Barry Edge who leases the sporting rights from the Crown. A major competition was held here in 1985 to mark the centenery. An attempt was made in 1931 however to ban fishing here because it provided water for the town of Blaenau Ffestiniog, the attempt failed. The dam was built in 1879 and gives the lake a maximum depth of 42'. Since 1993 Morynion also supplies Trawsfynydd with its water. In 1906 the poet Ellis Evans received his bardic name of Hedd Wyn during an eisteddfod held on the shores of the lake. Hedd Wyn was later to be immortalised in the Birkenhead National Eisteddfod in 1917 when his 'awdl' won the chair, he himself had been killed in the trenches a short time before not knowing of his success.

## LLYNNAU MYMBYR
*GR 7057*
*Height: 588'*
*Group: Glyderau*
*Area: 58 acres*

One cannot think of these twin lakes without thinking of Plas y Brenin, National Mountaineering Centre that stands above the lower lake. Originally built in 1800 as the Capel Curig Inn by Richard Pennant (of Penrhyn quarry and estates, Bethesda), it quickly assumed importance as an early tourist venue. The Shrewsbury to Holyhead Mail Coach used it as a staging post and even before Telford's 1815 construction of the A5 the 'Ancient Briton' coach brought tourists to Capel Curig. The journey to Holyhead could take as much as 14 hours! Among the specialities on offer were dried goat and trout from the lakes. The kitchen even had a roasting spit that was turned by a water wheel powered by the little stream. It was said that when the inn was later extended it could accommodate everyone in the parish twice over! One of the early and much respected Snowdon guides, Robin Hughes was based here. Thomas Roscoe and Walter Scott were one time guests. It was re-named the Royal Hotel in 1870 following Queen Victoria's visit. During the second world war it was used as a mountain warfare centre. In 1953 the hotel closed and became Plas y Brenin Mountaineering Centre in 1955.

A large stone which stood higher up the valley on the right of the road was removed to the inn at the beginning of last century. According to the stanza 'The Soldiers of Britain' it may have marked the grave of a Gwryd; other theories suggest it may have been the boundary stone of the old Irish settlement (see Llyn

*Llynnau Mymbyr*

Gwryd). The farmhouse at (GR 695573) is Dyffryn Mymbyr which is featured in Thomas Firbanks' 1940 classic 'I bought a mountain'. Years ago the Tylwyth Teg were active in the valley and a tale is told of a woman who lived by the lakes who left her baby with her mother while she went to work in the harvest. Unfortunately the old lady fell asleep and the Tylwyth Teg came into the house and swopped babies. The baby they left, although identical in looks was sickly, irritable and always crying and the mother quickly realised what had happened. She consulted with a 'wise man' from the Trawsfynydd district who told her to heat some salt on a shovel in the baby's room with the window open. When she did this the baby vanished and her own was returned none the worse for its experience.

There are some fine trout in the lakes, the top lake possibly having the best. Local anglers last century were prone to play down the quality of fish caught in Llynnau Mymbyr when they were compared with other mountain lakes. One can almost perceive a jealousy which is explained by the fact that fishing these waters was not easily available for the common locals, rather they were the reserve of the paying guest and the occasional netting for the hotel kitchens. Today the lakes are the domain of canoeists and other Plas y Brenin activities which has over the last forty years built up its own set of traditions and values. How apt for example that the rock overlooking the 'narrows' between the two lakes should be called 'Gibraltar' reminiscent of the entrance to the Mediterranean. A very dry summer will render the lakes seperate as the narrow channel between them is quite shallow, a few more centuries of silting should see the separation complete. Both lakes have a maximum depth of 29 feet.

## LLYN MYNYDD FOEL UCHAF
*GR 7020*
*Height: 1,120'*
*Group: Rhinogydd*
*Area: 1 acre*

This narrow little pool that seems to hug one of the low hills overlooking the Mawddach estuary is surrounded with disused gold mines. Initially the various test levels in the hillsides in this area were made in the search for lead. Gold was then discovered in small quantities which heralded the beginning of a number of ventures in search of this rich ore which was found mainly in white quartz. This search proved very expensive and although some public revenue was raised for the Foel Ispri mine the amount never reached the hoped for expectations. The Foel Ispri works eventually closed, only to re-open as a zinc blende mine. The 'new precipice walk' was the tramway for this mine, (see Cwmymynach). This did not prove to be a success either and in 1900 the whole lot was floated as 'Voel Mines, Meirioneth'; revenue was raised and some quite modern plant and equipment installed. By 1902 however the yields were still pitifully low and the concern closed in 1903. The remains of a small slate quarry can be seen just below the 'new precipice walk' (GR 707197) which only really ever scratched the surface. Ispri was a traditional giant, one of several in the area of Dolgellau; he made his home on the summit of the hill taking his name. The smaller pool just to the south of the lake was probably a reservoir for the works. There are no fish in either pool.

## LLYN NADROEDD
*GR 5943*
*Height: 1,738'*
*Group: Wyddfa*
*Area: 2½ acres*

Interestingly enough this is the only one of the three tarns that share this little cwm not to contain fish. Its exit stream tumbles over some quite precipitous rocks whereas both other pools share a stream that flows a little gentler down the mountain thus allowing the passage of fish. Nadroedd is Welsh for snakes but as for the reason it has been named thus I have been unable to fathom, (see Llyn Wylfa for a snake link). The lake level was artificially raised to supplement the water supply to the larger pool of Treweirydd but following the 1975 Reservoir Safety act the dam was breached and a

*Llyn Nadroedd*

channel cut to decrease the lake's capacity. There are some fine perched blocks and boulders in the area immediately around.

## LLYN NANNAU IS-AFON
*GR 7022*
*Height: 1,835'*
*Group: Rhinogydd*
*Area: ¼ acre*

A very small tarn on the eastern slope of Y Garn which is very shallow and devoid of any fish. It was beneath some rocks near a wall on Y Garn that two miners walking home one weekend in 1890 found a silver Chalice and Paten thought to have been hidden at the Dissolution of the Monastries. Cymer Abbey (GR 722195) was of Cistercian order founded in 1198, it was never a rich abbey and when destroyed in 1536 it only had four monks and the abbot (the abbot, Lewis ap Thomas later became Bishop of Shrewsbury). Many historians therefore doubt whether such a valuable find could have come from Cymer. Curiously enough it is inscribed as having been made by Nicholas of Hereford; there is no record of a goldsmith of that name in Hereford at that time. One theory is that they were commissioned by Edward the first in Chester in 1274 for the celebration of the founding of Vale Royal Abbey, a goldsmith by the name of Nicholas did exist in Chester in 1270. How they came to have been hidden near this insignificant little lake is a mystery. Since 1910 they have been at the National Museum of Wales, Cardiff. There is another small fishless pool some 500 yards south east.

## LLYN NANNAU
*GR 7420*
*Height: 800'*
*Group: Cadair Idris*
*Area: 2 acres*

This set of small pools were located in the grounds of Nannau estate to the north west of Dolgellau but are now largely drying up, they were created in fact as fish ponds. Sometime in the latter half of the eleventh century Cadwgan son of Bleddyn ap Cynfyn of

Powys established the estate of Nannau which at the time included most of the district around Cadair Idris. During the time of Llywelyn Fawr this estate became much smaller and closer in size to that which it is today. There have been many illustrious descendants of Cadwgan residing at Nannau, two perhaps in particular. Howel Sele who was a half cousin to Owain Glyndŵr was opposed to the rebellion and was even considered a danger by Glyndŵr. In 1402 Glyndŵr went to Nannau and captured him but was ambushed by Sele's men as he attempted to leave. Following negotiations through the Abbot of Cymmer the two men agreed to meet in the ground of Nannau to talk. During this meeting Hywel Sele made as if to shoot at a deer but instead drove his arrow at Glyndŵr. Having had the foresight to wear a chain vest the arrow did no real harm to Glyndŵr. A fight ensued which ended with Sele's death; his body was hidden in a hollow oak tree and the original house of Nannau burnt to the ground. The tree which was still standing in 1813 was sketched by Sir Richard Colt Hoare. Nothing now remains except a sun dial which marks the spot. Interestingly enough the tree which was known as 'Ceubren yr Ellyll' is still marked on modern OS maps at (GR 743199). Another descendant worthy of mention but contrasting in character was 'old' Sir Robert Vaughn who was an MP for 44 years. He did much for the district and was much thought of by the less well off. The Vaughn library of valuable manuscripts has thankfully been preserved for posterity. There are two other pools in the grounds of Nannau in the designated deer park. They are at (GR 746202) and (746201), they measure ½ acre and 1 acre and are at an elevation of 700'. The hill rising to the east is called Foel Offrwm and is the traditional home of a giant of that name. There are ancient settlements on its western slopes underlining perhaps the importance this corner where two rivers meet has had over the centuries. Two other pools totalling an acre are also situated within the Deer park (GR 746201).

## LLYNNAU NANT CWMANNOG
*GR 7662*
*Height: 370'*
*Group: Carneddau*
*Area: 0 acres*

These were in reality sediment pits for the 'Klondyke mine' (GR 762617) and no longer exist as pools. I include their mention purely because they appear on some OS maps.

## LLYN (CWM) NANTCOL
*GR 6026*
*Height: 210'*
*Group: Rhinogydd*
*Area: 2½ acre*

Although artificial, this reservoir, surrounded as it is by trees in this lovely narrow valley is quite an attractive pool. The dam which is a surprising fifty three feet in height was built in 1917 and is of concrete gravity construction. It produced the first electricity in the area soon after construction for a small number of houses which included the tiny chapel of Salem. Today a handful of houses receive their water supply from it whilst the electricity produced supplies the old Cooke's factory now sub let into units. It is owned by Cookes Chemicals who had an explosives factory at Penrhyndeudraeth. Before selling to ICI, the company retained a weedkiller plant at Llanbedr. The reservoir has a capacity of 32,000 cubic metres/6 million gallons. Four hundred yards north is the tiny chapel where the famous 'Salem' picture was painted by Curnow Vosper (see Hafod y llyn). Talsarnau and Artro Districts Angling Association hold the lease and there are both Brown and Rainbow trout present. The reservoir is also known as 'Cooke's Dam' or merely the 'dam'.

## LLYN NANTLLE UCHAF
*GR 5153*
*Height: 322'*
*Group: Moel Hebog*
*Area: 80 acres*

It is called 'uchaf' (highest) because before the quarrying took the area over there were two lakes, the other being the 'lowest'. It was drained to reduce the flooding in the Dorothea quarry pits. It is perhaps ironic that these deep pits are now flooded and are the reserve of amateur divers, many of whom get into difficulties. The quarry opened in 1820 and despite the flooding problems which began in 1864 it was perhaps the most profitable quarry in the area, it finally shut in 1968. Ward (1931) refers to two lakes, the lower one being silted up with quarry waste and unfishable. A painting by Richard Wilson in 1765 which is now in the Walker Gallery, Liverpool also clearly depicts two lakes. Edward the first apparently camped here in the summer of 1284 using the natural fortifications of the two lakes as an added security. In the Mabinogion story Lleu Llaw Gyffes was eventually found by Gwydion between the two lakes. He was in the form of an emaciated eagle following his deceitful murder contrived by Blodeuwedd, his wife, (see Llyn Morynion, Llyn Oerfel).

In addition to Nant-Lleu from the Mabinogion link there are two other explanations for the name. The golden haired water beast from Llyn y Gadair (Rhyd Ddu) was eventually caught and killed in this valley and the yell it gave is the 'llef' in Nant-llef. Another old belief was that the whole valley was once thickly wooded, hence the name Drws y Coed (gap through the trees) higher up the valley. One day a huge forest fire destroyed the trees and the cries of the trapped animals left such an impression on those who heard them that the valley was thus named, (valley of cries). After passing the lake whilst going uphill the valley begins to narrow, by looking carefully at the rocks on the right and using a liberal amount of imagination the figure of a human can be seen. Years ago this was pointed out to tourists as 'John Bull' or 'Old Meredith'. The famous Marged uch Ifan (see Llyn Padarn, Llyn Dywarchen) once kept a tavern at Telyrnia sometime in the 1750's/60's drawing much of the custom from the copper miners of Drws y Coed. Telyrnia (GR 521533) stood somewhere between the lake and the old tollhouse. There are trout in the lake and many years ago it is thought that the 'torgoch' or arctic char were also present. Edward Llwyd, the 17th century naturalist, conducted a survey and one William Rowlands claimed that they were present in Nantlle Uchaf.

## LLYN NEWYDD
*GR 7247*
*Height: 1,550'*
*Group: Moelwynion*
*Area: 12 acres*

Along with its sister lake Bowydd it was created to provide water for the Maen Offeren slate quarry (GR 715465). Both lakes occupy a shallow, wet basin on the uplands above Blaenau Ffestiniog. Although the quarry opened in the early 1800's it wasn't until the last half of the century that it became successful. Most of the quarrying was done underground and the water was used for powering saws as well as for counter weight to lift the slate out of the ground. In 1918 the waters were used to run a power station which was still in use quite recently. The dam was built in 1860 and consists of a clay and earth core with a masonry shell. At 22' the dam is capable of holding 100,000 cubic metres/20 million gallons of water. It is owned by Llechwedd slate company.

## LLYN NEWYDD (Rhos Quarry, Capel Curig)
*GR 7355*
*Height: 1100'*
*Group: Moelwynion*
*Area: 4 acres*

Known locally as Llyn Newydd this implies that the lake was constructed as an additional water source for Rhos quarry. The dam is about six foot high which must be close to the maximum depth of the lake, when full it had a capacity of 80,000m$^3$. Trout were put in some twenty years ago on one occasion and the fish present now are from that stock. Both the lake and surrounding land is owned by Rhos farm (GR 732568) and there is no right of way or access granted to the lake or the quarry.

## LLYN OERDDWR
*GR 5744*
*Height: 1,090'*
*Group: Moel Hebog*
*Area: ¾ acre*

Much of the area around this small pool is marshy and the summer months sees most of the lake covered in reeds and other growth and dries to form several smaller pools. There are some small trout present but they are seldom fished, the exit stream perhaps being better. Less than a mile north east of the lake the hillside of Muriau Gleision is traditionally where Owain Glyndŵr began training his soldiers. There is an old fort marked on the map (GR 586456) although its history is uncertain. A hut circle and the criss cross of ancient paths do seem to indicate that this upland corner may have been of some significance in the past. D. E. Jenkins (1899) indicated that the hut circles may have been used to guard the 'back entry' into Eryri, a route that effectively by-passed the easily defended Aberglaslyn Pass, they were apparently used at a later date as a venue for playing quoits by some of the men in the cwm. Jenkins also refers to a remarkable snake found at approximately (GR 594443) which was exhibited at London Zoo in the 1830's.

## LLYN YR OERFEL
*GR 7138*
*Height: 1,009'*
*Group: Trawsfynydd*
*Area: 9 acres*

Llyn yr Oerfel is located within three hundred yards of the Roman Amphitheatre (GR 708389) which would have included a modest sized fort and within four hundred yards of the old motte castle of Tomen y Mur (GR 705386). Sarn Helen the north-south Roman road also passes very close by. The original (pre-motte version) fort was built by the Romans around 78 A.D. it was strengthened about thirty years later and finally abandoned 140 A.D. The amphitheatre is thought to be the only example in Britain that was attached to a minor fort. The remains of the bridge that carried Sarn Helen over 'Nant Tyddyn yr Ynn' which drains the lake can also be seen a few yards below the present dam. The earth banks a little lower down are thought to be all that is left of some bath houses. Little is known about Tomen y Mur for the next few centuries until the year 1095 when the Normans under William Rufus made a determined forage into Gwynedd and took the fort. It may have been at this time that the mound was built but history tells us that his stay was in fact a relatively short one; the cold winter and the constant pressure by Gruffydd ap Cynan saw the Normans off. Henry the first also paid a fleeting visit to Tomen y Mur in 1114 but he too was seen off by Gruffydd who reigned supreme for 62 years. Folklore too has inevitably played its part. In the Mabinogion Lleu Llaw Gyffes and his wife Blodeuwedd make their home at Tomen y Mur. Lleu goes away for a period during which time Blodeuwedd takes Gronw Pebyr of Penllyn, Bala as her lover. They plot to kill Lleu, who, like Achiles is almost immortal. Blodeuwedd uses her guile to discover the means of killing him which involved not being indoors or out, not on the ground nor on horseback, and not being on either land or water. She then contrives a scenario that saw Lleu stepping off the back of a goat into a bath under the cover of leaves in the Cynfal Valley north of the castle. Hiding on Bryn Cyfergyd nearby was Gronw, at the precise moment he threw his spear and killed Lleu who was transformed into an eagle (see Llyn Nantlle). When he was eventually found by Gwydion (see Llyn Nantlle) and transformed back they set off for Tomen y Mur but Blodeuwedd had fled with her maidens (see Llyn Morynion). Gronw was then invited to face the same fate as Lleu but offered the added protection of being allowed to hold a rock between his body and Lleu's spear. Lleu's spear penetrated both the rock and Gronw killing him instantly. The rock which still has the hole caused by the spear was recently re-discovered and can be seen at (GR 716405). A mile to the north is the farmhouse of Cynfal Fawr the former home of Huw Llwyd who was a soldier, a poet and a sorcerer. He was born around 1568 and spent some time fighting in France before returning to the family home. His reputation as a wise man and 'seer' grew dramatically through a series of incidents and deeds attributed to his powers. He is said to have frequently visited a singular column of rock in the Cynfal gorge (GR 705411) called Huw Llwyd's pulpit in the middle of the night where he would shout and practise his incantations. His magic books were thrown into the gorge by his daughter at his death bed request where a pair of hands reached out to receive them into the water.

The lake which is heavily covered in reeds was a reservoir capable of holding almost 30,000 cubic metres/6 million gallons but following an inspection in 1986 it was decided to lower the level by about a foot and thereby not come under the judrisdiction of the 1975 act. Some twenty years ago it was used as a hatchery lake by the Prysor Angling Association. The reeds have only grown to such a prolific state in recent years. It still holds trout but owing to the vegetation fishing is difficult. The lake which is also known as Llyn yr Oerfa is crown property.

## LLYN YR OGOF
*GR 6346*
*Height: 1,170'*
*Group: Moelwynion*
*Area: 1 acre*

An extremely shallow tarn which has almost become a marsh. Nearby (GR 634466) is a feature known as the cave. It is in fact a chance meeting of two huge boulders that has been further adapted by man to create what is a very snug shelter. A very old north-south path passes seemingly through the lake and there are some ancient settlements half a mile north at a place called Bwlch y Battel (pass of the battle). It is traditionally where the forces of Ieuan ap Rhobert and the Earl of Pembroke fought during the War of the Roses. Ieuan was defeated and spent some time hiding in a cave on Moel Hebog (see Llywelyn). According to Jenkins (1899) numerous swords and daggers have been found on the site. The disused slate quarry two hundred yards south was owned privately by the owner/manager who lived on site. The slate was carted along the still existing track to the village of Croesor. There are no fish in Llyn yr Ogof. A small pool 400 yards south does not contain fish either. A very impressive perched boulder graces the skyline just to the north west above the lake, it is known as the quartz mushroom.

## LLYN OGWEN
*GR 6560*
*Height: 984'*
*Group: Glyderau*
*Area: 78 acres*

This is a natural lake which had its level raised by some two feet sometime during the early years of this century. This was done to provide extra water which in conjunction with other sources was taken out of the river Ogwen for the use of the Penrhyn quarry, Bethesda. It is still owned by the Penrhyn estates now managed from Porth Penrhyn, Bangor. It is a very shallow lake and is nowhere deeper than ten foot, because of this the capacity is only 100,000 cubic metres/25 million gallons. Most anglers over the years agree that the quality of the trout from this lake is excellent, many of the old local anglers making the specific point that they were far superior to those in Llynnau Mymbyr. They were apparently transported to London and other English towns wrapped in wet hay! The second Lord Penrhyn who was a keen angler stocked the lake with Loch Leven trout in addition to the extremely attractive native brownies. Today the fishing rights belong to the Ogwen Valley Angling Association and is the only one of their lakes which is regularly stocked with both Brown trout and Rainbow. Some years ago several newspaper articles appeared blaming the low flying exercices from RAF Valley for low fishing returns. The lake however continues to give good value for money. The area immediately around and just below the lake was known years ago as the 'Benglog', the three stage waterfalls commencing two hundred yards below the dam still retaining this name. At the foot of the first drop and old cattle shoeing station used by the drovers still survives despite its 'Home Guard' adaptation as a pill box during the war (GR 648605). Another 'pill box' stands hidden in boulders half way along the lake's north shore. Just above the former, traces of one of the original tracks up the valley can be seen

*Llyn Ogwen (top) with Llyn Idwal (right) and Llyn Clyd*

which was described by Pennant (1778) as 'the worse horse paths in Wales'. A little further up just beneath Telford's modern A5 the Capel Curig Turnpike Trust toll road runs parallel with traffic for some three hundred yards. This road had a short unpopular lifespan and suffered much vandalism by its users who were reluctant to pay for the privilege. The reconstructed foundation of its bridge is also there beneath the modern bridge. Looking up at the underside of the present bridge the extension which was added on to Telford's 1815 bridge some sixty years ago is clearly seen. The south side of the valley had a road too, constructed in 1797 by Lord Penrhyn, he later extended this to the Capel Curig Inn which he built in 1800 (see Llynnau Mymbyr). Locals will tell you that Penrhyn built this road following his failure to be elected as an M.P. Apparently the people of Conway voted against him. Following his defeat he swore that he would make grass grow on the streets of Conway. In opening up the valley and offering an alternative route to the perilous Penmaenmawr and Penmaenbach section he did in fact symbolically achieve his oath since much of the traffic was deprived from Conway. The earliest track took the north shore of the lake while all subsequent routes passed beneath Tryfan. A cave called Ogof Ifan Bach is located just off the old track and is one of two caves where tradition places Rhys Goch Eryri who like his friend Owain Glyndŵr had to hide from the English forces, (see Hafod y Llyn), the other cave is in a boulder field at the foot of Ysgolion Duon (GR 669638). On the south shore of the lake the steep rocky slopes of Tryfan rise majestically to their three thousand foot summit. Somewhere in this jumble of rocks there is a hidden cave containing treasure left behind by Irish settlers who were ousted from their stolen territory but were resolved to return, they never did and the treasure according to tradition awaits its discovery by an Irishman. Many years ago two brothers from the farm of Ciltwllan were searching this slope for a lost lamb when one of them happened across the cave. Inside there was a table with some large expensive looking bowls on it, the entrance was guarded by a vicious dog. He went to fetch his brother so that they could both tackle the dog but when they arrived back the cave could not be found. Another story tells of a young shepherd who found the cave in similar circumstances, there was no dog but he could not carry the heavy bowls so he covered the entrance lest anyone else should find it and went for help leaving a trail by whittling his stick. When he returned the following day not a single chip of wood could be seen, the Tylwyth Teg had gathered them all up. Tradition says that one day an Irish shepherd will see a black ram with a speckled face going into the cave and it will be he that claims the treasure. There are tales of hauntings too along the shore of Llyn Ogwen. There are more than one version referring to a ghostly coach which has been vaguely connected to the treasure in that it waits for someone to come out of the cave. Another story tells of the real coach travelling one night to the Royal Hotel, Capel Curig. It stopped to pick a man up by the lakeside who was playing cards whilst waiting. The horses became agitated and made extremely heavy weather of what was ostensibly a downhill section, they were covered in lather and breathing heavily with wide frightened eyes when they arrived. When the coach stopped the man vanished leaving behind a sickly smell of brimstone that hung in the air for ages.

The long northern ridge of Tryfan sweeping down towards the lake has been cut short by the glaciers of twelve thousand years ago to form a cliff that has become known as the 'Milestone Buttress'. Thousands of novice climbers' scrabbling boots have worn the rock smooth but it continues to be a popular crag. High up near its top and now barely distinguishable a rather worn white 'V' can be seen, this was apparently painted on the rock during the VE celebrations. The buttress was baptised because the tenth milestone from Bangor once stood at the roadside in front of it, sadly it was taken by somebody some twenty years ago during road improvements, wouldn't it be a pleasant enigma if it were suddenly to re-appear concreted back into place! Above the lower end of the lake Ogwen cottage (said to have been designed by Telford himself) is now an Outdoor Pursuit Centre owned by Birmingham LEA. A little further west Idwal Cottage Youth Hostel continues to flourish beside the car park and tea shack. Before the council decided to improve the site the tea shack used to be located by the side of the A5 just above where the two rivers Ogwen and Idwal join. It was a wooden affair built around an old caravan that had served tea there for over fifty years. Above the new 'shack' the disused Idwal Hone stone quarry is now used for cliff rescue drills and wet weather abseiling sessions by centre groups.

Considered by some to be the finest hone stone in the world it was also used for classroom writing slates. Both these products were in huge demand as far away as America. The quarry opened in 1796 and was owned by Lord Penrhyn. The patch of mature conifers between the car park and the road were planted to disguise the spoil heaps from the quarry. There is a boat house situated at the lower end of the lake.

## LLYN PADARN
*GR 5761*
*Height: 340'*
*Group: Wyddfa*
*Area: 280 acres*

Padarn was an ancient saint whose roots are long forgotten, the ruin of the church dedicated to him is just below the Victoria Hotel and the Snowdon train station. The most dominant feature that overlooks the lake however is Dolbadarn castle standing as it does on a rocky knoll between the two lakes. Llywelyn ap Iorwerth is thought to have built the castle at around the end of the twelfth/beginning of the thirteenth century. Later on his grandson Llywelyn ap Gruffudd (the last prince of Wales) kept his brother Owain Goch a prisoner here from 1255-1277 following the battle of Bryn Derwin. Following his own death and the downfall of the Welsh resistance in 1282 the castle was last used as a brief resting place for Dafydd, Llywelyn's other brother. He was also captured in 1283, reputedly near the summit of Bera Bach (GR 672678) from where he was taken and barbarically executed in Shrewsbury. The castle was all but destroyed by Edward, much of the material taken to Caernarfon for the erection of his own castle. Bingley during his described tour of North Wales (1798) made the suggestion that Ashetton-Smith should adapt the castle as an inn.

It is likely that many thousands of years ago Peris and Padarn were one lake but the silt and rock carried down by the river Arddu has effectively seperated them. The deepest part is 94' and it is one of only three Eryri lakes to have 'wild' arctic char (torgoch). These enigmatic fish feed in shoals in the cold depths of the lake and are caught in the following fashion. A spot is chosen (many of these spots are well kept and cherished secrets) and a line is lowered with baited hooks at regular intervals. When one is successfully hooked the angler is then able to determine the correct depth and site for that particular session. The char in Padarn are slightly larger than their counterparts in other Eryri lakes and catching one of a pound in weight is not uncommon. There are also excellent brown trout which are stocked by the Seiont, Gwyrfai and Llyfni Angling Association who hold the lease. The lake was for many generations a free lake in sharp contrast with its neighbour Peris which for years could only be fished by guests at the Royal Victoria· Hotel. The lake is also a popular venue for sailing and canoeing and the old slate tips on the south shore have for many years provided a wonderful arena for these activities for local outdoor centres as well as individuals. The area is known as the 'lagoons'. On the north shore the whole hillside is covered with deciduous trees of which the natural sessile oak is quite dominant; a still autumn day with blue skies makes the view across the lake from the Llanberis-Caernarfon road one of the prettiest in Eryri. The old bridge at the bottom end marks the spot where the salmon come every year to spawn as the lake subtley transforms itself into the river Rhyddallt before becoming the Seiont lower down as it picks up speed. At the upper end of the lake the beginnings of the huge Dinorwig slate quarry gashes into the hillside above. The impressive water-filled pit of Vivian quarry is the first of many chambers, tunnels and enormous pits that have been gouged out of Elidir Fawr over the last two centuries. The largest water wheel in the world can be seen in the old quarry buildings now transformed into a museum at this end of the lake. It is also from this large recreational complex that the little Padarn Steam train begins its lakeside journey along part of the original track used to transport the slate to Port Dinorwig· before the quarry closed in 1969. Many years before the quarry grew to become one of the largest in the world the lake was used to transport copper from the Nant Peris mines, and here there is an amusing tale to be told. Sometime between 1764 and 1770 a very remarkable woman by the name of Marged Uch Ifan came to live in Penllyn Cottage with her husband Richard. She came from Dyffryn Nantlle (see Llyn Nantlle) and was about seventy years of age. She had the reputation of being the best wrestler, rower, harpist, fox hunter and joiner in the district and despite her age this reputation was to stay with her for the next twenty years until she died in 1783 in her ninety first year. Her husband who died fifteen years before her was also an accomplished poet. Pennant who visited the area shortly before her death was disappointed in not finding her at home. Marged had the contract for transporting by boat the copper ore from the Nant Peris (Derlwyn) mines along both lakes to a small dock built at the side of a pool in the river Rhyddallt called Llyn Bogelyn from where it was carted to Caernarfon. Pennant stayed the night with Richard Farrington, one of the managers of the mines who most probably furnished him with her story. The Farringtons came from Eglwysbach in the Conwy valley and it is interesting to note that it was a T.B. Farrington who built a bridge across the Conwy in 1894 to carry the water pipes from Llyn Cowlyd. There have been many verses written in Welsh to celebrate this unique lady.

In the 1958 Commonwealth Games the rowing competitions were staged here at Llyn Padarn. An annual swimming race across the lake has also been held and a small sailing regatta was organised way back in the summer of 1889. A sad tragedy occurred here August 12, 1993 when a Wessex helicopter crashed into the lake killing three young cadets, a plaque on the shore commemorates this loss.

## LLYN PARC
*GR 7958*
*Height: 664'*
*Group: Betws-y-coed*
*Area: 22 acres*

This long narrow lake is the most easterly of the Betws lakes and lies in a north-south direction above and parallel to the Conwy valley. It is a natural lake which had its level raised around the time of the first world war to provide water for the Aberllyn lead and zinc mine. Some of the old levels actually penetrate beneath the lake, there is one huge chamber in particular which is called the 'cathedral stope', most of these old levels are now too dangerous to enter. In 1900 there were 200 miners employed in these mines which were to close in 1921. The lake was enlarged to a capacity of 89,000 cubic metres/18 million gallons, and was used to drive turbines for the mines. In the early 1960's an unfounded rumour was generated that water was seeping into Parc mine through an underground fault (see Llyn Sarnau and Pencraig for similar story). The concern that grew from this rumour reached a climax one night when someone opened the sluice gate and left the lake to drain to its original level. Unfortunately the result of this was a deluge of muddy water and debris that swamped Cwm Llannerch cottage and the railway line at (GR 709579).

A seven foot wall which was built by French Napoleonic prisoners of war can still be seen to the west of the lake. This was to keep the deer in what was then Gwydir High Park. The area around Llyn Parc is one of the last remaining strongholds of the Red Squirrel. In 1938 a huge forest fire which destroyed over 400 acres of trees actually 'jumped' across the narrowest part of the lake thus shattering the hope that it would act as a natural fire break. The conifers have since been replanted and a mature forest now surrounds the lake. A small but pretty gorge takes the exit stream down to join the Conwy about a mile below Betws-y-coed. The walk up to the gorge from Pont y Pair is a popular one with many hundreds of visitors every year and like its southern neighbour Llyn Elsi is the venue for an annual race organised in conjunction with the local running club 'Eryri Harriers'. There are no fish in the lake at present due to the poisonous level of lead from the mines but the lake is becoming 'cleaner' and it may well be in the not too distant future that trout could be re-introduced into Llyn Parc. It has a maximum capacity of 89,000m$^3$/29½ million gallons. Remains of the Aberllyn feeder pipe and concrete stanchions can be seen at various points below the lake. Some hundred yards below the dam a large stop cock is fenced off along with some accompanying metalwork just west of the approach path.

## PARRY'S POND (see Llyn Edno)

## LLYN PENARAN
*GR 8624*
*Height: 2,700'*
*Group: Bala*
*Area: ½ acre*

This, the second highest tarn in Eryri is only twenty five feet lower than Ffynnon Llyffant. It is one of three little pools found within a few hundred yards of the summit of Aran Benllyn but the only one marked on the map. Ward (1931) does mention one of the others as being 2,830' above sea level. In the dry summer of 1984 all three were still full of water whilst Llyn Bach (GR 8319) which is an acknowledged 'lake' on the OS map had dried up. There are no fish in any of them. There is an amusing little rhyme locally recited that gives the lake's dimensions and asks for its volume:

'Mae llyn ar ben yr Aran
Mae'n ugain llath o hyd.
A'i led yn bymtheg union,
'Nôl llathen Sion Pant Clyd.
Dwy droedfedd yw ei ddyfnder
Mae hyn yn ddigon siŵr,
A ddwedwch im' wŷr doethion
Sawl chwart sydd ynddo' ddŵr?'

I would roughly translate it thus:

'The pool on Aran's summit
is twenty yards along,
there's fifteen more across it
If Sion Pant Clyd's not wrong.
There's two clear feet of depth there
and this is known of old,
so tell me men of wisdom
The quarts this pool can hold?'

The little pool can be seen some two hundred yards north east of the summit on a little knoll. The last eagle in Eryri was supposedly sighted near the summit of Aran Benllyn.

## LLYN PENCRAIG
*GR 7758*
*Height: 700'*
*Group: Betws-y-coed*
*Area: 5 acres*

It is also known locally as 'Llyn gwaith y llyn' (lake of the lake works) due no doubt to its close connection with the lead mining enterprises dotting this area. It is a natural lake and according to Ward (1931) it was partially drained during one of these searches for lead ore. A nearby stream called Gwaen Llifon lends credence to the story that the lake was once much larger and called Llyn Llifon. There is also a vague reference to a sunken city legend being linked to it. Strangely enough there was a real deluge around 1950 that involved Llyn Pencraig. The old dam of Llyn Sarnau gave way one night and the flood water roared down and into the lake. Mrs Myfanwy Hughes who then lived in Ffridd (GR 779588) had the fright of her life when she heard the terrible roaring in the darkness outside her window. In addition to the lead mine there was also a Silica mine on the north shore of the lake. There is little to see (GR 777585) other than a couple of piles of white rubble amidst the conifers, brambles and little crags. Hafod yr Owen quarry to the south of the lake was a favourite spot for the miners to collect clay that they used to hold their candles on their hats and walls. The quarrymen of Blaenau Ffestiniog had a similar favourite spot to gather their clay from 'Ceunant Sych' below the town. It is not thought that there are fish in the lake other than minnows and other heron fodder due mainly to its seasonal change of level. During the summer the lake does not exist other than a marsh, in the winter months one would be pushed to find water deeper than 4'. A fine looking fir tree stands tall and proud out of the east end of the 'marsh'. A track running parallel to the lake's north shore has become very overgrown and difficult to trace. There are otters in the area around the lake.

## LLYN PENLLYN
*GR 5898*
*Height: 3'*
*Group: Cadair Idris*
*Area: 1 acre*

A series of lakes almost at sea level once ran along the coast between Aberdyfi and Tywyn. Today apart from marsh pools only one remains, Penllyn. In 1813 there were two large lakes almost ¾ mile in length. One was called 'Gwyrgledd Rhawniar' which was near the present day Rhowniar girls Outward Bound School. The other which was to the north was called 'Llyn y Borth' and was full of red fleshed trout whose cunning made them difficult to catch. There are no fish in Penllyn but the whole area is full of other wildlife.

## LLYN PENMOELYN
*GR 6615*
*Height: 900'*
*Group: Cadair Idris*
*Area: 2 acres*

A small pool belonging to Gallestra farm. Ward (1931) claimed there were small trout in it but at the time of writing the pool appears empty of fish. It is quite a shallow lake apart from one section near the middle which is a different colour, the owner assured me that this 'eye' was quite deep. It is sometimes called llyn llygad or the 'eye lake'. Another name for it is Llyn Pen Pared. It would have been somewhere amongst these little hidden valleys of trees surrounding the lake that the Tylwyth Teg cut the wood to make their magic harps in byegone days. One Morgan Rhys who showed some kindness to these little folk when they came to his door for food was rewarded by a gift of one such harp. He had always been an accomplished harpist but with his new harp anyone hearing the music could not stop dancing, his reputation spread far and wide. Morgan however began to abuse his new ability by making people dance for far longer than they wished to. One morning following a particularly long night of dancing he awoke to find his harp had gone never to return and people were of the opinion that it was the Tylwyth Teg who had taken it back. The remains of a small slate quarry nearby (GR 667154) was called the 'Brown Horse Quarry'. Ty'n Llidiart (GR 672155) was built at the turn of the century as a hunting lodge for Sir Watkin Williams Wynn and a rather poignant reminder of those days are pencilled on the walls of the barn in the form of pheasant rearing accounts. One of the young workers 'Tommy' signed his name on the door in 1910, he was to die in the Dardanelles 1916. A profusion of yellow water lilies adorn this beautiful little lake set in a crater from whose lips are views to rival any lake.

## LLYN PERFEDDAU
*GR 6526*
*Height: 1,532'*
*Group: Rhinogydd*
*Area: 2 acres*

Llyn Perfeddau like Llyn Hywel is owned by Mr A. Jones, Graig Isaf, in Cwmnantcol, (GR 639260). During the summer there is quite a lot of vegetation on its surface making it difficult to fish. There are brown and Loch Leven trout in the lake and permission to fish may be sought at the farm. The mountain on whose northern slope it nestles is called Y Llethr and despite what many people assume at 2,475' it is the highest peak in the Rhinogydd range. A disused manganese mine at (GR 649268) which closed in 1924 was once an elaborate affair with tramways, wire ropeways and accommodation barracks on the site. It is said that the Loch Leven trout were introduced into the lake by the manager of the manganese works who himself was a Scotsman. Two pewter dishes, one a jug with a horse's head carved in it the other a bowl were discovered near the old mine; they are both in the National Museum, Cardiff. This slope overlooks Maes y Garnedd the old home of Colonel John Jones of Oliver Cromwell's Army, (see Llyn Cwmhosan).

## LLYN PERIS
*GR 5959*
*Height: 340'*
*Group: Wyddfa*
*Area: 95 acres*

In 1974 work on the largest pumped storage scheme in Europe began in Llanberis. A series of tunnels were dug through the mountain of Elidir Fawr that allows water to flow from Llyn Marchlyn Mawr to generate electricity from turbines set deep within the mountain. It is estimated that when electricity is produced 92,000 gallons of water flows per second generating a staggering 1,300 megawatts in 10 seconds! The water, once used then continues its flow into Llyn Peris where it is stored until the night when cheaper nuclear generated electricity can be used to pump it back up. Some of the caverns dug inside the mountain are the largest man made chambers in the world. A huge, environmentally friendly scheme which has proved a success. Llyn Peris unfortunately had to suffer the indignity of first being completely emptied and then having its river of 12,000 years diverted through a tunnel constructed specifically to by-pass the lake. All the fish were re-located including the arctic char (torgoch) which were put in Llynnau Dulyn, Melynllyn, Ffynnon Llugwy and Cowlyd. Although the lake was not re-stocked the fish have re-appeared including the torgoch! The legendary tunnel of the torgoch which is reputed to join the Llanberis lakes to Cwellyn springs to mind! A new dam was also constructed at the lower end of the lake to ensure the minimal loss of water. This was completed in 1981 and receives a weekly safety inspection. This has somewhat changed the nature of the short river joining the two lakes; the traditional breeding ground of the torgoch. Interestingly enough salmon whose ancestors have fought upstream to spawn for thousands of years actually use the tunnel (those that escape the poacher anyway). For years the fishing rights were kept solely for guests at the Royal Victoria Hotel. Gallichan (1903) describes seeing 'monster trout' swirling from the depths beneath the spoil heaps to take an evening moth.

Above the lake's northern shore the spoil heaps of what was once one of the world's largest slate quarries lie mute and disused since its closure of 1969. It seems as if the whole of Elidir's southern flank is comprised of discarded slate. Closer inspection will reveal a labyrnith of tunnels, pits and trackways with numerous empty buildings, unsafe ladders and architectually handsome inclines and arches, broken machinery, hawsers and rusty wagons. So immense is the whole quarry that a whole day should be set aside to explore it. Originally the hillside comprised of several small enterprises but in 1787 the landowner, Ashetton Smith took over and amalgamated them to form the Dinorwig quarry. At its peak it is estimated that over fifty miles of rail track was laid just in the quarry itself with a workforce of almost three thousand men in 1882. Today many of the slate faces are used for rockclimbing, the tracks are used by the odd runner and mountain biker whilst the 'airspace' is used when conditions are right by a small group of parascenders (all without the official blessing of National Grid, the owners). The large pointed pinnacle above the lake that has been quarried into a spire was once much higher and is known as 'Y Ceiliog Mawr' (the large cockeral) and it was in the shadow of this that the castle scene of the film 'Willow' was filmed in 1986. The main external workings and offices for the power station are located by the lakeside at (GR 593601) where the old Wellington quarry was situated.

According to Pennant Peris was an ancient saint who had been a cardinal, he founded the church of Nant Peris. Nant Peris was the original Llanberis village. The church has an ancient well which was considered at one time to be sacred. The well used to contain two sacred trout whose appearance represented good luck to young sweethearts. At one time the fish were replaced whenever they died.

Anyone looking up at the mountainside from the lower end of the lake will see a cluster of rocks and crags at (GR 590586) just below the horizon. Liberal imagination will show the rocks forming the sillouhette of a woman's head staring westwards. She is the 'lady of Snowdon' whose eternal fate is to wait for her lover who will never return.

## LLYN PONT LLAERON
*GR 6904*
*Height: 970'*
*Group: Cadair Idris*
*Area: 0 acres*

This was a quarry reservoir for the Bryneglwys slate quarry. Pont Llaeron refers to a small but very ancient arched bridge crossing the river Llaeron about 2 hundred yards above the lake. Just below the bridge an impressive leat is cut to draw water from the stream and the remains of a smaller dam used to divert this water is still in situ. After some early foraging in the early decades of last century the quarry matured rapidly in the boom years of the 1860's. A Mr T.H. McConnel who was a large cotton mill owner from the mid-lands decided to invest in the quarry in the face of the American civil war which meant a decline in cotton shipments. A prosperous period followed for twenty years which saw a workforce of 300 men but by the time the lease was due for renewal in 1910 his son who was the new director had allowed the quarry to decline without investment. A brief closure and then Mr Henry Haydn Jones bought the quarry and re-negotiated the lease, it was this move which also secured the future of the Talyllyn railway. Haydn Jones kept the railway open for summer service even after the quarry closed in 1947. When Sir Haydn Jones (he was knighted in 1937) died in 1950 the Talyllyn Railway Preservation Society was formed to ensure the survival of this popular little tourist attraction. It was slate from Bryneglwys quarry that were used to roof Westminister Hall. The lake was stocked at one time with Brown Trout. Today, it is completely dry, the unusually broad earth dam having been breached, some say accidentally in 1963. The tower valve is still standing. The whole site is now afforested.

## PRENTEG POOL
*GR 5741*
*Height: 280'*
*Group: Moel Hebog*
*Area: ½ acre*

Was this the pool referred to by Gallichan as containing good fish I wonder? The pool originally provided water for Portreuddyn Slate Quarry (GR 578408) which closed in 1870. The slate quarried here was very hardwearing and a popular choice as doorsteps for many of the local houses, TanyBwlch Study Centre being one example.

## LLYN PRYFED
*GR 6632*
*Height: 1,780'*
*Group: Rhinogydd*
*Area: 4 acres*

There is no doubt that for such a small, high lake Llyn Pryfed has earned a healthy respect. Local farmers consider it to be extremely deep. Cliffe (1850) states it to be the most dangerous lake he knew.

*Llyn Pryfed*

The water is dark and peaty with the banks being comprised of miniature cliffs making it difficult to approach safely. An angler dropped his rod into it some years ago and it was never seen again. There are tales of large brown trout with staring eyes that unnerve the angler and is generally avoided by the serious fisherman. Ward (1931) even considers it to be one of the most innaccessible in Wales. In reality the trout are very average with some larger ones feeding possibly off the smaller ones. The whole area around the lake is composed of rock and heather with clefts and crag steps to catch the unwary making it potentially quite dangerous walking country. An interesting feature worth noting perhaps is an old water wheel on the side of Wern Cyfrdwy Farmhouse (GR 675334).

## LLYN PWLL Y GELE
*GR 7621*
*Height: 700'*
*Group: Dolgellau*
*Area: 6 acres*

Gele is the Welsh word for leeches and this seems a fitting name for such a vegetated pool. Bedwyr Lewis Jones refers to several other similarly named lakes and pools in Wales. There is Llyn Gelod (a variation of the plural) in the Llŷn peninsula, Llyn Gelan in Mid Wales, and Pwll Gelod in the south. It may have been the practise of using these blood sucking creatures by physicians in the old days that highlighted their presence by naming these pools after them. Many doctors kept a large jarfull in their surgeries supplied quite probably from pools like this one. A few years ago some young salmon (smolts) were turned loose in the hope that the pool would become part of their offspring's migratory itinery but there has been little evidence of success. The lake appears to have been enlarged by a small dam which has a 1956 date on it. It is teeming with minnows and several herons are always in attendance. There are numerous trout and some very attractive pockets of water lily. The level of the lake fluctuates considerably. In the winter water often flows over the dam but in the summer months a large expanse of mud is revealed as the surface area diminishes. Unfortunately the dam leaks and full capacity is not retained for long once the rain has ceased. There was evidence of large plastic sheeting having been laid to try and reduce this leakage July 1994. Its immediate vicinity is an extremely beautiful piece of countryside with decidious shrub and a public footpath adding to the attraction. The nearby renovated Llofft y Bugail house was built in 1789 by the same designer that built the Hywel Dda Inn which stands by the side of the Bala-Dolgellau road (GR 828239). The lake is owned by the Nannau estate.

## LLYN Y RHOS
*GR 7255*
*Height: 1300'*
*Group: Moelwynion*
*Area: 2 acres*
Along with a smaller reservoir 300 yards lower down (GR 727562) this pool provided water for the Rhos Slate Quarry (GR 729564). This large pit quarry opened in 1860 and by 1882 employed 45 men. At one stage as many as four water wheels were being used one possibly being the 40' Cyffty (see Llyn Cyffty) wheel installed in 1919. When the Foel quarry which is situated above (GR 717556) closed in 1880 the pit was flooded to provide even more water for Rhos. Rhos also continued to pay the owners of Foel for the use of their inclines until it too closed in the 1950's. The lower reservoir is now dry but the upper one is still very much a 'lake' and there is still much to see of the old quarry works although there is no public right of way to it. Both the lake and surrounding land belongs to Rhos farm, Capel Curig and although no right of way exists to this lake the farmer does allow access along the path towards Moel Siabod. The lake becomes very low during dry summers, the maximum depth at the dam being about 6'; there are no fish present.

Another lake ½ mile south east is known as Llyn Newydd (see under).

## LLYN RUCK
*GR 7201*
*Height: 600'*
*Group: Cadair Idris*
*Area: 2 acres*

The modest estate of Pant Lludw (GR 733015) has been in the hands of the Ruck family for many generations. It seems likely that part of 'managing' this estate at one stage involved either creating or developing this small pool which also bears the family name. The remains of a multi seater toilet above the present house implies a reasonable workforce sometime in its history. The ruined house of Gwel y Môr by the lakeside is known by the family as 'honeymoon cottage' and was built for the occasion of the marriage of one of the Rucks. It was he in fact who first stocked the lake with brown trout in the early 1930's and kept a detailed fishing log which is still in existence. More recently following an unsuccessful experiment with sea trout fry in another nearby lake Caeau Madog (GR 713010) where they became land locked some were removed and transferred to Llyn Ruck. They apparently fared no better here due to lack of suitable spawning grounds. Eels and water fowl monopolise this rhodedendron surrounded hilltop pool today. The surrounding land is farmed by Marchlyn. There is also the remains of a small reservoir at Cwm Ebol (GR 689017) which supplied the slate quarry nearby. Slate from these open pits were taken by cart and then tramways to a point on the river Dyfi (GR 702996) where they were loaded onto a ship. Nine men worked in the quarry in 1883. The remains of an old farmhouse (pre-quarry era) can be discerned in the old reservoir bed. A quartz mine (GR 695009) may also have used the tramways for a period. A small pool (GR 731028) in the forest a mile north of Llyn Ruck does not contain fish. In 1983 following the incorrect inclusion of a public right of way leading through Pant Lludw on the OS map the thoroughfare was quite rightly revoked and permission to visit the lake should be sought first. The Rucks have produced a number of book authors most notably perhaps Berta Ruck who wrote several romantic novels many of them containing a Welsh flavour in the 1920's. Norman Hunter the playwright leased Pant y Lludw and lived there for a number of years until about 1992. The lake is also known locally as Llyn Marchlyn.

## LLYN SARNAU
*GR 7759*
*Height: 799'*
*Group: Betws-y-coed*
*Area: 2½ acres*

Sarnau is the Welsh plural for roads or trackways, and when one considers the numerous tracks that cross in its vicinity it does seem an appropriate name for the new reservoir that was constructed sometime between 1850 and 1860 to provide water for the Vale of Conwy lead mine. The trackway going to Coedmawr pool for example was once a council maintained route. The lake itself is divided by a causeway and the old Roman road Sarn Helen passes very close by the lake. Its exact route is unknown but its best suggested course from the fort at Caerhun to Caer Llugwy brings it past Geirionydd, Glangors and just westwards of Sarnau. There are no fish in Sarnau and most summers will see it completely empty of water for weeks. This is partly due to evaporation and not enough replacement rain and partly due to a fault in the rock below the lake. Since 1955/6 when the No.3 level joined the Cyffty, Gorlan and Llanrwst mines water from the lake has seeped slowly through a weakness in the underlying rock and drained out through the level. A few years before this another incident had occurred that resulted in the lake becoming a very shallow one. The dam at (GR 779589) burst one night and a rush of water roared down the little Ffridd gorge to Llyn Pencraig, (see Pencraig). The numerous old mine shafts and ruined buildings that dot the area around the lake have now all been made safe and the shafts and levels fitted with bat gates that allow these nocturnal creatures to go in and out without human interruptions. Some of the older local residents still remember bonfires and skating parties on the lake. The lake was also known as Aber Meddiant for a short time after its construction.

## LLYN SERW
*GR 7742*
*Height: 1480'*
*Group: Migneint*
*Area: 1½ acres*

When one considers the illustrious past this lake had in sporting terms it is sad to learn of its present plight. Acid rain and lack of game management have taken their toll. Even the river, a meandering black mamba of deep pools and little cataracts only produces the odd hungry little trout. In Andrew Foster's day (head keeper of the Penrhyn estate on these moors for the last three Victorian decades) both lake and river were teeming with brownies so much so that poachers from Blaenau Ffestiniog considered the risk a viable one. Two were caught for instance on 17th June 1882 and marched to the Llyn Conwy Cottage for interrogation by Foster. There are other accounts of netting the river to provide Cambridge Angling Association with trout. Baits were laid at the lake in 1880 in the drive to rid the moors of seagulls who ate grouse eggs.

During planning stages for the giant Celyn reservoir it had been proposed to build a system of leats and tunnels to draw water from both the Conwy and Serw; this never came to fruition. Despite the bleak boggy terrain the Tylwyth Teg have left a legacy in the form of a legend concerning a wandering harpist. Somewhere on the long ridge running north east and seperating the rivers Serw and Conwy there is a hidden cave where the harpist was tempted inside by the little folk. Inside the mountain a labyrinth of passages connected halls where the sounds of music and mirth was overpowering. He lost track of time and of the way out. Sometimes on quiet days he can be heard playing his harp deep inside the mountain. A piece of land below the site of the cave is still called 'Dôl y Telynor'. Another tale tells of a tunnel leading from somewhere near Trwyn Swch (GR 816454) down to somewhere near Pandy Uchaf (GR 840482) where two of the Tylwyth Teg were seen in the 1840's — the last two to be seen in the area. A similar legend tells of a harpist, fiddler and piper who were on their way to

Cricieth to perform in a feast in the castle. Along the way however they met a gentleman who persuaded them to perform for him for a higher fee. He led them into a cave where they also became lost and separated. Eventually after weeks of wandering the harpist emerged out of some rocks in Nant Gwynant and was so shocked that he died. His burial sight can still be seen marked by a rock and is called 'Bedd y Crythor Du'.

Four hundred yards north of the lake (GR 777434) is an outcrop of rock called Cerrig Llwynogod (Foxes' rocks) and this contains a cave which can be gymnastically crawled through. The old county boundary of Caernarfon and Denbigh passes through the rocks and still has a marked boundary stone on their summit. A mile north west of the lake at the road junction the old well of Ffynnon Eidda erected by the first Lord Penrhyn marks the site of an old Inn called Tŷ Newydd y Mynydd. The last landlord of the Inn was a Richards. There were also four cottages near the old Inn but there is very little left on the site now. A word of caution should be said regarding the dangers of walking these very wet moors especially after wet weather, there are some extremely deep quagmires.

## LLYN STWLAN
*GR 6644*
*Height: 1,570'*
*Group: Moelwynion*
*Area: 22 acres*

Originally this was a small corrie lake which contained natural brown trout, and although it was never to have the reputation of Ffynnon Lloer or Idwal it was nevertheless fished by locals and members of the Cambria fishing society. Several thousand young trout were put in during the 1923/4 season for example. Then in the late 50's the Tanygrisiau pump storage scheme was created which was eventually opened by HM the Queen in 1961. This was the lake chosen as the top reservoir from which the water would drop a 1000' to turn the 360 megawatt turbines. Off peak the water would then be pumped back up using electricity from the grid. Such fluctuations in water level compounded with the strong current produced by the run off was considered unsuitable for fish and fishermen and all the fish were removed. As a compensatory measure the CEGB gave the Cambria 5,000 trout with which to stock Llynnau'r Gamallt. The lake's original name was Trwstyllon or Trwystyllan and if said quickly it can be seen where the Stwlan came from. It was also referred to in the old days as Llyn Drws Elen because the col immediately above which seperates Moelwyn Mawr and Bach was one of the ancient ways that people used to cross the mountains, it may also have been used by the Romans as a link route to Sarn Helen, (see Croesor for another connection). Just below the lake on the way down to the village of Tanygrisiau there is a shallow cave called Ogof Stwlan where a stone axe was discovered during the building of the pump storage scheme. The crags just above the road going up to the dam are very popular with rockclimbers, the rock is sound, quick drying and gives excellent friction for rubber soles. During the summer buses are run at regular intervals up to the dam for visitors to enjoy the view etc. The 119' dam is of a Gravity Buttress construction and provides a capacity of $207,300m^3/41\frac{1}{2}$ million gallons.

## LLYN TALYLLYN
*GR 7109*
*Height: 270'*
*Group: Cadair Idris*
*Area: 223 acres*

Without doubt one of the most famous fishing lakes in Wales which has been immortalised many times over by the writings of generations of fishermen. The original name was Myngil or Mwyngil as various documents going back as far as 1494 show, in recent years it has become the fashion to use this name once again. It was in 1844 that Colonel Vaughan of Hengwrt, Dolgellau built the Ty'n y Gornel hotel near the bottom end of the lake and supplied two boats. This was to become a mecca for fly fishermen; it was affectionately known as 'Jones', today it is still extremely popular. Welsh Water through their subsidary company Tir a Hamdden (Land and Leisure) bought the lake and hotel in 1988 and have continued to 'manage' the fishing. Between 1989 and

1990 9,000 trout were put in each weighing betweeen one and five pounds, 9,000 smolts were also put in during this period. One of the drawbacks of introducing fish that have been reared on fast growth food is that they tend to lose weight and become leaner when in their new environment, this was found to be true here. Trout that were put in weighing 5lb were caught a few months later weighing only 3lb. In the early days baskets were enormous, J.H. Cliffe writes that during an eight day period in 1855 276 trout were caught! It is quite a shallow lake with a lot of bed vegetation, a perfect environment for feeding. The natural trout have the reputation of having delicious flesh if cooked within a few hours of capture, but if left any longer they tend to lose their succulence. It is also one of the few lakes to have sea trout and salmon running through it. A 14 pound salmon was taken late in the 1986 season. Fly fishing only is allowed and at the time of writing there is a 12 inch size limit. Permits are available from the Fishery manager who is based at the hotel. Also at the lower end of the lake there is a very old church which amongst many things of interest has two in particular. On the right and in the corner as you enter the cemetery is the grave of Jenny Jones, the only woman who was at the battle of Waterloo. She went there with her husband who was one of the officers. Another curious thing to notice is that the cemetery has two entrances. Not so many years ago when a lot of rain had fallen to swell the many streams feeding the lake it was not an uncommon sight especially if the wind was north east to see the road completely flooded. During these occasions members of the congregation that came from the village of Corris could not actually enter without getting wet. It was because of this that the other gate was made at the back of the cemetery. Today, following work done to the outlet of the lake such problems no longer occur. Years ago church grounds were also used for games on the Sabbath a practise that was quite acceptable for a long period of time. But this gradually came to be frowned upon by the church and eventually there came a time when it was not allowed. Habits, especially pleasurable ones die hard and alternative venues were found for these Sabbath games. One such spot became famous for an incident that happened one Sunday when a group of young people from adjoining parishes met for their recreation. One version of the story has them cock fighting. A loud roaring and rumbling was heard followed by a loud crack and the devil himself appeared in the form of a donkey rearing on its hind legs on a slab of rock. Everybody scattered and the spot was avoided for many months afterwards. One day however two shepherds, one from Rhiwogof (GR 709100) and the other from Pencoed (GR 685111) ventured to see the slab of rock and were amazed to see the devil's hoofprints burnt deeply into the rock. It later became the custom for the shepherds from the district to carve their names on this rock, the oldest is 1564 but the oldest I could find was 1632. The rock is found on the footpath leading over from the Dysynni valley at (GR 689104). The rock is called 'Carreg y Gŵr Drwg', (Devil's Rock) 'Carreg Enwau', (Rock of Names) or 'Craig y Bugeiliaid', (Shepherd's Rock). It would have been along this path that Mary Jones walked the twenty miles to Bala barefoot around the year 1804 to buy a bible. Her cottage 'Ty'n Ddôl' has a plaque on it to commemorate the event (GR 674095). A little lower down the valley at (GR 668085) is Castell y Bere one of the last of the Welsh castles to hold out after the 1282 collapse, for years it was forgotten beneath oak scrub and brambles but is now 'presentable' thanks to 'CADW'.

At the upper end of the lake the old farmhouse Dôl Ithel once belonged to the 'Idris Table Water' company from where they ran their business of bottling the water of the river Gadair which is actually on the other side of the mountain. Idris Shandy cans can still be bought.

On land belonging to this farm in 1684 some enormous stone coffins were found containing the skeletons of huge men, there was a hazel rod lying next to each one with some of them still retaining their bark.

## LLYN TANYBWLCH
*GR 6440*
*Height: 410'*
*Group: Moelwynion*
*Area: 1 acre*

Also known as Llyn Trefor and Llyn Pant y Gysgfa it did supply water for Trwyn y Garnedd farm (GR 637402). It is owned by Till Hill economic forestry, a subsidary of Gallagher's Tobacco pension fund. It was stocked with Brown trout and some of the descendent still survive although not of great size. The dam was renovated in 1969 and in February of that year one of the workers was sadly killed on the dam's spillway. The lake may at the time of writing be a reserve water supply for the Ffestiniog railway by arrangement with the owners.

## LLYN TANYGRAIG
*GR 7120*
*Height: 412'*
*Group: Rhinogydd*
*Area: 1½ acres*

Up to a decade ago Llyn Tanygraig supplied the village of Llanelltyd with their domestic water supply. A natural lake which was enlarged to supply water power for the Crushing Plant of the Prince of Wales Gold Mine at Llanelltyd. It was here that a short lived bonanza occurred in 1853 when a particularly rich pocket yielding a thousand ounzes per ton was discovered. A leat to increase the catchment area to include the river Wnin was also constructed. The lake is owned by Mr W. Humphreys, Bryn Du, Llanelltyd who stocked it with brown trout for a period of three years and issued fishing permits up until 1991. The venture proved unsuccessful due to the impracticalities of bailiffing and rife poaching. The earth dam is still in very good condition.

## LLYN TANYGRISIAU
*GR 6844*
*Height: 600'*
*Group: Moelwynion*
*Area: 95 acres*

This was constructed in 1960 to hold the water coming down from Stwlan once it had done its job of turning the turbines at the Power Station. Before it was built the site was little more than a boggy valley which contained two very small river lakes called 'Llyn Ceg Twnel' (mouth of the tunnel lake) and 'Llyn Inclen' (lake of the incline). Both referred to the original Ffestiniog Railway which actually ran through the valley and through a 730 yard tunnel. Llyn Ceg twnel still existed until the new railway (early 1970's) was built. There was another pool by the name of Gelliwog which was also known to the angler. One of the old fishing lores concerning these lost pools was that when there was an electrical storm the fish would go for any bait and large baskets were often recorded during these occasions. When the hydro electric scheme was built the original 730 yard tunnel and track bed running through the valley were lost so that when the Ffestiniog Railway was re-opened as a predominantly tourist line a completely new section had been installed. A new 287 yard tunnel which was opened in 1977 ran parallel to the old one but a little higher up whilst a loop was engineered to gain sufficient height for the railway to by-pass the new lake. The Dduallt loop is the only one of its kind in Britain and was constructed mainly by volunteers. The lake is also known as Llyn Ystradau. It has become a well stocked and popular fishing venue despite the regular lowering and raising of the water level. A rise and fall of 18 feet has made it a necessity to ban waders by anglers because of the obvious danger involved. There is a thousand feet of height difference between this lake and Stwlan. The lake is owned by National Grid who took over from the CEGB when privatisation occurred. Ffestiniog Fisheries manage the fishing and permits are issued for the stock of Brown and Rainbow trout which are available. The dam like its upper partner Stwlan is of gravity concrete construction and provides a capacity of 200,000m³/40 million gallons.

## LLYN TECWYN ISAF
*GR 6237*
*Height: 260'*
*Group: Rhinogydd*
*Area: 7 acres*

A very pretty lake popular almost as much for picknicking as for the excellent coarse fishing it affords. It lies in a pocket of countryside at the top of some steep winding roads above the village of Talsarnau. There is a profusion of plant growth both within and around the lake with examples of more exotic species nearer the estate to the north east. Plas Llandecwyn actually owns the lake from whom fishing permits may be obtained. There are Rudd, Perch and Trout and it has the reputation for being an outstanding coarse fisherman's lake. Pennant made a mention of the water lilies in his 'Tour in Wales' (1789). A century later D.E. Jenkins (1899) writes an account of how the vicar of Llanfair who had to officiate once a month at Nanmor was drowned one night when he tried to negotiate the swollen river at the upper end of Traeth Bach. Much of this floodwater came from the Tecwyn lakes area. It was not unusual in those days for 'parishes' situated near estuaries and other geographical barriers to be disembodied. Following the incident which must have occurred near (GR 620377) Nanmor chapel was given to Beddgelert in exchange for a piece of land at Llaneuddwyn called 'Parsel tu hwnt i'r bont' (parcel beyond the bridge). A similar version is told (see Llyn Dyniewyd) which actually has the parishioners drowning rather than the vicar. Both legends are from the time before the cob at Porthmadog was built. Another tragic drowning incident is still spoken of by some of the locals, an incident that occurred in the 1930's. Three boys had gone to skate on the frozen lake when the ice broke and they fell into the freezing water. Two tried to swim ashore but the ice in that direction kept breaking and impeding their weakening progress, they were drowned. The third boy managed to clamber onto the ice nearer the middle of the lake which held firm for him to walk ashore and thus survive. This lake is extremely popular in summer and the limited space available for parking has to be paid for.

## LLYN TECWYN UCHAF
*GR 6438*
*Height: 509'*
*Group: Rhinogydd*
*Area: 31 acres*

Both lakes are joined by a fine cart track which passes the old Llandecwyn church on the left. William Evans' grave (see Llyn Llennyrch) is just over the wall. Pennant, who toured in 1789 was impressed with the milky white goats found on the cliffs abounding the lake and its approaches. The lower now redundant dam was constructed in 1896 whilst the upper one in 1920, receiving further alteration in 1938, it provides water for Penrhyndeudraeth, Porthmadog and Maentwrog districts. There is a maximum depth of 40' giving a capacity of 28,000 cubic metres/5½ million gallons. The fishing is leased by Talsarnau and Artro Districts Angling Association. There are Browns, Rainbows, Loch Levens as well as Silver Sea trout which are occasionally caught. An interesting old legend is told of Tecwyn Uchaf concerning a witch. Dorti lived on her own and seemed to have a way with animals as well as the 'knowledge' of how to mix and prepare herbs for all manner of ailments. But as with modern doctors when things go wrong they are also quite often blamed. Dorti was seen near some cattle shortly before they fell ill and died. The blame escalated into a witch hunt and eventually she had to flee pursued by the people she had once helped. Dorti was caught on the hill above the lake and placed in a barrel which had several nails protruding on the inside. She was then rolled down the steep shaly cliff to land screaming and dying at the lake shore where she died shortly after. She was buried at the spot and a cairn of white quartz rocks placed over her grave. Various rhymes and beliefs sprung up over the years concerning Dorti. One tradition stated that it was bad luck to pass her grave without placing a stone on the cairn or reciting the following nonsense rhyme:

Dyrti Dorti
Bara gwyn yn llosgi

Dŵr ar y tân
I olchi'r llestri.

Translated, it means : Dirty Dorti, the white bread is burning! Put some water on to boil to wash the dishes! The consequence of forgetting either of these rituals was to die within the year. Placing a stone at the time of a funeral seemed to bring good luck too. Another belief was that if anyone removed a stone from her cairn she would appear, embrace the thief and drag him/her into the lake to drown. The cairn was apparently moved in 1920 when the new dam was built. The unsightly pylons passing by the lake and a newly constructed track does rather spoil an otherwise pretty lake.

## LLYN TEGID
*GR 9134*
*Height: 529'*
*Group: Bala*
*Area: 1,123 acres*

Llyn Tegid or Bala lake as it is sometimes unfortunately referred to is Wales' largest natural lake. In a charter in 1200 by Owen Brogyntyn of Oswestry when he gave land and fishing rights to Cistercian monks of Basinwerk Abbey, Holywell the lake was called Pimblemere or Pemblemere. It was known to the Romans who had a fort at Caer Gai (GR 877315) and were thought to have mined for gold nearby. An inscribed stone thought to have been an altar was found in 1885. The inscription on it referred to one Julius Gaveronius and has been dated to AD 109, the then owner Sir Watkin Williams Wynn presented it to the museum at Chester. Arthurian links too cannot be ignored since tradition places him as a youth in his step-father's care here at Penllyn, the Tudor poet Spenser refers to Gai the step-father as Timon. Another old campaigner who retired to the shores of the lake was Llywarch Hen who reputedly lived to be 145 years old. He lost all 24 of his sons in the wars against the Saxons before retiring to live on the site of Plas Rhiwaedog (GR 947348) the present day Youth Hostel. In his early days he too is supposed to have fought alongside Arthur; later on in life he made his mark as a poet, the most quoted piece attributed to him being a lament on the downfall of his friend Cynddylan of

*Canoeists startled on Llyn Tegid!*

Powys. Gronw Pebyr (see Llyn yr Oerfel) of Mabinogion fame also had his castle near the bottom end of the lake. Of even vaguer substance the wicked and corrupted prince Tegid once had his palace on the valley floor before the lake came. He was persistently cruel and hard with his people and on the birthday of his first born he held a magnificent banquet inviting all his equally cruel friends and influential aquaintances, he even sent for the best harpist in the land but characteristically omitted to invite any of his own hard working people and tenants. The great day arrived and the banquet began, the harpist was sitting in the corner resting before his next stint when a little bird flew in and sang what he thought were the words 'Vengeance will come, vengeance will come!' it did this in a manner that seemed to invite the harpist to follow. This he did, the little bird all the time enticing him up the hill from bush to bush, knoll to knoll and away from the palace. Eventually when they were high above the valley the bird flew away and when the harpist looked around he was just in time to see the palace being engulfed by water which was to become Llyn Tegid. There are numerous versions around this main theme (many of which apply to other lakes in Wales and abroad) but one variation in particular merits a mention. When the stunned harpist returned to the shore of the new lake he was suddenly startled to see his harp break the surface brought up by two white fish and it was these two fish which were the first Gwyniaid in the lake. The Gwyniaid which are thought to have been a form of migratory whiting landlocked since the ice age have evolved to adapt to their 'new' environment to such an extent that they are now recognised as a seperate species. They are unique to Llyn Tegid. There is a tale told of a rather ungodly travelling poet called Charles who actively blasphemed against the faith on several occasions. One night whilst on his way to Trawsfynydd in the dark he wandered across the frozen lake along with several other people; (winters were winters in those days!) Suddenly the ice cracked and he fell through into the water from where his cries for help were heard for but a short time, it was curious that nobody else who were on the ice suffered the same fate. Another story concerning the lake in a frozen state is told of a stranger who arrived in the town one night. He enquired casually whose was that enormous field he had just walked over. When told that he had actually walked over the lake he apparently died of shock! Another famous Welsh legend associated with the lake is the legend of Ceridwen and Taliesin (see Geirionydd). Ceridwen was a sorceress who had three children, her daughter Creirwy was one of the most beautiful girls in the land, her one son Morfran was a strong handsome young man but her other son Afagddu was sickly and hideously ugly. She decided to prepare a cauldron of special herbs that when they had simmered for a full year and a day would provide Afagddu with the gift of wisdom and the ability of second sight. Gwion Bach was chosen to ensure the fire did not go out and the mixture did not boil dry. This he did most conscientiously but when there was only a day of boiling left some of the mixture splashed on to his finger, it was hot and he immediately put his finger in his mouth. The result shocked him, for he could suddenly see the future and he saw Ceridwen's intention to kill him when his work was over; he decided to run away. Ceridwen pursued him but Gwion turned into a hare, Ceridwen promptly turned into a greyhound. Gwion then turned into a fish and dived into the river, she transformed herself into an otter and swam after him, he then tried the guise of a bird but Ceridwen turned into a hawk and came ever nearer; in desperation Gwion turned into a grain amidst thousands of other grain in a barn. She could not find him so she turned herself into a hen and started eating the grain, eventually Gwion was eaten and Ceridwen transformed herself back into a woman. But the story was only just beginning; with the grain in her body she became pregnant and in the course of time Gwion was re-born as a baby. Evil as she was she could not bring herself to actually kill her own child so she decided to wrap him up in a leather bag and throw him into the sea and let the waves do her work. At this time a rather unfortunate character by the name of Elfin lived on the west coast of Wales. He was the son of a wealthy prince but everything he attempted usually ended in failure, he was world's most unlucky person. An example of his bad luck was the share his father had given him from his estate — Cantre'r Gwaelod; which is the tract of land supposedly buried under the sea! He did however own a fish trap weir or a 'goret' as it was known in Welsh. Shortly after Ceridwen threw the baby into the sea Elfin was due to empty the goret. But true to his luck there wasn't a single fish to be found, nothing except the leather bag. It was at this point that Elfin's luck began to change. Inside of course was Ceridwen's baby and Elfin named him Taliesin. As Taliesin grew his wisdom and foresight contributed in no small way to Elfin's fortune and at the same time one of Wales' most famous bards grew into folklore. He is supposedly buried at (GR 672913) and anyone willing to spend the night alone upon his grave will, by the morning either have the gift of the poet or have become insane, (see Bochlwyd, Gadair and Du'r Arddu).

A more recent legend associated with the lake is that of 'Teggy'. Over the last twenty years there have been a few sightings of an unexplained creature swimming in the lake; naturally there have been tongue in cheek comparisons with the Loch Ness phenomena hence the name 'Teggy'.

The town of Bala has, through the ages always found a significant niche for itself in the order of town importance. At one time the town was famous for its woollen products, most notably perhaps stockings. It is said that George the third obtained his woollen stockings from Bala as recommended by his doctor for his rheumatism; the particular stockings were supposedly knit by the vicar of Trawsfynydd's daughter! It was Mary Jones' epic twenty mile barefooted walk in 1804 to purchase a bible that prompted Thomas Charles to establish the British and Foreign Bible Society. For the next century and more the town was to be a focal point for many other of Wales' religious intitiatives. In 1837 the first of two theological colleges was established and there were to be two religious revivals.

The lake which was bought by Merionethshire County Council in 1965 now belongs to Gwynedd C.C. There is a permanent Lake Warden employed to oversee the recreational use of the water which apart from fishing includes swimming, boating, yachting, canoeing and windsurfing. There are several species of fish in the lake. There is the previously mentioned Gwyniaid which are caught only by net; there has never been an instance of one caught with rod and line. According to Bradley (1899) the Gwyniaid sometimes flung themselves in panic onto the gravel when chased by pike. Along with examples of every species in the lake the Gwyniaid can be seen 'pickled' in the White Lion hotel bar. The largest Gwyniad caught weighed 2lbs and was almost 16 inches/40cms long. It was caught in 1906 and was presented to the British Museum by Sir Watkin Williams Wynn. These strange fish are thought to live between 50-90 feet down in the colder waters but according to Gallichan (1903) they were found on the shingle after storms having been battered by the waves. Similar examples are found in some lakes in Ireland where they are called 'pollans' as well as in the Lake District but all these are slightly different due to the different environments they have had to adapt to over the last twelve thousand years or so. The pike grow up to 30lbs, and traditionally were introduced to the lake in 1803. Trout of up to 14lbs are caught and it seems there are a mixture of sub-species. While some seem to have their red spots completely missing others boast a very pink flesh. Eels of up to 7lbs are sometimes caught. Grayling were introduced in 1770 and although still occur in the lake they are mostly caught in the river below. There are roach, rudd, chubb, loach bream and perch. The perch grow up to 10lbs. Spawning salmon pass through the lake but according to tradition do not loiter as they seek the upper Dee and Lliw. Traditionally even the river Dee itself does not 'mix' with the other waters and from a vantage point on Garth Fawr (GR 875285) in certain weather conditions the river can indeed be seen snaking through the lake mantaining its identity. Locals also believe that the best salmon prefer to go up the river Tryweryn. At one time when the river emptying the lake flowed beneath the old bridge (Pont Mwnwgl y llyn) a strong south west gale with heavy rain meant some ferocious floods all the way down the Dee valley (see Llyn Lliwbran). Today this problem has been solved and the water level of the Dee is controlled and maintained by Llyn Brenig and Llyn Alwen on the Hiraethog moors as well as Llyn Celyn and Tegid; water for domestic consumption for a large area of north east Wales and the West Midlands is taken out near Chester. Little wonder perhaps that such a large tract of water lying in the same direction as the prevailing wind caused such flooding and Edward Llwyd to say in 1698

"'tis certain that the Dee flows more upon wind than rain, but especially when both concurre!'

The deepest waters lie just off Llangower point where the banks shelves steeply and therefore constitutes a danger for swimmers.

As with many of these glacial 'Ribbon' lakes it was at one time a much longer sheet of water extending quite possibly beyond the village of Llanuwchllyn. The Urdd Outdoor Adventure Centre, Glan Llyn lies near the upper end of the lake, one of the first such centres in Eryri. It was obtained for the nation by the efforts of Sir Ifan ap Owen Edwards in 1950 who also founded the Urdd movement. The Welsh language and culture is very strong in the whole of this valley and has an excellent tradition. It was at Llanuwchllyn that the last Welsh lady costume was worn near the turn of the century.

Other attractions to the town and area include the first ever narrow gauge railway to be laid on an old British Rail track bed. It runs the length of the lake on its south shore and opened in 1972. A new leisure centre opened in Bala in 1993 which adds to the considerable itinery possible for the visitor.

## LLYN TERFYN
*GR 6647*
*Height: 2,035'*
*Group: Moelwynion*
*Area: ½ acre*

This is a very small tarn nestling beneath a series of small crags on the uplands north west of Blaenau Ffestiniog. Its size tends to fluctuate depending on the rainfall, at times it almost runs dry. There are no fish in it. The word 'terfyn' means boundary and in this instance it is a very fitting name as both the old county and the parish boundaries met at the lake and indeed the local government district boundary also passes quite close. Were it not for this fact it is quite likely that it would have remained an anonymous pool like others nearby, some of which are actually larger.

## LLYN TEYRN
*GR 6454*
*Height: 1,237'*
*Group: Wyddfa*
*Area: 5 acres*

Thousands of walkers going to or coming from Snowdon pass Llyn

Teyrn each year and many more turn back when they have reached it for it is at this point that Snowdon comes into view to reveal the real magnitude of the task of climbing it. Various offers have been put forward to explain the name 'teyrn'. Ward (1931) suggests it may originally have been 'treryn' which he explains as 'a fighting place' which could have links with the King Arthur legend (see Llyn Glaslyn) or the Irish settlement story (see Llyn Gwryd). Teyrn has also been put forward as a meaning linked to monarchy, a name that may have been given to the lake by the princes who hunted and fished from their base in Beddgelert. This particular pool may have been a royal hatchery or specially stocked for the princes' pleasure. The lake lies just above the entrance to Cwm Dyli which is almost a valley because of its length which stretching as it does almost three miles to the summit cliffs of Snowdon itself. At one time the parish could boast the highest hearth in Wales which was Hafoty Cwm Dyli as well as having the lowest in the form of Tafarn y Delyn which was situated below Aberglaslyn bridge at the then tidal limit.

The miners track which passes above the lake on its way to the now disused copper mines of Llyn Glaslyn was used to transport the ore to the road at Penypass. A row of ruined cottages by the lakeside were once used as barracks for the men who worked here during the week. One legend states that miners from Brittany used these barracks but had to flee when the Napoleonic wars broke out. Legends have a habit of containing coincidences — Brittany-Llydaw! Penypass is today a Youth Hostel nearing its thirtieth year as a special grade hostel used by thousands every year. Up to the early sixties it was the Gorphwysfa hotel, the focal point of Geoffrey Withrop Young's famous Easter parties during the early years of the century. Rawson Owen who died in 1962 had been the landlord for sixty years and although much controversy surrounded his relationship with the locals he made the paying guests of the climbing world always welcome. In the same way that Pen y Gwryd made itself the mecca for climbers in the middle years of this century so too did Gorphwysfa for the first three decades when the great cliffs of Lliwedd yielded its many routes and much of the very essence of climbing was born here. Before the inn was built there were two cairns of stones at the head of the pass and Edward Llwyd relates a curious tale about them. The guide who was to lead him up Snowdon (circa 1698) walked around one of these mounds nine times all the time reciting the lord's prayer! When they were eventually demolished, the stone being used for the building of the inn and two small cottages a stone chest (cist faen) was found in the middle of one of them containing an old clay pipe and a flintstone! The lake still contains smallish trout although it is no longer stocked. Another name for it is Llyn y Coblynod; this may have mining connotations as many of the early miners would swear that the sounds of 'coblynod' (goblins) tapping with their hammers were responsible for leading them to the richer veins.

## LLYN TONFANAU & POOLS
*GR 5603*
*Height: 3'*
*Group: Cadair Idris*
*Area: 3 acres*
A shallow sea level pool of little significance or interest, it lies between the National Park and the sea! Sea birds, water fowl and holiday makers now share what was once a larger pool.

## LLYN Y TOMLA
*GR 7549*
*Height: 1,450'*
*Group: Migneint*
*Area: ½ acre*
It is quite likely that the name is derived from a word meaning a heap or mound, possible of dung. There is a mountain called Tomla on the Berwyn range and dung connotations are also not unknown (see Llyn Biswail and Tri Graenyn). This tiny pool however lies in a very shallow saucer on a slight col to the south east of Ro-wen above Penmachno. It has marshy ill-defined banks and becomes very low in dry weather, there are no fish there. Of interest some three miles to the north east at (GR 769524) is Tŷ

Mawr, Wybrnant which was the birthplace of the Bishop William Morgan who in 1588 the same year as the Spanish Armada finished translating the Bible into Welsh. This was arguably the most important single act that ensured the survival of the Welsh language, it is advisable to take a 'gate opener' with you along the approach road. A mile to the west the course of Sarn Helen the Roman north-south road can be traced. Half a mile north west on the summit of Ro-wen another small pool features which is little more than a knee deep puddle.

## LLYN TRAWSFYNYDD
*GR 6936*
*Height: 700'*
*Group: Trawsfynydd*
*Area: 1,180 acres*

The lake was formed by the building of a main dam between 1924 and 1928 to provide water for the Maentwrog hydro-electric power station which was built at the same time. The catchment area is enormous and numerous leats and ditches were also dug at the time to improve the drainage but the main river that was damned was the river Prysor which begins its journey at Llynnau Conglog Mawr/Bach. Before 1924 the valley contained some twenty four smallholdings, a few cottages and a chapel but a large patch of marsh in the middle was called y Gors Goch (red bog). The lake was initially referred to as Llyn Maentwrog and from the beginning showed much promise as a fisherman's lake. One of the results of diverting the water along pipes was to leave the spectacular gorge of Ceunant y Llennyrch almost dry, a fate that has been shared by other Eryri gorges. Cwm Dyli (GR 650543) and Dolgarrog (GR 765675) to name but two. Then in the early 1960's the lake was practically drained once again, this time to prepare for the construction of Britain's first inland nuclear power station. As the lake was also enlarged further strengthening and damming to retain the additional water was necessary. As water from the lake was to be heated by the radioactive rods for steam to drive the turbines it was necessary to ensure a proper circulation of water around the lake. The idea was to construct connecting bund walls between the few small islands in the lake to prevent any eddying or backwater hot spots forming; the first generation magnox type power station opened in 1965. Water took between five and eight days to circulate all the way around the lake. The nuclear power station has now been de-commissioned and work on its partial removal has started. Maentwrog power station is still going strong despite a major pipe burst about a decade ago causing a large landslide to block the road. The main Ceunant Llennyrch dam was completely renovated in 1992.

Trawsfynydd is possibly most often thought of by the Welsh as the home of Elis Evans the poet known as Hedd Wyn. Hedd Wyn was killed on Pilken Ridge 31st July 1917 without ever knowing that he had won the chair of the National Eisteddfod that was shortly to be held in Birkenhead. The solemn ceremony of placing a black veil over the chair in many ways symbolised the tragic waste of other young lives lost in the Great War. His statue stands in the square in Trawsfynydd and his home 'Yr Ysgwrn' is still occupied by his family. In 1994 a film about his life was nominated for an Oscar, the first Welsh language film to do so. Five hundred yards to the west of Ysgwrn is another old farmhouse with a story, Plas Capten (GR 718342). According to tradition a Captain John Morgan who fought with Charles the first against Cromwell had to flee from Holt castle, Clwyd following un unsuccessful campaign. He returned here to his home then known as Gelli Iorwerth but it was considered too risky for him to stay very long. It is said that he hid in a cave in some rocks between the village and Y Gors Goch and was fed daily by an old woman. One day however he was betrayed to Cromwell's troops and was ordered out of his cave. When he emerged he was made to lie on a slab of rock and shot. A cauldron of gold and other valuables was found on Plas Capten land sometime after his death no doubt hidden in haste before his retreat to the cave. Another old house which stands on the eastern shore (GR 703365) called 'Y Goppa' has a strange tale to tell. The house has a tradition of going back as far back as 1608. One of the ladies of the family had fallen in love with Hwfa one of the workmen. The match was doomed and the liason a passionate and secret one, a sure recipe for tragedy. One evening she kept a tryst arranged by one of the pools in the valley only to find Hwfa's clothes by the side and her lover drowned in the water. It was never revealed whether his death was suicide, accidental or murder but she never got over her grief and soon died of a broken heart. Her ghost was seen for years at the spot calling for her lover. Another ghost troubled the farmhouse Bryn Goleu (GR 718349) at one time until a particularly spirited lady by the name of Gweno Hen Barlwr agreed to spend a month in the house for ten shillings (50p) and her keep. On the first night all her candles were blown out, the house started shaking violently and all the doors would open and shut, but Gweno constantly kept a bible with her and she drew strength from this. In the middle of the night a white horse appeared with a lady on its back which bade her to follow them. Gweno did this and was led across the fields to a particular spot that was indicated; a number of articles were found but more significantly the ghost was never seen again. A particularly tragic story is told of one Annie Hugh of Holborn who fell in love with the son of a rather shady couple who moved to live in Bryn Hir, one of the houses now beneath the lake (GR 697357). Despite the boy's father's attempts to end the relationship it continued to blossom and eventually he paid one Jac Pegi who was another unsavoury character from Dolgellau to kill Annie, which he did. Records show she was buried on the 4th April 1753. The son went away and was never heard of again but the parents, who were under suspicion were never to know another night's peace. Nightly banging noises alternated with sad wailing of a girl disturbed them constantly, all the animals died one by one and eventually under such stress the wife also died. Permission to bury her in the cemetery was refused so strong was the feeling of outrage over Annie's death. And then the story took on another twist; Jac Pegi turned up one night at Bryn Hir and the following morning his body was found in a pool in the river Prysor still known as 'Llyn Jac Pegi'. The father also went away very soon afterwards. It is said that Annie's ghost is still seen in the area around her old haunts. Finally it may be of interest that a very old golf course of sorts was once regularly used at the point where the Bala road joins the village by-pass.

The lake has been a very successful angling venue and has hosted several international competitions. There is a lake Management committee which leases the fishing rights to Prysor Angling Association. There are rudd, perch, brown and rainbow trout and chinese grass carp. An article in the Daily Post on 30th April 1992 reported a 42lb carp which was found on the shore seemingly to have been struck by a boat propeller, this is by far the heaviest fish to come out of the lake. There are however several anglers who claim to have hooked something only to have their lines snapped like cotton. These giants can only be attributed to the relative warmth of the lake's water caused by the nuclear plant, the water temperature has for three years been normal due to the inoperation of the station which ultimately led to its closure. Owing to this warmer water the season began earlier here at Llyn Trawsfynydd usually on the first of February. It is a 'put and take' lake where reared fish are stocked and most of them caught during the season.

It seems that the present de-commissioning of the nuclear station which will result in many local job losses in only the latest of a series of penalties that the people of 'Traws' have had to pay over the years. In 1903 the army moved to Bron Olau to set up a training establishment only to move to Rhiwgoch in 1905 dispersing the farm population that formed the community in those areas. Then in 1926 the lake was created drowning as much as thirty homes. And then forty years later the dubious honour of hosting a nuclear power station with all its inherent dangers were thrust upon them. Once de-commissioned Trawsfynydd will then have a radioactive temple whose contained poison will remain a cloaked threat for many many years. A small pool in a basin on the slopes of Moel y Griafolen (rounded hill of the Mountain Ash) at (GR 675351) also makes a contribution by way of a stream to Llyn Trawsfynydd. At the time of writing a huge latex castle supported along its 100 yard length by scaffolding stand on one of the islands. It was constructed only to remain for a month by Columbia

Pictures of Hollywood for their film 'First Knight'. Richard Gere, Sean Connery and Julia Ormond are the stars.

## LLYN TREWEIRYDD (see Llyn Ffynnon y Gwas)
### GR 5854

## LLYN Y TRI GRAEANYN
### GR 7513
*Height: 1,000'*
*Group: Cadair Idris*
*Area: 0 acres*

The second of two lakes described in this book that no longer exist, and only some four miles from the other, Llyn Maes y Pandy. Both lakes were often mistaken for each other as they were both on the roadside and both sometimes referred to as Llyn Bach. Llyn y Tri Graeanyn also went by other names, its direct translation 'three pebble pool' was used by the many visiting anglers staying at Ty'n Gornel Hotel. The three pebbles referred to are the three giant boulders which lie by its site. Idris the giant supposedly removed them from his shoe one day whilst on his way to his home on the summit of Cadair Idris. Other names for this little pool were Llyn Pen Morfa (Edward Llwyd 1698), Llyn y Bwlch and Llyn Bisodd y Gawres. The latter name translates as the 'giantess' piddle pool' a name that appeared on maps issued by the war office half a century ago. Black with peat it had the reputation for being bottomless and even when proved different as the following anecdote will show folklore insisted on it remaining bottomless. It was in the early years of this century that a farmer was walking a small herd of bullocks to Dolgellau market. One of the bullocks decided to stop for an unscheduled drink at the little lake but in the confusion of trying to retrieve it the poor beast stumbled headlong into the lake and waded across scarcely wetting his underbelly! A combination of a dry summer in 1921, a minor rockfall from the crags above that winter and a road improving operation in 1926 saw the little lake off, it never recovered. It is included in this book for two reasons, numerous references to it by early travellers would make omitting it unforgivable, and secondly an incident that occurred last century

*The mysterious trout of Llyn y Tri Graeanyn*

is worth relating. On the morning of the eighth of June 1882 a traveller on his way to Tywyn spotted a large dorsal fin breaking the surface. This, even to a non-fisherman was astounding as it was generally accepted that no fish lived in the lake. No stream left or entered Llyn y Tri Graeanyn, it was left to rainwater to keep it topped up. The traveller in question called at the Ty'n y Gongl (the recognised mecca for anglers) and imparted his news to a rather incredulous almost condescending group. One Dr Frere Webb however decided to 'pop' up to see and using a live minnow as bait had landed a 5lb brown trout within minutes of arriving. It was never resolved how the fish got there, whether anyone had put it in, who, and how long had it been there. A life size picture of the fish can be seen on the wall of the bar at the hotel to remind anglers of one of the more amusing mysteries the sport has produced in this area. Above the lake the ominous looking crag is called Craig y Llam (rock of the leap) and it has two stories to explain this name. One involves Idris the giant again who used to leap across the valley from here on his way to the mountain (unless he had some pebbles in his shoe of course). The other story goes back to the time when wrongdoers were killed by being hurled over a cliff, this was one such cliff used for the purpose (see Llyn Ffynhonnau for another). On one occasion however the victim very courteously asked to shake the hand of the magistrate as he had been touched by the fairness of his trial. This the magistrate agreed to do but once their hands grasped the condemned man let out an almighty yell and leaped to his doom taking his condemner with him! Another interesting little story concerning the lakeside involves a gipsy caravan being drawn by two horses many years ago. It was quite stormy and as they neared the top a lightning struck to cause the horses to panic with the result that the caravan turned over fatally injuring both horses. They were both put down and buried at the lakeside and since then the rushes growing at the spot where they were buried have always been a slightly different shade of green. Today the little lake is just a bed of usually dry rushes and the lower slopes of Craig y Llam a rough stone quarry.

## LLYN TRYWERYN
*GR 7838*
*Height: 1,267'*
*Group: Bala*
*Area: 20 acres*

When George Borrow passed this way in 1854 he stopped for some refreshment at Tai Hirion (GR 811398) and in the conversation he had with the lady of the house which is well documented in Wild Wales he was told that pike of up to fifty pounds in weight had been caught in Llyn Tryweryn. Although the weight is almost certainly exaggerated it does give us an indication of the reputation these fish had at that time as any exaggeration must be considered plausible in the opinion of the teller. There are no pike present today but there are plenty of Brown Trout stocked from time to time by Bala Angling Club. No stocking has taken place for two years as there is some concern regarding the PH level and it is intended to 'lime' the lake in the near future. Tai Hirion was built in 1630 in the classic traditional Welsh longhouse style. Above and 800 yards west an ancient arch bridge constructed of dry stone also bears the name 'Pont Tai Hirion' and is thought to form part of Sarn Helen, the Roman road. Further south and a short mile east of the lake (GR 802384) is the site of Nant Ddu cottage which was rented by James Innes and Augustus John for the summers of 1911 and 1912. Both these artists made significant contributions to the world of art but it must surely be Innes' obsessiveness with the mountain Arennig Fawr that is best remembered. In 1911 he buried a casket of love letters on the summit of the mountain following a doomed love affair with one Euphemia Lamb who actually stayed at Nant Ddu in 1911. Although a brilliant painter his personality was unsettled and he was to die at the age of twenty seven. John continued to stay in the area. A mile to the north of the lake (GR 786401) are Creigiau Ednyfed themselves on the slopes of Carnedd Iago the ancient meeting place of three 'cantrefi' (see Llyn Dywarchen). Ednyfed Fychan was one of Llywelyn Fawr's stewards who supposedly fought a battle against Elisan ap Madog of Penllyn in 1202 here at the rocks. Llywelyn gave him a shield depicting the bloody heads of three Englishmen on it. The old track that carried the 'Great Western Railway' passes very close to the lake's north shore, it was dismantled following the 'Beeching' cuts in 1961.

## LLYN TŴR GLAS
*GR 6632*
*Height: 1,750'*
*Group: Rhinogydd*
*Area: 2 acres*

Generally thought to be fishless, this tarn is found on the jumbled rock plateau of the north Rhinogydd. Some claim to have seen fish rising but the consensus seems to be that this is very unlikely. Tŵr Glas (blue/green tower) is the name of the nearby knoll where it is said an old watchtower once stood. Very little remains now but as this upland region bears enough evidence of past occupation, this elevated spot with a view is a plausible place for such a structure to have once stood.

*Llyn Tŵr Glas*

## LLYN TY'N MYNYDD
*GR 7658*
*Height: 800'*
*Group: Betws-y-coed*
*Area: 1 acre*

Another artificial lake constructed to provide water for the large water wheel of Cyffty Lead mine. The low earth dam is still in situ but breached and the lake is silting up dramatically with very little water actually remaining. A 2″ diameter pipe leaving via the old dam may provide domestic water supply for Ty'n Mynydd house a little below. Interestingly enough once the water had been used at Cyffty it was then sold to "Pool" Lead and Zinc mine to power their turbines. These were situated some five hundred yards below Swallow Falls (Rhaeadr Ewynnol) and a series of leats were used to carry the water. Today it is the haunt of water fowl and a specially constructed watching hide has been erected on the lake's east shore.

## LLYN WRYSGAN
*GR 6745*
*Height: 1,250'*
*Group: Moelwynion*
*Area: ⅓ acre*

A tiny pool perched on the very lip of the cliffs and quarry faces overlooking Tanygrisiau. It has a twin walled dam which was constructed to provide water for the quarry below. The probable date of construction was 1874. The pool is now much smaller and does not actually reach the dam any more. An interesting explanation of the word 'wrysgan' is given by G. J. Williams in his 1882 book 'Hanes Plwyf Ffestiniog'. He claims the word is a corruption of 'ysgefnydd' which means the easy way to reach a height, to zig zag perhaps; this probably refers to a short cut from the village which passed the pool on its way to the col which gave access to Cwm Croesor. An old well situated close to the chapel in Tanygrisiau is called Ffynnon Wrysgan Fawr, this is said to be haunted. There are no fish in the pool.

## LLYN WYLFA
*GR 6716*
*Height: 700'*
*Group: Cadair Idris*
*Area: 6 acres*

This very shallow lake was part owned by and provided water for the Garth Angharad Hospital (GR 667165) up to the hospital's closure July 1993. The other half of the lake is owned by Mr G. Griffiths, Gallestra. Mr Griffiths remembers his father referring to the lake as the abode of snakes and claims it is so shallow that it can easily be waded. There are certainly eels present as well as brown trout. A nearby knoll is called Tŵr Glas (see Llyn Tŵr Glas) which may be linked to the lake's name 'gwylfa' meaning watching place. Less than a mile to the east a beautiful wooded valley contains King's Youth Hostel. There is what appears to be a small quarry just to the west of the lake which was possibly slate or manganese. The lake is also known locally as Llyn y Ffridd Fawr.

# BIBLIOGRAPHY/REFERENCES

E. Hyde-Hall, *A description of Caernarvonshire*, 1809-11, Caerns. Historical Society.

A.J. Richards, *A Gazeteer of Welsh slate industry*, 1991, Gwasg Carreg Gwalch.

A.H. Dodd, *A History of Caernarvonshire*, 1968, Caernarvonshire Historical Society.

Vernon Hall, *A Scrapbook of Snowdonia*, 1982, Stockwell, Devon.

Edited by Geraint Bowen, *Atlas Meirionnydd*, 1972, County Press, Bala.

E.H. Owen and Elfed Thomas, *Atlas Sir Gaernarfon*, 1954, Gwenlyn Evans Cyf., Caernarfon.

Thomas Pennant, *A Tour in Wales*, 1789 (1991 re-print by Bridge Books, Wrexham).

Donald Shaw, *A to Z of Betws*, 1990, Gwasg Carreg Gwalch.

D.E. Jenkins, *Beddgelert, its facts, fairies and folklore*, 1899, Clark, Edinburgh.

Charles Squire, *Celtic Myth and legend*, 1902? Gresham publishings, London.

A.G. Bradley, *Clear Waters*, 1915, Constable.

A.G. Bradley, *In Praise of North Wales*, 1925, Methuen.

*Climbers' club guidebooks, (Various)*,

Evan Isaac, *Coelion Cymru*, 1938, Cambrian News, Aberystwyth.

*Country Quest Magazine* 1960 - (Various).

Dewi Tomos, *Crwydro Bro Lleu*, 1990, Gwasg Carreg Gwalch.

*Cymru (Magazine)* edited by O.M. Edwards 1874-1927 (Various).

Emrys Evans, *Dal Pysgod*, 1989, Gwasg Carreg Gwalch.

T.P. Ellis, *Dolgellau and Llanelltyd*, 1928, Outlook Press, Newtown.

Lou Stevens, *Fly Fishing*, 1988, Blandford press.

W.M. Gallichan, *Fishing in Wales*, 1903, Robinson and Co.

Askew Roberts, *Gossipping Guide to Wales*, 1891.

Merched y Wawr, *Hanes Bro Trawsfynydd*, 1973, Gwasg Gwynedd, Nant Peris.

Rev. Owen Jones, *Hanes Cymru*, (Vol.1 and 2), 1875, Blackie and sons, Edinburgh/London.

G.J. Williams, *Hanes Plwyf Ffestiniog*, 1882, Hughes and son, Wrexham.

Hugh Derfel Hughes, *Hynafiaethau Llanllechid a Llandegái*, 1866 (Re-printed by Cyhoeddiadau Mei 1979).

Thomas Firbanks, *I bought a mountain*, 1940, Harrap and Co.

*Journals of the Merioneth historical and record society* (Various).

*Llafar Bro*, Blaenau Ffestiniog local paper. (Various.)

*Llafar Gwlad*, Magazine edited by J.O. Huws.

Myrddin Fardd, *Llên Gwerin Sir Gaernarfon*, 1908, Cwmni Cyhoeddwyr Cymraeg 'Swyddfa'r Cymru'.

J. Bennet and R.W. Vernon, *Mines of the Gwydyr forest*, Parts 1-6, 1989-92, Private publications.

W.T. Palmer, *More Odd corners in North Wales*, 1945, Skiffingtons, London.

Chris Barber, *More mysterious Wales*, 1986, Paladin.

J.S. Foster, *Mountain, moorland and river*, 1938, North Wales Weekly News.

J.D. Evans, *Myfyrion hen chwarelwr*, 1978, Cyhoeddiadau Mei.

Chris Barber, *Mysterious Wales*, 1983, Paladin.

Cledwyn Fychan, *Nabod Cymru*, 1973, Y Lolfa.

Edward Doylerush, *No Landing place*, 1985, Midland Counties publication.

Rev. W. Bingley, *North Wales, scenery, antiquities and customs*, 1804, Longman and Rees, London.

William Williams, *Observations on the Snowdon mountains*, 1802, Collingwood, Oxford.

W.T. Palmer, *Odd Corners in North Wales*, 1937, Skiffingtons, London.

Dafydd Guto Ifan, *O'i ben i'w gynffon*, 1979, Cyhoeddiadau Mei.

*Proceedings of Llandudno*, Colwyn Bay and district field club. (Various.)

Emrys Evans, *Pysgod dŵr croyw*, 1983, Gwasg Dwyfor.

Roger Redfern, *Rambles in North Wales*, 1968, Robert Hale, London.

M. Hughes and W. Evans, *Rumours and oddities from North Wales*, 1986, Gwasg Carreg Gwalch.

John Cantrell and Arthur Rylance, *Sarn Helen*, 1992, Cicerone press, Cumbria.

D.L.F. Hoare, *Snowdon, that most celebrated hill*, 1987, Private publication.

Edited by G. Rhys Edwards, *Snowdonia National Park*, 1958/1973, HMSO.

G.W. Young, G. Sutton, W. Noyce, *Snowdon Biography*, 1957, Dent and sons, London.

North, Cambell and Scott, *Snowdonia*, 1949, (New Naturalist series) Collins, London.

*Snowdonia, a historical anthology*, 1994, Gwasg Carreg Gwalch.

Simon Jones, *Straeon Cwm Cynllwyd*, 1989, Gwasg Carreg Gwalch.

Robin Gwyndaf, *Straeon Gwerin Cymru*, 1988, Gwasg Carreg Gwalch.

Showell Styles, *The climber's bedside book*, 1969, Faber and Faber, London.

Fay Godwin and Shirley Toulson, *The Drovers' roads of Wales*, 1977, Wildwood House, London.

G.W. Hall, *The Gold mines of Merioneth*, 1986? Griffin publications, Herefordshire.

W. Bezant Lowe, *The heart of Northern Wales*, 1912, Private publication.

(Giraldis Cambrensis) Ed. Ll. Williams, *The itenary through Wales*, 1908, Dent and co. London.

Jonah Jones, *The Lakes of North Wales*, 1983, Wildwood House, London.

Frank Ward, *The Lakes of Wales*, 1931, Butler and Tanner, London.

Alan Hankinson, *The Mountain men*, 1977, Heinemann Educational books.

H.R.C. Carr and G.A. Lister, *The Mountains of Snowdonia*, 1925, Crosby Lockwood and son, London.

David Bick, *The old copper mines of Snowdonia*, 1982, Pound house, Gloc.

David Hubback, *Time and the valley*, 1987, Gwasg Carreg Gwalch.

*Transactions of the Cymmrodorion*. (Various.)

*Transactions of the Caernarvonshire Historical society*, (Various.)

Ian Niall, *Trout from the hills*, 1961, Heinemann.

Dewi Jones, *Tywysyddion Eryri*, 1993, Gwasg Carreg Gwalch.

Philip Gwyn Hughes, (Ed. R.J. Moore-Colyer), *Wales and the drovers*, 1943/1988, Golden Grove, Camarthen.

Edited by M.J. Blake, *Wartime wrecks of interest in Snowdonia*, 1970's in various booklets, private publications.

D. Parry Jones, *Welsh Legends*, 1953, Batsford, London.

George Bolam, *Wild life in Wales*, 1913, Palmer, London.

George Borrow, *Wild Wales*, 1855, (1896 edition) Murray, London.

Dewi Tomos, *Yn llwybrau Lleu*, 1981, Cyhoeddiadau Mei.

Twm Elias, *Y Porthmyn Cymreig*, 1987, Gwasg Carreg Gwalch.

Hugh Evans, *Y Tylwyth Teg*, 1934, Gwasg Brython, Liverpool.

John Owen Huws, *Y Tylwyth Teg*, 1987, Gwasg Carreg Gwalch.

Apart from numerous articles and odd snippets of information obtained over the years whose sources are long forgotten my thanks are due to the following . . . some of whom unfortunately are no longer with us.

Wil Fred James, Gellilydan; Dafydd Guto Ifan, Bethel; Gwynant Hughes, Dyserth; Dewi Talardd, Beryl Griffiths and Ifan Garej, Llanuwchllyn; Goronwy Pugh, Rhiwogof; Jack Williams, Bontddu; D.O. Jones, Ysbyty Ifan; Dafydd Roberts, Caerwys; Shaun Sheltinga, Betws-y-coed; The Ruck family, Pennal; Dewi Evans, Bala; John Evans, Werngron, Llanbedr; Griffith Griffiths, Dolgellau; Ian Woolford, Llanrwst; Wil Davies, Highways, Gwynedd County Council; Cynan and June Jones, Nanmor; Gareth Davies, Warden of Tanybwlch; Hywel Hughes, Dyffryn Conwy; Edwin Noble, Dolwyddelan; Terry Lloyd, Water Bailiff; Dr Tom Davies, Aberdovey; Emyr Lewis, Llanbrynmair; Tom Jones, Bryncir; Tom Kirkop, Pwllheli; Howard Huws, NRA; Glyn Hughes, Welsh Water; Michael Bayley Hughes, Mold; Vic Osborne, Harlech; Dafydd Hughes, Porthmadog and others who are too numerous to mention.